A Variorum Edition of

The Works of Geoffrey Chaucer

Volume II

The Canterbury Tales

Part Ten

The Manciple's Tale

Paul G. Ruggiers

General Editor

Donald C. Baker

Associate Editor

The Variorum Edition

Part Ten
The Manciple's Tale

Hengwrt Manuscript, folio 108v, National Library of Wales, Aberystwyth

A Variorum Edition of The Works of Geoffrey Chaucer

Volume II
The Canterbury Tales

Part Ten

The Manciple's Tale

Edited by Donald C. Baker

University of Oklahoma Press : Norman

Library of Congress Cataloging in Publication Data

Chaucer, Geoffrey, d. 1400.
   The manciple's tale.

   (A Variorum edition of the works of Geoffrey Chaucer; v. 2. The Canterbury tales; pt. 10)
Bibliography: p. 129
   Includes index.
   I. Baker, Donald C. II. Title. III. Series: Chaucer, Geoffrey, d. 1400. Works. 1979; v. 2. IV. Series: Chaucer, Geoffrey, d. 1400. Canterbury tales; pt. 10.
PR1866.R8   1979, pt. 10 [PR1868]   821'.1   83-14734
ISBN: 0-8061-1872-5

The paper in this book meets the guidelines for permanence and durability of the Committee on Production Guidelines for Book Longevity of the Council on Library Resources, Inc.

For
Beth

Contents

Illustrations

General Editor's Preface

A *Variorum Edition of the Works of Geoffrey Chaucer* is a collaborative effort of forty-two medievalists whose chief interest is the work of Geoffrey Chaucer and his time. Originally projected exclusively as a commentary upon the entire canon of Chaucer's poetry and prose, the *Variorum Chaucer* was expanded in 1979 to include a series of facsimiles representing the tradition upon which subsequent editors of the printed editions of his work have based their texts. Thus the *Variorum Chaucer* rests upon the two great foundations of text and commentary.

I

The facsimile series, the prime support for the various texts provided by the *Variorum Chaucer,* was inaugurated in 1979 with the publication of the facsimile of the Hengwrt manuscript (Peniarth 392D) of *The Canterbury Tales.* The series was begun with this particular manuscript on the obvious ground that it was our base manuscript for *The Canterbury Tales* and that the treatment of *The Canterbury Tales* was the part of the project that initially commanded our greatest attention. An explanation of the reasons for the choice of the Hengwrt manuscript as base text is given in the introductions to the publication, along with a full description of the manuscript by A. I. Doyle, Keeper of Rare Books and Reader in Bibliography, University Library, Durham; and M. B. Parkes, Tutor in English Language and Lecturer in Palaeography, Keble College, Oxford. In brief, with reliance upon the Hengwrt manuscript as the base text for *The Canterbury Tales* and with the provision of a running comparison between the transcribed Hengwrt and Ellesmere manuscripts, the *Variorum Chaucer* returns to the sources from which virtually all modern editions of *The Canterbury Tales* have emanated.

Reliance upon the Hengwrt manuscript as a base text does not free the editors of *The Canterbury Tales* from the survey of the manuscript tradition, but rather places each under the obligation to survey both the manuscripts and the printed editions, emending in the light of both sources. The practices that govern the treatment of *The Canterbury Tales* generally set the norms for the establishment of the text for the other parts of the Chaucer canon.

Other parts of the facsimile series include Tanner 346 *(The Legend of Good Women, The Book of the Duchess, The Parliament of Fowls, Anelida and Arcite);* Bodley 638 *(The Legend of Good Women, The Book of the Duchess, The Parliament of Fowls, The House of Fame, Anelida and Arcite);* Pepys

Library 2006 *(The Legend of Good Women, The Parliament of Fowls, The House of Fame, Anelida and Arcite, The Tale of Melibee, The Parson's Tale, Chaucer's Retraction);* Trinity R.3.19 *(The Legend of Good Women, The Parliament of Fowls, The Monk's Tale);* St. John's College L.1 Cambridge *(Troilus and Criseyde);* and Morgan 817, *olim* Campsall *(Troilus and Criseyde).*

II

The commentary series is built upon a model evolved over many years: critical and textual introductions, newly established texts for the poems, collations providing evidence both of the manuscripts and of the printed editions, textual and explanatory notes, and bibliography. It is our conviction that so full an apparatus will constitute a summary of the commentary, both textual and evalutive, that has accumulated over the past six hundred years, as well as afford a starting point for future scholarship.

It should be noted that the textual apparatus, melding evidence from both manuscripts and printed editions, will enable the user of the *Variorum Chaucer* to see at a glance the changes through which the various Chaucer texts have passed over the course of six centuries.

III

The *Variorum Chaucer,* when complete, will follow the plan here offered provisionally:

Volume   I: *The Canterbury Tales: A Facsimile and Transcription of the Hengwrt Manuscript* (and the facsimiles listed above; seven parts)
Volume   II: *The Canterbury Tales* (twenty-five parts)
Volume   III: *Troilus and Criseyde* (seven parts)
Volume   IV: *The Vision Poems (The Book of the Duchess, The House of Fame, The Parliament of Fowls, The Legend of Good Women;* (four parts)
Volume   V: *The Minor Poems* (two parts)
Volume   VI: *The Prose Treatises* (two parts)
Volume VII: *History of the Printed Editions*
Volume VIII: *Concordance and Rhyme Index* (two parts)

IV

The collational system of the Variorum Edition is, of course, related to that of John M. Manly and Edith Rickert (*The Text of the Canterbury Tales,* 8 vols., 1940). That relationship and an explanation of the Variorum approach to Manly and Rickert's work are presented in some detail in our Preface to *The Miller's*

Tale (volume 2, part 3, of the Variorum Edition, the first of *The Canterbury Tales* to be published) and require no restatement here. Similarly, the rationale for the conservative modern punctuation supplied for all texts of *The Canterbury Tales* is provided in our Preface to *The Miller's Tale.*

PAUL G. RUGGIERS
General Editor

Norman, Oklahoma, 1983

DONALD C. BAKER
Associate Editor

Boulder, Colorado, 1983

Preface

This edition of the *Manciple's Prologue* and *Tale* has been very long in the making, not because of any difficulties inherent in the material but rather, owing to the shortness of the *Prologue* and *Tale,* because it was selected as the original model for the fascicles of the *Variorum Chaucer* and has during the intervening thirteen or fourteen years been recast again and again as the editorial board has sifted and transformed the original concepts upon which this vast project was based. It could have been published much earlier, but I felt that such a small mouse as the first publication of the Variorum Edition might have appeared a bit ridiculous after such mountainous laboring. Nevertheless, the mouse has been worth the labor of its editor. Although by no means the richest of Chaucer's work, the *Manciple's Prologue* and *Tale* are very instructive examples of Chaucer's art; they are, like almost all of Chaucer's other work unique, and in attempting to understand them, I feel that I have gained insights in this corner of Chaucer's mind and art that I could not have gained from some of the greater work. I hope that the insights I have gained can be accessible to the user of the edition, for I have certainly spared no effort to make the apparatus as full as possible and to make the text as accurate as it is possible to make Chaucer's text. As is inevitable, some valuable commentary will have slipped through my hands, even with so short a piece of work, and I offer my apologies in advance to any outraged reader who finds his own views slighted or ignored. *Mea culpa.*

The materials in this edition have been read many times, principally by the General Editor and my old friend and teacher, Paul Ruggiers, but also by colleagues, many of whom began as mere names but became friends: to name only a few, Tom Ross, Derek Pearsall, Derek Brewer, Vance Ramsey. I must also thank for their patient labor the staff of the *Variorum Chaucer,* particularly Donald Rose, Lynne Levy, and Lane Goodall.

Naturally an account of such work would be incomplete without the usual acknowledgments to the great libraries: the British Library, the Bodleian, the Cambridge University Library, the National Library of Wales. Closer to home, the Norlin Library of the University of Colorado has been of much help in its photocopying, borrowing of materials, and making space available for work. My friend and colleague, Michael Preston, of the University of Colorado Center for Computer Research in the Humanities, has prepared a concordance of the *Manciple's Prologue* and *Tale* which assisted me a great deal in isolating some aspects of Chaucer's use of his language.

"Errours endlesse traine" must inevitably include this edition in spite of the many, many hours spent by myself, Paul Ruggiers and his staff, and my patient wife, Beth, to whom the edition is dedicated. That model editor of the University of Oklahoma Press, Doris Radford Morris, whose crisp letters I learned to dread as well as appreciate, has done her best. But for the errors that remain, I stand alone responsible.

DONALD C. BAKER

Boulder, Colorado

A Brief Guide to the Use of This Edition

The Introduction provides a critical commentary, including a survey of criticism, arranged by categories, of the *Manciple's Prologue* and *Tale* from the earliest substantial mentions of the work to 1980-81, and a Textual Commentary, describing each manuscript and printed edition used in preparing this edition, and evaluation of its significance for the text of the *Manciple's Prologue* and *Tale.* The Textual Commentary also includes a set of tables of correspondences for the manuscripts (including the first printed edition of Caxton, used by Manly and Rickert as a manuscript text) and one for the printed editions (in which the first Caxton is also included).

The text, as will be described, is based upon the Hengwrt manuscript, amended where necessary and lightly punctuated according to modern norms. The letters *u/v, i, j, ʒ*, and *þ* are given their modern equivalents. Below the Text are the Collations (where original spelling is retained) from the ten "base" manuscripts and the twenty-one printed editions which were collated, and the melded Textual Notes and General Notes, which are devoted to text, meanings, style, structure, sources, and the like. The edition also provides a Bibliographical Index and a General Index.

Abbreviations and Sigils

ABBREVIATIONS OF CHAUCER'S WORKS

Note: Following Manly's lead, to permit the scholar the widest latitude of reference, abbreviations are provided suited to specific reference needs; for example, *Monk-Nun's Priest Link* as well as *The Nun's Priest's Prologue; Second Nun-Canon's Yeoman Link* as well as *The Canon's Yeoman's Prologue;* and *Knight-Miller Link* as well as *The Miller's Prologue.*

ABC	*An ABC*
Adam	*Adam Scriveyn*
Anel	*Anelida and Arcite*
Astr	*A Treatise on the Astrolabe*
Bal Compl	*A Balade of Complaint*
BD	*The Book of the Duchess*
Bo	*Boece*
Buk	*The Envoy to Bukton*
CkT, CkP, Rv-CkL	*The Cook's Tale, The Cook's Prologue, Reeve-Cook Link*
ClT, ClP, Cl-MerL	*The Clerk's Tale, The Clerk's Prologue, Clerk-Merchant Link*
Compl D'Am	*Complaynt d'Amours*
CT	*The Canterbury Tales*
CYT, CYP	*The Canon's Yeoman's Tale, The Canon's Yeoman's Prologue*
Equat	*The Equatorie of the Planets*
For	*Fortune*
Form Age	*The Former Age*
FranT, FranP	*The Franklin's Tale, The Franklin's Prologue*
FrT, FrP, Fr-SumL	*The Friar's Tale, The Friar's Prologue, Friar-Summoner Link*
Gent	*Gentilesse*
GP	*The General Prologue*
HF	*The House of Fame*
KnT, Kn-MilL	*The Knight's Tale, Knight-Miller Link*
Lady	*A Complaint to His Lady*
LGW, LGWP	*The Legend of Good Women, The Legend of Good Women Prologue*

ManT, ManP	*The Manciple's Tale, The Manciple's Prologue*
Mars	*The Complaint of Mars*
Mel, Mel-MkL	*The Tale of Melibee, Melibee-Monk Link*
MercB	*Merciles Beaute*
MerT, MerE-SqH	*The Merchant's Tale, Merchant Endlink-Squire Head-link*
MilT, MilP, Mil-RvL	*The Miller's Tale, The Miller's Prologue, Miller-Reeve Link*
MkT, MkP, Mk-NPL	*The Monk's Tale, The Monk's Prologue, Monk-Nun's Priest Link*
MLT, MLH, MLP, MLE	*The Man of Law's Tale, Man of Law Headlink, The Man of Law's Prologue, Man of Law Endlink*
NPT, NPP, NPE	*The Nun's Priest's Tale, The Nun's Priest's Prologue, Nun's Priest Endlink*
PardT, PardP	*The Pardoner's Tale, The Pardoner's Prologue*
ParsT, ParsP	*The Parson's Tale, The Parson's Prologue*
PF	*The Parliament of Fowls*
PhyT, Phy-PardL	*The Physician's Tale, Physician-Pardoner Link*
Pity	*The Complaint unto Pity*
Prov	*Proverbs*
PrT, PrP, Pr-ThL	*The Prioress's Tale, The Prioress's Prologue, Prioress-Thopas Link*
Purse	*The Complaint of Chaucer to His Purse*
Ret	*Chaucer's Retraction* [*Retraction*]
Rom	*The Romaunt of the Rose*
Ros	*To Rosemounde*
RvT, RvP	*The Reeve's Tale, The Reeve's Prologue*
Scog	*The Envoy to Scogan*
ShT, Sh-PrL	*The Shipman's Tale, Shipman-Prioress Link*
SNT, SNP, SN-CYL	*The Second Nun's Tale, The Second Nun's Prologue, Second Nun-Canon's Yeoman Link*
SqT, SqH, Sq-FranL	*The Squire's Tale, Squire Headlink, Squire-Franklin Link*
Sted	*Lak of Stedfastnesse*
SumT, SumP	*The Summoner's Tale, The Summoner's Prologue*
TC	*Troilus and Criseyde*
Th, Th-MelL	*The Tale of Sir Thopas, Sir Thopas-Melibee Link*
Ven	*The Complaint of Venus*
WBT, WBP, WB-FrL	*The Wife of Bath's Tale, The Wife of Bath's Prologue, Wife of Bath-Friar Link*
Wom Nob	*Womanly Noblesse*
Wom Unc	*Against Women Unconstant*

MANUSCRIPTS

Collated Manuscripts

Hg	Hengwrt, National Library of Wales, Aberystwyth (now Peniarth 392D)
El	Ellesmere, Henry E. Huntington Library, San Marino, California (now 26.C.9)
Ad³	Additional 35286, British Library (Ashburnham Appendix 125)
Cp	Corpus Christi 198, Corpus Christi College (Oxford)
En¹	Egerton 2726, British Library
Gg	Cambridge University Gg.4.27, Cambridge University Library
Ha⁴	Harley 7334, British Library
He	Helmingham, Princeton University Library
La	Lansdowne 851, British Library
Pw	Petworth, Petworth

(Dd   Cambridge University Dd.4.24, Cambridge University Library, is Out for all *ManP* and *ManT,* and En¹ is substituted for it in the base-ten manuscripts collated.)

Manuscripts Employed to Supplement the Collated Manuscripts

Ne	New College D.314 (to supplement He when Out), New College (Oxford)
Tc²	Trinity College R.3.15 (Cambridge)

Other Manuscripts Cited by Manly and Rickert

(Some are cited in the Introduction and Notes but are not collated.)

Constant Groups (as cited by Manly and Rickert)

a	= Dd+		*Cn*	= Cn Ma
b	= He *Ne*		*Cx¹*	= CX¹ Tc²
c	= Cp La+		*En³*	= En³ Ad¹
d	= *Pw*+		*Mm*	= Mm Gl
Bo¹	= Bo¹ Ph²		*Ne*	= Ne *Cx¹*

Individual Manuscripts

Ad¹	Additional 5140, British Library
Ad²	Additional 25718, British Library

Bo[1]	Bodley 414, Bodleian Library
Bo[2]	Bodley 686, Bodleian Library
Bw	Barlow 20, Bodleian Library
Ch	Christ Church (Oxford) 152
Cn	Cardigan (now Deene Park)
Dl	Delamere (now Takamiya 32)
Ds	Devonshire
En[2]	Egerton 2863, British Library
En[3]	Egerton 2864, British Library
Fi	Fitzwilliam Museum (Cambridge) McClean 181
Gl	Glasgow Hunterian 197 (U.1.1), Glasgow University Library
Ha[2]	Harley 1758, British Library
Ha[3]	Harley 7333, British Library
Ha[5]	Harley 7335, British Library
Hk	Holkham 667
Ht	Hatton Donat. 1, Bodleian Library
Ii	Ii.3.26, Cambridge University Library
Lc	Lichfield 2
Ld[1]	Laud 600, Bodleian Library
Ld[2]	Laud 739, Bodleian Library
Ln	Lincoln Cathedral 110 (A.4.18)
Ma	Manchester Eng. 113 (John Rylands Library)
Mg	Ms 4, Morgan Library
Mm	Mm.2.5, Cambridge University Library
Ne	New College (Oxford) D.314
Nl	Northumberland
Ox	Oxford (Manchester 63 and Rosenbach)
Ph[2]	Phillipps 8136 (now Rosenbach 156)
Ph[3]	Phillipps 8137
Ps	Paris, Bibliothèque nationale fonds anglais 39
Py	Royal College of Physicians 13
Ra[1]	Rawlinson Poet. 141, Bodleian Library
Ra[2]	Rawlinson Poet. 149, Bodleian Library
Ra[3]	Rawlinson Poet. 223, Bodleian Library
Ry[1]	Royal 17.D.15, British Library
Se	Selden Arch. B.14, Bodleian Library
Sl[1]	Sloane 1685, British Library
Sl[2]	Sloane 1686, British Library
Tc[1]	Trinity College (Cambridge) R.3.3
Tc[2]	Trinity College (Cambridge) R.3.15
To	Trinity College (Oxford) Arch. 49

PRINTED EDITIONS

(In chronological order; for complete citations see the Bibliographical Index.)

CX[1]   William Caxton, [*The Canterbury Tales*], 1478. *STC* 5082. CX[1] is not given manuscript status in the Collations as it is in Manly and Rickert, though it is included in the table of manuscript correspondences and of correspondences for the printed editions. Collated from a facsimile published by University Microfilms (Ann Arbor, Michigan) and from two copies in the British Library.

CX[2]   William Caxton, [*The Canterbury Tales*], 1484. *STC* 5083. Collated from photocopy.

PN[1]   Richard Pynson, [*The Canterbury Tales*], 1492. *STC* 5084. This and all successive printed editions through SP[1] were collated from photocopy. All others were collated from copies in the present editor's collection.

WN   Wynkyn de Worde, *The boke of Chaucer named Caunterbury tales,* 1498. *STC* 5085.

PN[2]   Richard Pynson, *Here begynneth the boke of Caunterbury tales dilygently and truely corrected and newly printed,* 1526. Pt. 3 of an edition of the works. *STC* 5086.

TH[1]   William Thynne, *The Workes of Geffray Chaucer newly printed with dyuers workes whiche were neuer in print before,* 1532. *STC* 5068.

TH[2]   William Thynne, *The workes of Geffray Chaucer newly printed, with dyuers workes whych were neuer in print before,* 1542. *STC* 5069.

TH[3]   William Thynne, *The workes of Geffray Chaucer newly printed, with dyuers workes whiche were neuer in print before,* 1545. *STC* 5071.

ST   John Stow, *The workes of Geffrey Chaucer, newly printed with diuers addicions, whiche were neuer in print before,* 1561. *STC* 5075.

SP[1]   Thomas Speght, *The Workes of our Antient and Lerned English Poet, Geffrey Chaucer, newly Printed,* 1598. *STC* 5077. There seem to have been two issues of SP[1], with minor differences. Both were examined in photocopy.

SP[2]   Thomas Speght, *The Workes of Ovr Ancient and learned English Poet, Geffrey Chaucer, newly Printed,* 1602. *STC* 5080.

SP[3]   Thomas Speght, *The Works of our Ancient, Learned, & Excellent English Poet, Jeffrey Chaucer,* 1687.

UR   John Urry, *The Works of Geoffrey Chaucer,* 1721.

TR   Thomas Tyrwhitt, *The Canterbury Tales of Chaucer,* 1775. There was a second printing of TR (1798), set in larger type than that of the first. Both are identical in every way in *ManPT,* save for variants in line 224.

WR   Thomas Wright, *The Canterbury Tales of Geoffrey Chaucer,* 1847-51.

SK   W. W. Skeat, *The Complete Works of Geoffrey Chaucer,* 1894.
RB[1]   F. N. Robinson, *The Complete Works of Geoffrey Chaucer,* 1933.
MR   John M. Manly and Edith Rickert, *The Text of the Canterbury Tales,* 1940.
RB[2]   F. N. Robinson, *The Works of Geoffrey Chaucer,* 2d ed., 1957.
PR   Robert A. Pratt, *The Tales of Canterbury, Complete, Geoffrey Chaucer,* 1974.
FI   John H. Fisher, *The Complete Poetry and Prose of Geoffrey Chaucer,* 1977.

In addition, *ManPT* was collated in the following editions, which are cited in the Notes and elsewhere but not in the Collations (for complete citations see the Bibliographical Index):

A. C. Baugh, *Chaucer's Major Poetry,* 1963.
E. T. Donaldson, *Chaucer's Poetry: An Anthology for the Modern Reader,* 1958.
G. Plessow, *Des Haushälters Erzählung aus den Canterbury Geschichten Gottfried Chaucers,* 1929.
A. W. Pollard et al., *The Works of Chaucer* (Globe Chaucer), 1908.

OTHER ABBREVIATIONS

Books

DNB	*Dictionary of National Biography,* edited by Sir Leslie Stephen and Sir Sidney Lee. London: Oxford University Press, 1917-.
MED	*Middle English Dictionary,* edited by Hans Kurath et al. Ann Arbor: University of Michigan Press, 1952-.
OED	*Oxford English Dictionary,* edited by James A. H. Murray et al. 12 vols., later supplements. Oxford: Oxford University Press, 1884-1928.
STC	*A Short-Title Catalogue of Books Printed in England, Scotland, and Ireland, . . . 1475-1640,* compiled by A. W. Pollard and G. R. Redgrave. London: Bibliographical Society, 1926.

Journals

AnM	*Annuale Mediaevale*
ChauN	*The Chaucer Newsletter*
ChauR	*Chaucer Review*

EIC	*Essays in Criticism*
ELH	*Journal of English Literary History*
ELN	*English Language Notes*
ES	*English Studies*
HLQ	*Huntington Library Quarterly*
JEGP	*Journal of English and Germanic Philology*
LeedsSE	*Leeds Studies in English*
MÆ	*Medium Ævum*
MLN	*Modern Language Notes*
MLQ	*Modern Language Quarterly*
MLR	*Modern Language Review*
MP	*Modern Philology*
MS	*Mediaeval Studies*
N&Q	*Notes and Queries*
Neophil	*Neophilologus*
NLWJ	*National Library of Wales Journal*
NM	*Neuphilologische Mitteilungen*
PBA	*Proceedings of the British Academy*
PELL	*Papers on English Language and Literature*
PLL	*Papers on Language and Literature*
PMLA	*PMLA: Publications of the Modern Language Association of America*
PQ	*Philological Quarterly*
RBPH	*Revue Belge de Philologie et Histoire*
RES	*Review of English Studies*
RR	*Romanic Review*
SAC	*Studies in the Age of Chaucer*
SB	*Studies in Bibliography: Papers of the Bibliographical Society of the University of Virginia*
SP	*Studies in Philology*
SRo	*Studi Romani*
SSF	*Studies in Short Fiction*
TLS	*[London] Times Literary Supplement*
TPS	*Transactions of the Philological Society*
UTQ	*University of Toronto Quarterly*
YWES	*Year's Work in English Studies*

Other Abbreviations, Notation

EETS	Early English Text Society
SATF	Société des anciens textes français

Standard abbreviations for classical and medieval works are employed.

Part Ten
The Manciple's Tale

Introduction

Unlike most of Chaucer's other didactic tales, *The Manciple's Tale* has undergone a number of remarkable shifts in critical acceptance. Not only is *The Manciple's Prologue* presented in a style markedly different from that of the *Tale* (a style more characteristically in the tradition of low realistic comedy with its goodly share of coarse, even brutal humor), but the *Tale,* with its slim plot of infidelity and discovery to which is appended a coda of moral admonitions dealing with control of the tongue, by its noteworthy change in style and genre offers a stiff challenge in interpretation to scholars. There has in fact resulted a considerable debate, given the variety of ostensibly antagonistic elements, about the artistic value of the entire performance. It is not surprising that the questions raised by the poem remain only provisionally answered: questions of genre, of fitness of style, of narrator's voice, of suitability to the teller, and of focus.

In spite of scholarly perplexities *The Manciple's Tale* is delivered in what are unmistakably several of Chaucer's voices, its topics echoing themes treated elsewhere in *The Canterbury Tales:* not only the lesson of the guarded tongue but the commentary on freedom in marriage and the paradox of liberty in love (Ruggiers 1965: 247–48). Equally important, *The Manciple's Prologue* and *Tale* function within the closing argument of the Canterbury pilgrimage as a whole: the quarrel of the Cook and Manciple, the Host's hearty intervention, the restoration of amity, the large statement about self-control—all lead by perceptible degrees to the weighty sermon of the Parson and make clearer Chaucer's larger intentions for *The Canterbury Tales* as a whole. Thus, whatever the particular challenges of *The Manciple's Prologue* and *Tale* taken separately, they function extraordinarily well within the poem and provide one more insight into the unfolding plan of the work as a thematic whole.

CRITICAL COMMENTARY

The Critical Commentary is intended to deal with all problems arising, from whatever considerations, in *The Manciple's Tale* and the commentary that has been devoted to those problems, as well as matters of interpretation and criticism and significant statements by scholars and critics devoted to the tale. The approach is both chronological and thematic; that is, sections are devoted to particular matters that seem to deserve separate consideration, and the commentary surveyed will be dealt with chronologically. No attempt has been made to mention every instance in which *The Manciple's Prologue* and *Tale* have been referred to in print, each instance in which a general comment upon the works has been made, either that they are good or bad. The commentary that has been gathered here attempts to address at some length matters of interest and importance therein, though occasionally very brief comments come in for attention because they mark a departure from or development of appreciation of the works. An attempt has been made to create a coherent essay from which the nature of the consideration granted *The Manciple's Prologue* and *Tale* may be gathered by the reader. Inevitably, some good comments of a general kind have reluctantly been omitted, for otherwise no coherence would have been possible. An attempt has been made, however, to record in the Bibliographical Index most works in which any appreciable mention of *The Manciple's Tale* occurs.

Sources and Analogues

There is no source or analogue for *The Manciple's Prologue,* and it is misleading to speak of a source for *The Manciple's Tale.* The story, properly speaking, has at its core the tale of Phoebus, his talking bird, and Phoebus's unfortunate wife, which is derived ultimately from Ovid's *Metamorphoses* (2.531-632). This Chaucer almost certainly knew, as Tyrwhitt, Skeat, and all commentators have assumed. Chaucer had very probably also read the relevant section of the *Ovide moralisé* (lines 2030-2548), as Skeat (1894:5.439) and others have argued. Quite possibly, as Stillwell has proposed (1940), Chaucer was acquainted with the version of the Phoebus story in Machaut's *Le Livre du voir dit* (lines 7773-8110), though Wimsatt (1968:84) disputes that any filiation has been demonstrated. Gower's redaction of the story in the *Confessio Amantis* (3.768-835) has attracted most attention as either analogue or source. All these works are printed in full or with intervening summaries in Bryan and Dempster (1941: 699-722) with an introduction and discussion by Work.

There is a remote possibility that Chaucer was familiar with the *Integumenta Ovidii* (which stresses the bird's cry as presaging rain and tempest, though this work attributes the bird's ability to the period before Phoebus slew his wife, and in Chaucer's poem the ability to "crye agayn tempest and rayn" [line 30] is given to the bird by Phoebus as part of his punishment).

An analogue to the story with which Chaucer was perhaps familiar is in *The Seven Sages of Rome* or possibly its French original, *Li Romans des sept sages,* with their similar stories of the deceived husband and his magpie, in which tempest and rain are also mentioned. The brief bit from the *Integumenta Ovidii* and the relative part of the *Seven Sages* are printed in Bryan and Dempster, and the passages from the French version as well as from the *Seven Sages* are printed in Furnivall et al. (1872-87:439-50). The latter collection also prints a number of analogues from the folklore of the Near East, but these have little interest except in a very general way, for Chaucer obviously "knew" none of them. Plessow had suggested, and printed in his edition (1929:110-11, 116-17), analogues from the *Gesta Romanorum* (the story of the three cocks) found in Herrtage's edition of *The Early English Version of the Gesta Romanorum* (1879: 174-77) and an exemplum in Wright's edition of *La Tour Landry* (1868:22).

Various claims have been made for the effect upon Chaucer of these stories. Although all scholars are agreed that Chaucer knew the Ovidian version of the *Metamorphoses,* all are agreed also that it was probably not an immediate "source." Plessow provides a general comparison in his edition (1929:94-102), and Shannon sums up the relation between the two accounts as follows (1929:324-25):

In the *Manciple's Tale* Chaucer has modified Ovid's story in some respects. He does not mention the name of Coronis, Phoebus' wife, and he represents the crow in his cage at the house of Phoebus telling his master on his return home of his wife's adultery. In Ovid, the raven went on a journey to tell his master of the circumstance. In the *Manciple's Tale,* the wife sent for her "lemman" while Phoebus was away from home. Ovid says nothing of this. Chaucer follows Ovid pretty closely in describing the conduct of Phoebus after he is convinced of the truthfulness of the crow's report, but he omits the appeal of Coronis for her unborn child, and adds some reflections upon too hasty suspicions. Though the metamorphosis in this tale is slight,—the mere changing of the color of the bird's feathers,—Chaucer's use of it is noteworthy. The change in the color of the fruit of the mulberry tree in the Pyramus and Thisbe story is just as slight, and yet he rejects it in the *Legend of Thisbe,* and habitually, in borrowing from the *Metamorphoses,* he omits the transformations of persons into birds or animals.

The emphasis of the two poets in telling this tale is very different. Ovid is intent upon showing the punishment of the raven for his loquacity. Chaucer, true to his usual purpose of interpreting Ovid's fables in terms of the life of men, stresses the propensity of human nature, exemplified by Phoebus' wife, to follow its own bent, even without a justifiable excuse.

This seems a very fair account of the matter, and Hoffman generally agrees (1966:194-95). Both Fyler (1979) and McCall (1979) emphasize Chaucer's humanizing qualities in his treatment of classical myth in general, over and above the extent to which classical myth was normally, in the Middle Ages, acclimatized to its new milieu. Norton-Smith, further, emphasizes a structural use of Ovid, in the joining of *The Manciple's Tale* by an "Ovidian bridge" (1974:151) formed by the recollection of a story in the *Ars amatoria* of the drunken Silenus falling off his ass in a religious procession, which he finds analogous to the fate of the Cook in *The Manciple's Prologue;* the invocation of Bacchus at the end of the *Prologue* by the Host, recalling that the religious procession in which Silenus had difficulty was in honor of that god (and followed by him), and the attaching by Chaucer of his Ovidian fable from the *Metamorphoses* in the form of *The Manciple's Tale.*

The most remarkable of the differences between Chaucer and Ovid are, as Shannon says, the omission of the wife's name in Chaucer (Coronis is named in the French analogues and in Gower) and Chaucer's omission of the business of the unborn babe who turns out to be Aesculapius, who is, of course, saved (a part of the story fully developed in the French analogues but not in Gower). And Chaucer adds another metamorphosis (interesting in view of his lack of interest in metamorphosis per se): the bird who has had a magical voice, capable of rendering any other voice or note, is reduced to crying against tempest and rain (this is not in Ovid but is found in a general way in Gower). Harwood (1972:269-70) in particular emphasizes the crow's loss of musical prowess. As a matter of fact, the only thing, except for the general plot outline, that Ovid and Chaucer really share is the moral against heedless speech, and, as Shannon asserts, this is more generalized (and far more extensive) in Chaucer than in Ovid.

The account of the story in the *Ovide moralisé* is rather more in keeping with Chaucer's approach to the material in its much more fully developed arguments against jangling that are inserted into the story at various points, interrupting the narrative, in a manner similar to Chaucer's account but not to Ovid's. This general assessment is true also of Machaut's *Le Livre du voir dit,* whether or not Chaucer was familiar with it (see Stillwell 1940; Wimsatt 1968:84). And there are some close parallels of individual lines among the three works (see Explanatory Notes). But there remain very important differences between Chaucer's and these French versions. Both French versions follow Ovid in the details of naming Coronis, of relating the birth of her child; both emphasize the bird's waiting for his reward, and the ironic reversal of his being turned black then becomes much more emphatic. Likewise, Chaucer's setting for the poem, derived probably from the *Metamorphoses* or the *Ars amatoria* (see Explanatory Notes), is not found in the French analogues.

In spite of Severs's accumulation (1952:2) of twenty-one similarities that Chaucer's poem shares with either or both the *Ovide moralisé* and *Le Livre du voir dit,* one remains with the impression that, although Chaucer may have known both accounts, and almost certainly knew at least parts of the *Ovide,* the French poems were not likely at his side while he was composing *The Manciple's Tale.*

In his account of *The Seven Sages of Rome,* Work (in Bryan and Dempster 1941:716-17) places emphasis upon the word "lemman," which it shares with *The Manciple's Tale,* as well as the fact that in both poems the wife sends for her lover; the husband returns to the caged bird (a magpie in the *Seven Sages*), where he is told the bad news (in the Ovidian versions the bird flies to Phoebus); and the bird greets his returning master in direct discourse, beginning "By God." Although Cadbury (1964:542-43), following Tatlock (1907:203n.), argues that some devices of characterization seem to be drawn by Chaucer from the *Seven Sages,* the evidence is not convincing. The one point that does seem to tell is the emphasis in the *Seven Sages* on an antifeminist tone (Cadbury 1964:542), which, indeed, is adopted by the Manciple in spite of his transparent protestations. The rest of the parallels seem too slight to be significant. There are as many in the *Seven Sages'* French original, *Li Romans des sept sages* (Furnivall et al. 1887:442-47).

Cadbury also observes (1964:539-40) that Chaucer may have drawn upon Pierre Bersuire (Petrus Berchorius), the *Ovidius moralizatus* (really the fifteenth book of his *Reductorium morale,* which had a separate existence as the *Liber de reductione fabularum et poetarum enigmatum*), or, more probably, the *Libellus de deorum imaginibus,* derived from Bersuire. Wilkins (1957:520) observed that Chaucer could not have known Bersuire directly, though he argues that Petrarch may have used him for *Africa.* Cadbury claims that, whereas "neither Ovid's version nor any other source contains the sympathetic description of the god that characterizes Chaucer's tale" (1964:540), the *Ovidius moralizatus* does contain all the elements that Chaucer employs: the dragon is pictured under the feet of Phoebus, the god has a bow and arrows in his hand, and tribute is made to the god's musical gifts. Cadbury asserts (1964:541), ". . . it is certain that Chaucer knew the work by the time of the House of Fame." That Chaucer probably knew the *Ovidius moralizatus,* or the *Libellus de deorum* derived from it, is also urged by Steadman, who thinks Chaucer used it for *The Knight's Tale* (1959:620-24). Work (in Bryan and Dempster 1941:699-700) surveys the other interpretations and moralizations of the Ovidian material in the late Middle Ages. Hoffman remarks (1966:195), ". . . it is not surprising to find that in the Middle Ages, Ovid's myth was traditionally read, at least on one level, as an exemplum warning against garrulity."

The most obvious parallel that Chaucer almost certainly knew (whether before or after he wrote *The Manciple's Tale*) was Gower's version in the *Confessio Amantis.* Gower's account is far shorter than Chaucer's and differs in many details (Gower has Phoebus slaying Coronis with a sword), but it is not in narrative or detail that we sense the similarity; it is rather that Gower's account begins with "Mi sone," a formula so noticeable in Chaucer's poem and, as we shall see (Explanatory Note to line 318), in much wisdom literature. In Gower it is so striking as perhaps to justify Hazelton's sweeping assertion (1963:22-25) that Chaucer is here parodying Gower. Although it has no bearing upon whether Chaucer was or was not parodying Gower, one is perhaps struck more by the differences between the two stories than by the similarities, except in a very general sense that they are the same plots and derived ultimately from the same original: all references to music are absent from Gower (in Chaucer's tale, as we have noted, music is very prominent indeed: see Harwood 1972:270), and Gower does not blacken the reputation of the "yong kniht" as does Chaucer in his comparison of the wife's "lemman" with the "lewedest wolf," etc. There is a flavor of courtly convention and assumptions in Gower's story that is decidedly absent from *The Manciple's Tale* (Schlauch 1937:210-11).

Harwood (1972:269-70) provides a useful list, for my purposes, of the material of the story that Chaucer does *not* share with any of the various originals and redactions that have been urged by various scholars as the source or sources of *The Manciple's Tale:*

I should like to begin by listing the major differences between the shape of the narrative in the *Manciple's Tale* and in the principal analogues. These differences cannot be accounted for, I think, either by supposing that the meaning of the tale is summed up in a warning against loose talk or by remembering that we have in the narrator someone who calls himself "a boistrous man" (211). In redacting the story, (1) Chaucer adds from Book I of the *Metamorphoses* reference to Phebus' slaying of the murderous Python. (2) While Machaut mentions Phebus' harp, Chaucer devotes six lines to Phebus' "mynstralcie," emphasizing his singing, . . . (3) Chaucer not only elaborates on Phebus as an ideal courtly lover in at least a dozen lines of quite generalized description, (4) he differs from the analogues, which eulogize Coronis, . . . by degrading the nameless "wyf" through an implicit comparison with the earlier object of Phebus' bow, the Python, and with transparent hints of her natural depravity. (5) Coronis' partner, simply a *iuvenis Haemonio* in Ovid . . . , a *damoisiau* in the French analogues . . . , and a "kniht" in Gower . . . , is made a "man of litel reputacioun" (199) . . . . And Coronis' choice of him therefore implies a serious insult to Phebus absent from the analogues. (6) Apparently only in Chaucer's version is Phebus responsible for having taught the bird to speak. (7) Chaucer deprives the bird of such an independent existence as might lie in being itself the recipient of an extended warning . . . or in having such independent motives as the hope of reward, as in the same three analogues. (8) Chaucer omits the "wyf's" pregnancy with Phebus' child, which in Ovid, the *Ovide moralisé,* and Machaut is the evident motive . . . for Phebus' repentance. (9) In Ovid and the *Ovide moralisé,* the remorseful Phebus works . . . to revive the wounded girl; in Machaut . . . he succeeds "par maniere si soutive" that her body regains the appearance of life. . . . Chaucer omits all this. (10) Although in Machaut, once the raven has been turned from white to black, Phebus bids him farewell by saying "Jamais ne ferra que jangler" . . . , the color change is altogether subordinated in the *Manciple's Tale* to the vengeance taken by Phebus upon the bird's voice, a punishment not even mentioned in [the analogues].

In my discussion I have been most concerned with those matters of the story that Chaucer's poem does not share with possible sources or analogues; the similarities have been previously presented and are argued by Work, Stillwell, Cadbury, and others, and will speak for themselves. What needs to be emphasized, as Harwood has done, is that none of the works discussed could possibly have been a "source" for *The Manciple's Tale.* The whole tone of Chaucer's poem is different from the tones of the analogues. Indeed, the most striking similarity to be found (other than the vocative formula that *The Manciple's Tale* shares with Gower's version) is in the overall shape of *The Manciple's Tale* and the stories in the *Ovide* and the *Voir dit,* for in these latter the story is rather rambling, interrupted by moral commentary, as in Chaucer's poem (see Campbell 1972: 140-41). Gower's version, too, begins and ends with the moral, but it is much briefer than Chaucer's and the French versions.

If there is a *source* in any specific sense for Chaucer's poem, it has been lost. It is far more likely, as most now recognize, that *The Manciple's Tale* was in its imaginative conception an amalgam of the Phoebus stories with which Chaucer was familiar, the medieval tradition, in short, an amalgam that probably originated not in Chaucer's returning to any of the stories but in his recalling those details from his reading and listening that suited his own purposes in telling the story. As Shannon remarks (1929:325), the resultant tale is rather more social and human in its import than are the Ovidian versions. Chaucer's not naming Phoebus's wife is not necessarily an inventive stroke; it would not have greatly lessened his effects if he had merely named her in passing, for many of his readers would have recalled her name in any case. Although the anonymity of Phoebus's wife does tend to suggest women in general, most probably Chaucer had forgotten it and did not bother to return to Ovid to rediscover it. Even the most central curiosity, that all Chaucer's predecessors feature a raven or a magpie whereas Chaucer's bird is a crow, would seem to suggest that the story formed itself in Chaucer's mind from bits and pieces and general impressions: perhaps the misremembered name of Phoebus's wife, Coronis (or Cornide in Gower), from which "cornix" suggested itself; or the use by Ovid of the cornix, or crow, warning the raven against disclosing Coronis's infidelity (*Metamorphoses* 2.547-49). The crow appears in this role also in the *Ovide* (Bryan and Dempster 1941:704, lines 2162-2338) and the *Voir dit* (Bryan and Dempster, p. 712, lines 7810-25). Phoebus's musicianship Chaucer had emphasized before (*The House of Fame,* lines 1232 etc.), and it must have seemed only natural to employ it again. He was certainly familiar with the general emblematic representation of Phoebus transmitted by such works as the *Ovidius moralizatus.* But there is finally nothing to indicate clearly that for any part of the tale itself Chaucer ever turned to any particular work anew.

Many sources or analogues have been noted for various passages in the non-narrative parts of *The Manciple's Tale.* The most obvious ones are the passages of the *Roman de la Rose* in which the exempla of the bird, the cat, and the she wolf are found, as well as lines 7037-57 of the *Roman,* in which a passage urging the holding of one's tongue is found; these are printed by Work (in Bryan and Dempster, pp. 720-22) and are found in the Explanatory Notes in the present edition. The exemplum of the bird in the *Tale* (lines 163-74) was, of course, derived by Jean de Meun from Boethius's *Consolatio,* which may have been Chaucer's more immediate remembered "source" here, though Robinson (1957: 764) denies it. Koeppel long ago (1891:44-46) opined that the passages about holding one's tongue might also have been derived from Albertano of Brescia's *De arte loquendi et tacendi,* and Hazelton (1960:376-80) has argued the *glossulae* upon the *Distichs* of Dionysius Cato as a possible source for some of the material against jangling; and, of course, Cato himself is the obvious source for at least two of the passages, as indicated not only by similarity of language but also by acknowledgment in manuscript glosses. Likewise, there is a probability that Chaucer knew this work of Albertano; not only did Chaucer derive his *Melibee* from Albertano's *Liber de consolationis et consilii* (1873), but marginal glosses to *The Manciple's Tale,* lines 335-38, give the exact wording and spelling found in *De arte loquendi et tacendi* for the proverb used (see Explanatory Notes).

Plessow (1929:114) suggests a passage in *The Book of the Knight of la Tour Landry* (Wright 1906:204-205) for parallels for the kind of proverbial wisdom against jangling; there does not seem to be any likelihood of direct knowledge on Chaucer's part, though the vocative formula "my fayre doughters" might be vaguely suggestive.

Mustanoja has proposed (1965:250-54) that a passage in a poem attributed to Abelard, "Carmen ad astralabium filium," might possibly be the original for the advice against telling a husband of his wife's infidelity in the *Tales,* lines 311-13.

And, of course, one must not neglect in this survey the brief passage in *The Manciple's Tale* (lines 147-54) in which Chaucer clearly draws upon one of his favorite works, Jerome's *Epistola adversus Jovinianum,* a debt that in this case is put out of doubt by the Hengwrt gloss.

Hazelton (1960:378) observed that a fairly complete overall model for the whole harangue against jangling in the last part of the *Tale* can be found in a ballade of Deschamps. This poem, entitled by the poet's editor (Raynaud 1893:8, 165-67) simply "Autre Balade, pour sa langue refrener," takes as its text the first verse of Cato's famous *Distich* 1.3: "Virtutem primam esse puto conpescere linguam" ("I think the first virtue is to curb the tongue"). This poem is a good example of the sort of admonitive literature to which *The Manciple's Tale* belongs, and a literature with which Chaucer was certainly familiar. Since the poem is Deschamps's, Chaucer may well have known it. It is true that much of the Manciple's harangue is here, but really parallel wording, except for the famous passages from Cato ("la premiere vertu") and Horace ("Car quant mot est de bouche yssu"—"For where a word has issued from the mouth")—see Explanatory Notes to lines 332, 335—is just not to be found; in addition, the Manciple's harangue seems to have rather more cynicism behind it.

It must appear that the whole *Tale,* in addition to the story within it, is a composite of many remembered things, some from obvious sources that Chaucer and any other educated medieval writer would have known, but more generally absorbed from a tradition of wisdom literature "lerned yonge." The form into which Chaucer casts his work has no real parallel with that of any other work. In even the one work upon which, in the opinion of many (e.g., Hazelton 1963), Chaucer was turning a parodic eye, Gower's version of the Phoebus story, the parallelism is largely limited to the vocative formula "My sone," which tends to make the whole *Confessio Amantis* rather dreary going in spots; and in Chaucer's poem the formulas are all gathered at the end of the poem, whereas in the

Confessio the formula introduces the tale itself. In our present state of knowledge, one can only conclude that *The Manciple's Tale* is in every sense, medieval and modern, an "original" composition.

The Date of The Manciple's Tale

There has been general agreement that *The Manciple's Prologue* is a late production, certainly, by its very nature, at least within the time frame of the composition of *The Canterbury Tales*. The disagreement, however, over the date of *The Manciple's Tale* has been perhaps more extreme than over the date of any other part of *The Canterbury Tales*. Furnivall thought it late, even 1399 (1868: 36). Skeat (1894:5.436) was not emphatic but apparently was, with Tyrwhitt, content to assume it fairly late, considering *The Manciple's Prologue* after *The Cook's Tale* and remarking no difference of date between them. Manly (1926a) has been most preoccupied with the early date of *The Manciple's Tale,* arguing there and in Manly and Rickert (1940:2.449) that the *Tale* must have been quite early because it was a student's piece, full of rhetorical stuffing ill-digested. He wrote (1926a:17-18):

Instead of attempting to realize his characters psychologically and conceive their actions and words as elements of a dramatic situation, he padded the tale with rhetoric. Thus he thrust into it and around it 32 lines of *sententiae,* 36 of *exempla,* 18 of *exclamatio,* 14 of *sermocinatio,* 3 of technical transition, 17 of *demonstratio,* and 63 of *applicatio—* all external and mechanical additions, clever enough as mere writing, but entirely devoid of life. If the tale had been written as a school exercise, to illustrate the manner in which rhetorical padding could be introduced into a narrative framework, the process of composition could not have been more mechanical or the results more distressing.

Manly (1926a) and Plessow (1929:161) also argued that *The Manciple's Tale* was early as evidenced by the heavy dependence upon material from the *Roman* (see Explanatory Notes). Plessow (p. 161) observed that close relationship with the *Roman* argued for an early date for the *Tale,* and since most scholars placed Chaucer's translation of his part of the *Roman* into the English *Romaunt* at earlier than 1380, some even as early as 1370, it followed that a date of no later than 1383 or 1384 seemed about right. Dempster (1932:85-86) concluded that the total absence of dramatic irony from the *Tale* suggested an early date, before Chaucer's powers matured: "He tried to draw from both that source [a fabliau-type story] and the *Metamorphoses,* but was not entirely successful in fusing the elements together or in grasping the story as a whole. Without such grasp no dramatic irony was possible; indeed, no ironic contrast could even suggest itself to the poet's mind" (p. 86).

Lumiansky (1947:562) remarks that, since the Manciple assures us (line 187) that his exempla pertain only to men, not to women, who are above such nature

11

and actions, Chaucer seems to be anticipating the exempla that are *The Legend of Good Women;* a similar brief statement appears in *Troilus and Criseyde* (5.1772-85). This leads Lumiansky to conclude that *The Manciple's Tale* was probably composed before either of these works. Owen (1958:465) generally agrees.

Of specific evidence for the date of *The Manciple's Tale* there is not a great deal. Manly and Rickert, as we shall see in the Textual Commentary, argue for an early date on the basis of manuscript evidence; but this, I urge, is insufficient for such a conclusion and does not support a circular argument. The manuscript evidence is merely that there is a slightly more complex history of transmission for the *Prologue* than for the *Tale.* Manly and Rickert attempted to construct an argument (1940:2.449) that the *Prologue,* "with its involvement of three personae in the action" was, because of its complexity, evidence of artistic maturity, whereas the *Tale* "in matter, in style, and in its indebtedness to the *Roman de la Rose*" was a product of Chaucer's 'prentice period, available to the organizers of the commercial exemplar in a stable text. These arguments are open to question.

We can, perhaps, because of the "titlelees tiraunt" reference (line 223), rule out most of the last year of Chaucer's life, when Henry IV was threatening Richard's throne or had actually usurped it; Chaucer, as his moral balades demonstrate, was no coward, but he would scarcely have risked such a gratuitous offense to the man who might be or indeed already was his king (particularly a man with whom Chaucer had had such close court connections).

The cat exemplum (lines 175-82) with its *milk/silk* rhyme does indeed seem to echo, as Koeppel long ago argued (1891-92:261-62), the bird exemplum in *The Squire's Tale* with the same rhymes (lines 613-14), and if there were a definite date for the latter, we could perhaps be more affirmative about *The Manciple's Tale;* as Robinson notes (1957:717), line 73 of *The Squire's Tale,* ". . . for it is pryme," certainly seems to suggest that that tale was written in the context of *The Canterbury Tales,* i.e., the very late 1380s and the 1390s. If Chaucer's poem is, as Hazelton industriously argues (1963), a parody of Gower's Phoebus story, then *The Manciple's Tale* would seem at least to postdate 1390 (see Gower 1900:1.xxi).

Plessow's arguments about the material in the *Roman* are, of course, irrelevant, except to prove that Chaucer could not have written *The Manciple's Tale* before he knew the *Roman,* which has never been in doubt; so many of his late poems, particularly *The Wife of Bath's Prologue,* quote and echo the *Roman* that this material can be really of no concern in arguing the date of *The Manciple's Tale.* To some extent much of the debate about the date of the poem has been simplistic and circular: if one likes it and considers it "realistic" (so long the key word in appreciation of Chaucer) or "dramatic" (so important a consideration with Manly), then it can be reasonably late; if one does not like it, or considers it overly serious, rhetorical, or didactic, then it must be early. As Payne so well put it (1963:151): "Perhaps the circularity of such argument needs asserting again; we date the poorer tales earlier because they are poorer, and then argue that they are poorer because they were written earlier." The nature of Manly's rhetorical argument has been in general fruitfully attacked by Payne (1963), Murphy (1964), Knight (1973) and others.

It is in fact welcome when a critic dismisses *The Manciple's Tale* as a shoddy or weak performance without being concerned with its date, as did Lawrence (1950:147) and Malone (1951:232). Gardner (1977:294-95) reluctantly comes to admire the poem for reasons that Chaucer might not appreciate:

For sixty-two lines . . . , the Manciple speaks of the importance of not speaking . . . , babbling lines that might serve as a model of art so bad that, finally, it's good. . . . This late, intentionally clumsy poetry has not been much admired until recently. Perhaps it was not much admired in Chaucer's day; we will probably never know. But whatever his friends and patrons may have thought of it, writing such poetry, and chuckling over its awfulness, was one of the pleasures of the poet's peaceful old age.

Since the poem has become more appreciated, whether because it is good or good-bad, and since "rhetorical" has ceased to be a word of abuse, modern criticism has generally assumed a date in the 1390s for it.

There is at least one other approach, however, to a general determination of date, though it is an essentially negative one. I would argue that the structure and tone of *The Manciple's Tale* strongly suggest a date within *The Canterbury Tales* period of, say, 1388 to 1399, and probably somewhat later than earlier. The story in the *Tale,* unlike the stories of *The Legend of Good Women,* is really nothing. As Manly has tabulated at length, the narrative amounts to only a handful of lines (1926:17-18). What is worth noting about the structure of *The Manciple's Tale* is that the narrative simply provides opportunities for the "moral" reflections of the Manciple. These are always cast in argumentative form; the Manciple, as has often been noted, frequently addresses his audience, interrupting his own narrative—much more is interruption than narrative— apologizing, arguing, insinuating. Other than for a developed *Canterbury Tales,* I can imagine no context in or for which *The Manciple's Tale* might have been created. This is not the case for others of the Canterbury pieces that might have had and almost certainly did have in one form or another an earlier existence, such as *The Knight's Tale* and *The Second Nun's Tale.* In none of these and other possibilities is the narrative actually conceived for a secondary audience, i.e., a "dramatic" audience (even such as that assumed by Manly), and an audience such as that provided by the other pilgrims. Although these other works that did have a previous existence, particularly *The Knight's Tale* and *The Second Nun's Tale,* may be provided with associations at the beginnings and ends, the material itself presumes only a primary audience, i.e., the audience (or readers) of Chaucer the poet.

The Manciple's Tale, on the other hand, is a performance in which the primary audience is the witness as the Manciple deals directly with a secondary, fictional audience, the audience of his fellow pilgrims. It is, I would argue, with the possible exception of *The Pardoner's Tale* and *The Wife of Bath's Prologue,* that piece of *The Canterbury Tales* which is the most direct, the most assuming of a fictional secondary audience. It is quite unlike any poem of Chaucer's not among *The Canterbury Tales.* To argue that the story of *The Manciple's Tale* itself was, as Manly urges (1926*b*:257-58), written for a separate, early purpose and merely equipped later with nonnarrative material to make it fit into the context of *The Canterbury Tales* would be to assume that Chaucer would have for some purpose written a tiny narrative poem (a generous estimate is that 106 lines of the 258 may be fairly described as narrative, and even much of that is, as Manly claims [1926*a*:17-18] rhetorical development) and then expanded it to fit. Even such an argument would be forced to acknowledge that much of what was most distressing to Manly was in fact added late, to pad out the story and make it into a respectable member of *The Canterbury Tales.* There is no known context, among Chaucer's surviving work, into which or out of which such a tiny narrative redaction of the Ovidian Phoebus story could have developed. If it is not of *The Canterbury Tales* period, proponents of an earlier date must also provide that context in what we understand of the development of Chaucer's work. The only context that I can imagine that would fit an early date is a totally speculative one: that the original of *The Manciple's Tale* may have been intended for one of the illustrative stories for which *The House of Fame* was to have provided a frame, if, indeed, that was the purpose of *The House of Fame.* Granted that totally unsupported supposition, a tale about jangling would fit in a frame of stories concerned with "tydynges" (Manly long ago suggested such a purpose for *The House of Fame* [1913:73-81]).

About the date of *The Manciple's Prologue,* as we have seen, there has been universal assumption that it is fairly late, obviously from conception a part of *The Canterbury Tales.*

My conclusion from a study of *The Manciple's Prologue* and *Tale* is that, however different their styles, Chaucer composed them fairly close together. I conclude that they are closely linked in theme and character; the stylistic differences between the two are no more than the normal differences between a narrative introduction and exemplary elaboration of a character and point of view, in spite of the acute observations of Speirs (1951:199-200) and Knight (1973: 182), little more difference, in short, than is to be found between the apparently rambling ruminations of the Wife of Bath in her Prologue and the tightly woven tale that she tells, for instance. As we will see, the textual evidence is not of sufficient substance to decide the issue, though it seems to imply that the two pieces were composed at different times (true, one should think, for almost all the tales and links of *The Canterbury Tales*).

Relation to The Canterbury Tales

This is a matter that is easily divided into two separate concerns: the physical relation of *The Manciple's Prologue* and *Tale* to *The Canterbury Tales,* in the order of the tales and in the presumed organization of the pilgrimage itself, and the thematic relation of *The Manciple's Prologue* and *Tale* to the rest of the tales. The former concern will be dealt with first, though, of course, there will be some overlapping between the two concerns.

In the Textual Commentary I discuss the manuscript evidence of the physical relation of *The Manciple's Prologue* and *Tale* to the rest of the tales as a purely textual concern. Furnivall (1868:36-44) disagreed with Bradshaw (Baker 1981: 3-4) that there was any clear evidence that Chaucer intended *The Manciple's Tale* and *The Parson's Tale* for the return journey to London, though he did not discount the possibility. He argued that the evidence of the manuscripts, though not making *The Manciple's Prologue* and *Tale* inseparable from *The Parson's Prologue* and *Tale,* did indicate that *The Manciple's Tale* was a part of the "down journey." As for the *Parson's Tale,* "All that we can say is this: the Parson's Tale was evidently meant by Chaucer as the wind-up of either the down journey or the back one" (p. 38). In spite of Lydgate and others, "We have nowhere any hint of the back journey in his [Chaucer's] Work. . . . I prefer to take the (Parson's) Tale as written for the last of the down journey, but not finally revised by Chaucer to make it fit the time of the foregoing Manciple's Tale, and the short distance from Harbledown to Canterbury" (p. 38). Bradshaw, as cited above, preferred the Manciple to begin the "back journey" and *The Parson's Prologue* to end it before the pilgrims reached Southwark. Ten Brink (1892:2.182) cautiously concluded that *The Manciple's Tale* seemed "more probable" as the first piece for the journey home. Manly gave impressive weight to this argument (1931:615), concluding that *The Manciple's Tale* and *The Parson's Tale* had been attached to one another in such a tentative way by Chaucer for "future convenience." Furnivall had appealed (1868:36) to the evidence of Lydgate's *Story of Thebes,* devised as the first tale of the Canterbury pilgrims' return journey, in support of his view, but as Hammond (1908:317) aptly remarks: "Here, however, we must observe that Lydgate read Chaucer's work so carelessly that in the prologue to the same Story of Thebes he alludes to the quarrel of the Pardoner with the Friar."

As did Manly, Root also (1929:493-96) argued for *The Manciple's Tale* as the first performance of the homeward journey, taking the business of the Host's japing and playing as an indication that the pilgrims had just "started out on the road back to Tabard Inn" (p. 495). "If it is unlikely that a new tale should be called for within a mile of the journey's goal, it is in every way appropriate that the pilgrims should not begin the homeward series of tales until they had begun to settle down to their journey" (p. 496). Root further observed, anticipating

15

Manly's interpretation of the manuscript evidence, that "if the *Manciple's Tale* was intended for the beginning, and the *Parson's* for the conclusion of the home-ward journey, one may venture the guess that this fact explains their juxtaposition in all the manuscripts" (p. 496). One must interpolate here that they are not in fact juxtaposed in all the manuscripts (see Textual Commentary) but that the manuscript evidence in general bears out their close physical relationship. Root argues that this interpretation eliminates the difficulty about "Bobbe-up-and-down." Work, however (1932:62-65), strongly defended the other side of the argument, pointing out that, while either interpretation—that of *The Manciple's Tale* as the penultimate performance of the outward-bound journey or the beginning one of the homeward journey—had its difficulties, *The Parson's Tale* had about it an air of "finality" that suggested Canterbury rather than Southwark, and the pilgrims' "pious agreement 'to enden in som vertuous sentence' suggests an approach to the shrine of St. Thomas rather than to the final carousal at the Tabard" (p. 62). Further, the geographical haziness with which Chaucer records the pilgrims' entrance into a "thropes ende" suggests the distant Canterbury end of the journey rather than any place outside London where the geographical references had been so explicit. He also remarks that it is curious that the two pilgrims chosen for the two homeward-bound tales (if that is the interpretation) should be among the few who have told none of the outward-bound (Owen, of course, 1951, 1958, assumes other homeward-bound tales as well). Work concludes that Chaucer did not live to eliminate the confusing time reference in *The Parson's Prologue* and that this is a relatively minor detail, "whereas the whole schedule of tales, tellers, and distances would be thrown into confusion by the acceptance of the Ten Brink-Root theory" (p. 65).

Tatlock, in one of the seminal articles on the manuscript tradition and structure of *The Canterbury Tales* (1935), evinces suspicion of the return-journey theory and in any case describes the evidence as convincing that Chaucer created, at some point, *The Manciple's Tale* and *The Parson's Tale* as a unit (p. 125). Lawrence (1950) also concludes that there is no real evidence for the return-journey theory and relatively little to deny the two tales as a unit, however it came to be written. Pratt (1951), in his important article on the order of *The Canterbury Tales,* does not wish to become involved in this particular argument, contenting himself with the manuscript and internal evidence for the order of the tales and accepting the H-I fragment relationship without further speculation.

Owen in several articles (particularly 1951 and 1958) and a book (1977) has continued to press for the concept that we have in the surviving *Canterbury Tales* bodies of materials intended for both the outward and the return journeys, which he assumes to have involved five days altogether, and he assigns *The Manciple's Tale* to the first day of the homeward journey, the beginning of the fourth day, as he describes it. His argument essentially restates, with aesthetic support, the arguments of Ten Brink-Root and Manly.

16

Criticism since about 1950, with the notable exception of Owen, has tended to concede the present relationship of *The Manciple's Tale* to *The Parson's Tale* as what Chaucer intended, or, if not what he finally intended, then what he left, and that we must deal with the relationship as it stands.

Indeed, as we shall see, more recent criticism has been very happy with the juxtaposition of the two tales. Shumaker (1953) finds a parallel between the relation of *The Manciple's Prologue* to *The Manciple's Tale* and the relationship of *The Parson's Prologue* to *The Parson's Tale,* and a parallel between this parallelism and the relationship of *The Canterbury Tales* as a whole to Chaucer's *Retraction.* The Manciple's jangling in his *Prologue,* Shumaker argues (p. 152), makes *The Manciple's Tale* an ironic retraction, and Chaucer was aware of the implications of this for himself as narrator of *The Canterbury Tales.* Ruggiers (1965:247) observes that "attention to the ugly and the cruel has great value here as the last emphasis in the links upon human folly and recalcitrance before the sober tone of the Parson's 'merry' tale on repentance, vice and virtue." Whittock (1968) remarks upon the deliberate contrast intended between *The Manciple's Tale* and *The Parson's Tale,* and Harwood (1972) argues that *The Manciple's Tale* is a "curtain-raiser—a kind of satyr play—before the Parson leads the pilgrims from 'ernest' into a 'game' that is other than the sleep of fools." Howard (1976) makes the *Manciple-Parson* link the cornerstone of his interpretation of *The Canterbury Tales:* it is anticipatory to the Retraction and draws together the principal themes of *The Canterbury Tales.*

Relation Between The Manciple's Prologue *and* The Manciple's Tale

Just as there has been considerable disagreement among scholars and critics about the relationship between *The Manciple's Tale* and *The Parson's Tale* and *The Canterbury Tales* as a whole, so the relationship between *The Manciple's Prologue* and the *Tale* has been the subject of much discussion. As will be seen in the course of the Textual Commentary, Manly (Manly and Rickert 1940:2.449) flatly refused to believe that *The Manciple's Prologue* and the *Tale* had any intrinsic relationship; the *Tale* was much older, and was refurbished a bit in the later stages of the creation of *The Canterbury Tales,* and the *Prologue,* written in Chaucer's later style of "lively realism," was written as an introduction. I will observe that, apparently influenced by this aesthetic prejudgment, Manly and Rickert found evidence of manuscript affiliation to support the earlier date of the *Tale,* to go along with its rhetorical padding and bits and pieces of the *Roman,* a judgment that I question on the basis of the evidence presented. Manly's was the general view for quite some time, as is reflected in the comments of Lawrence (1950) and Malone (1951) and in the careful, perceptive criticism of Speirs (1951), who remarks upon the contrast between the "vividest of the comic dra-

matic interludes" (p. 199) and the *Tale,* which "exhibits a formal, almost man-
nered, wit; it is occasionally as if [Chaucer] were nearly anticipating the kind of
sophistication his couplet verse was to undergo at the end of the seventeenth
century" (p. 199).

More recent criticism has been, by and large, content with the joining of
Prologue to *Tale,* seeing, in one way or another, a close connection between the
two. Rejecting Hulbert's view (1948) that the *Tale* is, because of its Greek set-
ting, the rather learned rhetorical development, and the moral disquisition, "com-
pletely incongruous with the dishonest Manciple" (p. 576), Severs argues (1952:
11):

> A tale enforcing such a lesson, a tale exalting expediency rather than morality, seems
> to me altogether appropriate to the Manciple. From both the General Prologue and the
> Prologue to his own tale, we learn that the Manciple is cunningly dishonest in his pur-
> chasing and in his accounts: though he is but an ignorant man, his wit enables him to
> deceive and defraud a heap of learned men in the temple where he is employed. Would
> not such a cunning, practical, successful rascal be the very sort of man to tell a tale stress-
> ing that virtue is no guarantee of worldly comfort and that one should act not according
> to what is good and just, but according to what is practical and profitable?

He further agrees with Schlauch (1948) that the *Tale* implies a condemnation of
courtly love and that "it is an attitude which one would expect from the 'boystous,'
'lewed' Manciple, who has no respect for mere rank in itself" (p. 5).

Shumaker (1953) sees in the relation of *The Manciple's Prologue* and the *Tale*
"fictive demonstration and explication" (p. 152), a view that, though often couched
in quite different terms, has dominated commentary on the problem since, par-
ticularly in the essays of Cadbury (1964), Coghill (1966), Harwood (1972), and
Scattergood (1974). The *Tale* is seen as a demonstration and development of or
contrast with the *Prologue* and its principal themes, particularly "rakelnesse" and
the danger of a loose tongue, and the power of language to divide or unite. Birney
(1960) argues for a consistency of character in the Manciple, the ironically "gen-
til" man, between the *Prologue* and the *Tale.* Elliott (1954) and Donner (1955)
both argue for the *Tale* as in part a development of the Manciple's fears of the
possible revenge of the Cook upon him; the *Tale* is a sermon against jangling,
an evil habit in which the Manciple has indulged to his subsequent dismay, and
the Manciple's fable of the crow and its moral is intended to suggest to the
Cook (who may be tempted to jangle about the Manciple) the dangers of such
behavior. Both see the Manciple's subsequent story as a sort of mea culpa. Spec-
tor (1957) does not dismiss the relationship suggested between *The Manciple's
Tale* and the Cook but suggests that the moral passages of *The Manciple's Tale*
may also be a response to *The Canon's Yeoman's Tale,* which in most manuscripts
and all modern editions immediately precedes fragment H *(The Manciple's Pro-
logue and Tale),* parodying the Canon's Yeoman's insistence that he is not learned;

18

Spector also suggests (p. 26) that, in view of the Host's encouragement of the Canon's Yeoman to betray the Canon, the Manciple's advice to keep quiet is directed at that worthy and is, indirectly, a slap at the Host himself for having upbraided the Manciple in *The Manciple's Prologue.* Zacher (1976:121) and Burlin (1977:243) also assume a close thematic link between *The Manciple's Tale* and *The Parson's Tale.*

By no means, however, is the satisfaction with the relationship of *The Manciple's Prologue* and *Tale* universal. Knight, at the end of a long and perceptive analysis (1973), concluded that, whatever the merits of the two separately, their styles tended to draw them apart. The convictions of Manly are powerfully on record, and Fisher has (1977:337-38) published his opinion that the contrast in styles and matter of *Prologue* and *Tale* suggest that the *Prologue* was a late addition to a tale written earlier.

Inevitably this general question must be touched upon in the broader survey of criticism dealing purely with the art, or lack of it, in *The Manciple's Prologue* and *Tale,* but it seemed useful to outline here the tradition of reaction to the joining of the two.

Survey of Criticism

I have observed in the preceding sections that in modern times criticism of *The Manciple's Prologue* and *Tale* (as a unit) has come to be much more generally appreciative than it was in the first half of this century. The *Prologue* has always had its share of admirers, but until the last thirty years it was possible for anyone who wished to write about the *Tale* to begin his article with the observation that little had been written upon it, and that little rather unappreciative. It is true that not much had been written upon it, for apparently it had little appeal to the eighteenth-century reader and the moralistic critics of the nineteenth, the latter rather surprising. But it had not been entirely ignored; a brief but appreciative statement by Tyrwhitt is worth noting: "[Chaucer's] skill in new dressing an old story was never, perhaps, more successfully exerted" (1798:1.111). Considering that Chaucer's art lay to a considerable extent in new-dressing old stories, this is praise indeed from no mean source. The first important discussion, though brief, that takes up the problems of *The Manciple's Tale* was that of Wordsworth, who, in a letter to Dora Wordsworth of 1840, expressed a view of the morality of the *Tale* that could with profit be consulted today by many who have written upon morality and *The Manciple's Tale:*

Tell Mr. Quillinan, I think he has taken a rather narrow view of the spirit of the Manciple's Tale, especially as concerns its *morality.* The formal prosing at the end and the selfishness that pervades it flows from the genius of Chaucer, mainly as characteristic of the narrator whom he describes in the [General] Prologue as eminent for shrewdness and clever worldly Prudence. The main lesson, and the most important one, is inculcated as a Poet ought chiefly to inculcate his lessons, not formally, but by implication; as when Phoebus in a transport of passion slays a wife whom he loved so dearly. How could the mischief of telling truth, merely, because it *is* truth, be more feelingly exemplified? The Manciple himself is not, in his understanding, conscious of this; but his heart dictates what was natural to be felt and the moral, without being intended, forces itself more or less upon every Reader. Then how vividly is impressed the mischief of jealous vigilance, and how truly and touchingly in contrast with the world's judgements are the transgressions of a woman in a low rank of life and one in high estate placed on the same level, treated.

Wordsworth's modernization of *The Manciple's Tale,* incidentally, was never published by him because of his concern for the sensitivity of friends (Wordsworth 1958:4, App. B, p. 472).

Ten Brink at the end of the century found *The Manciple's Tale* genially attractive: "The Manciple's Tale takes us back to the old mythology. It treats in a very clever way a subject which has been frequently dealt with since the Metamorphoses of Ovid. . . . In the Manciple's discourse we see a talent for brisk narrative . . . united with a strong moralizing vein" (1892:2, pt. 1, p. 181).

Tupper, in two essays (1914 and 1915), made the Manciple one of his principal illustrations in a double theme: that *The Canterbury Tales* constituted, among other things, an exemplification of the seven deadly sins and, in addition, a running commentary upon the kinds of quarrels in which the pilgrims involved themselves. Upon the first theme, Tupper argues (1914:102-103):

The Manciple's Tale, which, as Gower's use of the theme attests, is so well designed to illustrate the Chiding phrase of Wrath, is supplemented quite in the *exemplum* manner ("Lordinges, by this ensample I you preye"), by a long "morality" against Chiding (H 300-362). For this Chaucer is indebted not only to Albertano of Brescia's treatise, *De Arte Loquendi et Tacendi,* but to his own Parson's sermon, in its section upon Wrath (I, 647 f.). That Chaucer's purpose in both tale and morality is the same as Gower's is, moreover, established by the close resemblance between his "application" and that of his friend (*Confessio,* III, 831-835). . . . Significantly enough, both Chaucer and Gower deem Chiding one of the divisions of Wrath, whereas in many medieval catalogues of the Sins, this fault is classed apart from the Deadly Seven as a Sin of the Tongue. Chaucer, however, seems to have recognized the claim of Chiding to especial treatment, since he had already illustrated the general theme of Wrath in his Friar-Summoner tales.

In the second essay Tupper remarks upon the economic basis of the Cook-Manciple encounter (1915:264-65):

We have seen that a Manciple chiding a Cook fulfills the conditions of contemporary trade-relations. And the purchaser assails the enemy of his class with the weapon of an ancient tradition. Indeed class-satire may be said to have its beginnings in an attack upon the Cook, for he is certainly the oldest of all social types in comedy. Between the Friar-Summoner and the Cook-Manciple quarrels lies this great difference. In the case of the first, the churchmen's tales are as brimful of class rivalry as their prologues; in the case of the second the quarrel is healed before the Manciple begins his story; hence there can be no place for a professional feud. The narrator concerns himself therefore with the two other motives that divide with class-satire the dominance of the Canterbury collection, the Deadly Sins and the woman-question. . . . Very sharply defined is the contrast between the Manciple's own chiding tongue that riots among the very epithets forbidden a chider of drunkenness by the Parson (I, 623 f.) and the rebuke to wicked speech implicit in his tale of Phoebus and the Crow. . . . Moreover, the inevitable theme of the relation of the sexes finds large illustration both in the story of cuckoldry and in the labored analysis of a futile and fatal jealousy (H 145-195). In the deliberate treatment of these two absorbing problems, the preliminary quarrel is quite forgotten.

Lowes (1915) responded to Tupper's first article on *The Canterbury Tales* and the seven deadly sins by stoutly denying any such kind of allegorical intention in the tales. For *The Manciple's Prologue* and *Tale* he particularly argued that Tupper had got his terms wrong and that "Cheste" of "Chiding" is not in question at all. In both Gower and Chaucer, he argued, it means "dispute" or "quarrel." "When Mr. Tupper states . . . that the Manciple concludes his tale of Chiding by a copious use of the Parson's words 'against that fault' (p. 116), he is running counter to the facts" (Lowes 1915:333).

We have already seen a good deal of Manly's commentary on the rhetorical structure of *The Manciple's Tale* (1926a); a briefer and more pointed dismissal of the *Tale* is found in another work published by Manly in the same year (1926b: 258-59):

Of the thinly drawn figures the Manciple is perhaps, after the Second Nun, the thinnest. He is not an individual; he is not even a well-drawn, rounded type; he is merely a stalking horse from behind which Chaucer shoots a playful arrow at his learned masters of the Temple—capable of managing great estates but not wise enough to defeat the low cunning of their servant. The tale he tells is not appropriate to him and is indeed a very early chip from Chaucer's workshop, hewn off when he was still struggling to master the rhetorical principles and practices of Matthieu de Vendome and Geoffroi de Vinsauf. The only time the Manciple exhibits any trait of humanity—in any sense of the term— is when he offers a drink from his gourd to the quarrelsome Cook.

Manly's cold dismissal of *The Manciple's Tale* seemed to dominate consideration of it for at least twenty-five years. In his students' edition of *The Canterbury Tales* of 1938, Manly included *The Manciple's Prologue* but omitted *The Manciple's Tale* because of its lack of interest (Donaldson in his edition of 1958 also omitted the *Tale* but without saying why).

Plessow (1929), in his careful assemblage of material to shed light on *The Manciple's Tale*, nevertheless does not reveal any particular appreciation of this minor work of Chaucer's. He is content to analyze the rhetorical structure of the *Tale* and to conclude, with Manly, that it must have been one of Chaucer's earlier pieces, stuffed with rhetoric and bits and pieces of the *Roman* (1929:159, 161).

As we have seen, Dempster (1932:85-86) analyzes the *Tale* for evidence of dramatic irony and finds none, in spite of the plethora of possibilities.

Lawrence (1950) and Malone (1951) are inclined to dismiss the *Tale.* Lawrence remarks (1950:147):

The *Manciple's Tale* is usually considered one of the least important in the whole work. It is short, conventional, and in no way especially appropriate to a thieving steward. It has sometimes been thought that it was written early; this conjecture may be true, but, of course, Chaucer may have done inferior and routine-like writing in his latest years. Possibly he had this story in his desk and utilized it at this point. Had he composed it especially for the Manciple, he would probably have made it suggest more clearly the marked characteristics of that worthy. But whatever is lacking in the tale itself is more than compensated for in its prologue.

Malone likewise concludes (1951:232):

The tales given to the manciple and the physician both have a vague appropriateness, but hardly more. The cunning manciple tells a story dealing with duplicity, and the learned physician draws from learned sources. But if the manciple had told the physician's tale one could still say that he told a story dealing with duplicity, and if the physician had told the manciple's tale one could still speak of his tale as more or less learned in character. One can find no compelling reason for the assignments to these two pilgrims of the particular tales they told.

Ussery (1971:130-34) in fact goes to some lengths to argue quite soberly against Malone's assertion that the Manciple and the Physician could have interchanged their tales with no one being the wiser. Ussery analyzes the differences in morality, rhetoric, and diction. He concludes that *The Manciple's Tale* is essentially a fabliau of a low moral tone, more suited to the character of the Manciple than to that of the Physician; its rhetoric is one of the low style, except for parody, again more suitable to the character of the Manciple than to that of the Physician: and the diction of the *Tale* is distinctly low, again more suitable to the Manciple. But Ussery appreciates the quality of the *Tale,* observing that its art is finished and effective.

Speirs, whose book (1951) introduced the fashionable "close reading" to the text of Chaucer, observed (p. 199):

The *Manciple's Prologue* and *Tale* are the last verse pieces in the MSS., but remain without any connections with any other tale or prologue. The episode of the drunken Cook who falls in the mire . . . is one of the vividest of the comic dramatic interludes. The realism is again close to that of the popular sermons on the Seven Deadly Sins; but the tone, as the episode concludes—the Cook being given another drink to humour him— is very different.

Speirs remarks approvingly upon the "formal, almost mannered wit" of *The Man-*

ciple's Tale (p. 199) and concludes by commenting, "We cannot say that the work of La Fontaine is more sophisticated" (p. 200). Speirs in his few but pointed comments seems to gather up the older, historical scholarship represented by the Tupper-Lowes argument with a newer interest in Chaucer's variety of styles.

And a very good critic indeed, returning to the quarrel about Chaucer's use of rhetoric, is dismissive of *The Manciple's Tale*. Everett (1950:172) observes:

It is a descent from [the Pardoner's] tale to the Manciple's. Yet, in its method, the *Manciple's Tale* resembles the Pardoner's, and even more closely the Nun's Priest's, and I doubt whether it is any more dependent for its form on rhetorical devices than they are. When, therefore, it is condemned as being over-rhetorical, it would seem to be condemned for the wrong reason. The real difference between it and the other two tales is that, in it, Chaucer appears to have been interested in rhetorical devices only for their own sake; there is no motive for the amplification of the story of Phoebus and the crow.

Everett had earlier (p. 158) drawn attention to the difficulty of rhetorical analysis, remarking that what Naunin labels *repetitio* in lines 318ff. Plessow calls a *conduplicatio,* and in fact Geoffrey de Vinsauf's definition of either term would cover it.

A good barometer of the critical atmosphere of the past thirty years is provided by the distinguished scholar Coghill. In his *The Poet Chaucer* of 1949, a little book enormously influential among students who are taking up the study of Chaucer and for whom the book was intended, he remarked (pp. 127-28) that he was not dealing with the tales of the Physician, Manciple and Parson: ". . . the Parson because his tale is in prose, the Physician and Manciple because I see no qualities in their tales that are not better exemplified in others, sardonic as is the last named." In the second edition, published in 1967, this paragraph is omitted, and *The Manciple's Tale* is treated at some length, though largely in summary, but with a very appreciative remark on the last sixty lines, which are "a wonderful reiteration of the . . . moral, phrased in the elaborate and forceful figure of rhetoric, known as conduplicatio" (p. 130). Coghill's revised estimate of *The Manciple's Tale* is most apparent when it serves as the cumulative illustration in his essay "Chaucer's Narrative Art," contributed to the collection *Chaucer and Chaucerians,* edited by D. S. Brewer (1966). Coghill assesses the *Tale* thus: "This little masterpiece seems to issue from Chaucer's most sardonic maturity" (p. 136).

It is scarcely an exaggeration to say that nearly everything written about *The Manciple's Tale* from the 1950s onward has been generally favorable (see Hussey 1971:14 for an exception, harking back to Manly, and also Gardner 1977: 294-95). It should be interesting to trace how the *Tale* has progressed from being, as Manly told his audience, "so insignificant and so little read that I cannot even assume that all of you recall the plot (1926*a*:16) to "this little masterpiece."

Apart from the aesthetic value of *The Manciple's Tale* itself, one generalization is, I think, quite sound: the *Tale* suffered particularly in the early part of the twentieth century from comparison with its *Prologue;* this is seen clearly in the controversy about the relative dates of the two pieces. *The Manciple's Prologue* was just the sort of Chaucer that was everywhere appreciated and deemed "lively" and "mature," that is, the sort of work that Chaucer wrote as he became like us. Rhetoric was regarded as just mechanical padding and was more or less ignored when in the service of lively realism, as in *The Wife of Bath's Prologue,* but felt to weigh heavily when it was so clearly isolated as in the structure and development of *The Manciple's Tale* (see Gradon 1971:273-331 for a good, broad discussion of medieval "realism"). Further, the *Tale,* with its moralizing, was unappreciated in an age that found nothing to admire in *The Tale of Melibee* or in *The Man of Law's Tale.* In fact, the moralizing repelled many commentators.

The years since the early 1950s have seen a rediscovery of the moral Chaucer so appreciated, apparently, by the fifteenth- and sixteenth-century reader, with criticism given a new focus by the Robertsonian "school" of analysis, and the same period has seen a new study of the traditions of medieval rhetoric (see Murphy 1964 and Knight 1973), a study that, one must say with all due respect to such a great scholar as Manly, is far more sophisticated and sensitive than was his brief essay. Both developments have caused the elevation of *The Manciple's Tale* in critical esteem. Furthermore, as Brewer has remarked (1966, Foreword), *The Manciple's Tale* in particular has benefited from that sharper attention to language and style which has generally marked modern Chaucer criticism. The new emphasis upon style, given such a boost by Muscatine's seminal book of 1957 (though Muscatine's own comments on *The Manciple's Tale* are few), and the sharper attention to language of which Brewer speaks are not only evidence of a closer attention to style and language in medieval literature but also part of a closer attention to style and language generally, in which structuralist and other interests have played an important part. In fact, as we shall see, the most recent criticisms of the *Tale* have focused upon it as a statement *about* language.

Even if not all scholars today are willing to grant that it is a "little masterpiece" and if that praise seems a little strained, *The Manciple's Tale* is no longer relegated to the shavings heap under Chaucer's workbench. It is studied seriously as an important part of *The Canterbury Tales,* however complete or incomplete the scholar may regard the larger work, and it is seen as a subtle and effective use of rhetorical structure and ornament. One must observe, however, that much of the appreciation shown the *Tale* in recent times is based upon the assumption that it is not, cannot be what it is presented as being, a moral tale told against jangling derived from a bit of Ovidian mythology. Much recent criticism has concerned itself with seeing the *Tale* as a parody of other things, a joke upon the Manciple himself, a joke upon the other pilgrims, and finally a joke upon us.

Future scholarship and criticism for a very long time to come must begin with Severs's thorough and sane analysis (1952). Severs focuses his attention on Chaucer's sources, upon the way in which he uses his material, and upon the suitability of the result to the character of the Maniciple as it is described in *The General Prologue* and revealed in his own *Prologue.* Severs recognizes that we do not know exactly what "source," if any, Chaucer used for the *Tale* and proceeds to analyze the important differences between Chaucer's poem and the various ana logues. He thinks that Chaucer is much closer to the French versions—the *Ovide moralisé* and Machaut's *Le Livre du voir dit*—than to Ovid, or to the English analogues, *The Seven Sages of Rome* and the *Confessio Amantis,* but that it is no simple manipulation of any of them. He emphasizes the extremely negative attitude toward Phoebus's wife in Chaucer's poem as opposed to the way in which she is presented in other versions; in Chaucer she is given no name, nor is she described, and there is no pleasant mist of courtly love thrown over her affair with her unworthy lover as there is, for instance, in Gower. Too, the most redeeming feature of Phoebus's wife in Ovid and in the French versions—her death while giving birth to Phoebus's child—is omitted by Chaucer. In *The Maniciple's Tale* the sympathy is for Phoebus, with what Severs calls a secondary sympathy for the crow. Severs sees two parts to the poem: the tale itself, which he takes to have the implied moral against rash action, and the Maniciple's interpretative sermon, which preaches against jangling and talebearing, even though it be of the truth. Severs explains the apparent contradiction in moral by arguing that the Maniciple changes the basis of his own judgment from morality to expediency: "Up to line 307 his attitude has been based upon judgements of right and wrong; after line 307, it is based upon judgements of wise and foolish" (p. 10). That is, the wife deserves to suffer, the crow is loyal and truthful, and all that, but the practical results of the crow's action are very unfortunate.

To Severs this switch of moral is very appropriate to the Maniciple: he is not a learned man, but he is enormously practical. The story is short, quite suitable to his purpose as an exemplum against overmuch jangling, aimed likely at the Cook, whom he had angered and who, if aroused sufficiently and sober enough to be coherent, could repay the Maniciple's "boisterousness" by telling the pilgrims of the Maniciple's graft in supplying the scholars for whom he worked. Severs concludes (pp. 10-11):

I believe that Chaucer planned the shift [of the moral] and that he intended the two parts of the poem to form an artistically consistent unit. I believe, too, that the whole constitutes a dramatically appropriate utterance of the Maniciple—indeed, that its artistry becomes fully comprehensible only when we consider it in its peculiar appropriateness to the Maniciple. A tale enforcing such a lesson, a tale exalting expediency rather than morality, seems to me altogether appropriate to the Maniciple.

Severs argues that we should not expect the brilliant characterization and depth of *The Miller's Tale* in what is essentially an exemplum, drawn in black and white rather than in full color. But he concludes that the fragment is quite effective and coherent and that it should be judged upon its own considerable merits.

25

Shumaker (1953) interprets the moral of the *Tale* as a warning not only against jangling but against loose speaking generally and sees this advice as taken seriously by Chaucer himself, for it is followed by *The Parson's Prologue* and *Tale* and the *Retraction.* Shumaker does not believe that the Manciple's moral is either ironic or superficial. It is picked up, he thinks, by the Parson's words to the Host: "Thou getest fable noon ytoold for me" (*The Parson's Prologue,* line 31). Shumaker therefore sees fragments H and I as a unit, together with the *Retraction,* and generally in the spirit of the latter. Of course, in Shumaker's view, *The Manciple's Tale* is a perfect contrast to its *Prologue,* for in the latter the Manciple is unable to control his own loose talking, and in this Shumaker thinks that Chaucer the poet was aware of his own situation (p. 152):

The Manciple knew perfectly well his ethical responsibility to guard his tongue; nevertheless he was unable, as Chaucer now also felt himself to have been unable, to inhibit sufficiently an instinctive drive to verbalize his perceptions. . . . the fifth element, the *Manciple's Prologue,* can be brought into organic relation with the other four elements of Fragments IX and X [H and I] and the Canterbury group made round and complete. The *Manciple's Tale* is an excellent preparation for the *Parson's Prologue,* and the *Manciple's Prologue* dramatically illustrative of the *Manciple's Tale.* The *Parson's Prologue,* in turn, is excellent preparation for the *Parson's Tale,* and the *Retraction* a fitting conclusion for all four. There is a clear continuity of theme: fictive demonstration and explication in the *Manciple's Prologue* and *Tale,* action in accordance with the established principle in the *Parson's Prologue* and *Tale,* and finally, in the *Retraction,* an announcement that the author is willing to sustain his moral thesis unconditionally, outside the limits of his aesthetic structure. All the parts of Fragments IX and X [H and I] cooperate to say, "I have written too much, and unwisely, and I confess my fault before God and men."

Brewer (1953:175-76): is less appreciative:

The story seems not to have caught fire in Chaucer's imagination, and its treatment is somewhat mechanical. Its main interest lies in yet further comments on the inexhaustible theme of truth in love, spoken with a directness unusual in Chaucer. The Manciple says he is a man of plain speech . . . , and that there is no difference between an unfaithful wife of high degree, and one who is poor . . . . This is unassailable truth, even if not quite the whole truth, and Chaucer, who never approves of adultery or promiscuity, may be taken to have agreed with his mouthpiece. It is a statement sufficiently forthright to command our respect for the author who lived in the loose and amorous court of Richard II. . . . There is some energy in these denunciations, though they are not connected very satisfactorily with the plot. The tale ends with fifty repetitious lines on the wisdom of a still tongue, which, though relevant to the plot, are hardly poetry.

Elliott (1954:513) has a pointed observation on a much-discussed theme, the relation of *The Manciple's Tale* to *The Manciple's Prologue* and to the dramatic situation:

This exemplum is a warning to the Cook not to tell what he knows of the Manciple's dealings. But the Manciple realizes that the intoxicated Cook is in no condition to interpret the fable for himself so he adds a moral which is one fourth as long as his story. The long, repetitious moralizing is a puzzling bit of writing until it is understood as directed toward the inebriated Cook. . . . The "Tale" is ideally suited to the Manciple, and the "Prologue" and "Tale" are so closely connected that either would seem incomplete without the other.

Lumiansky (1955:239-49) replies to the argument of Hulbert (1948:576) that the setting of the tale is unsuitable to the unlearned Manciple with its "learned" quotations and its "classical" material:

The "Greek setting" of the tale is almost nonexistent. . . . Certainly the Manciple is a suitable teller for a story of cuckolding. Furthermore, the digressive comment on the folly of jealously guarding wives, on the perversity of both animal and human natural desires, on the necessity for plain speech, and on the danger of talking too much does more to mar the rhetorical development of the narrative than to give it a learned air. In fact, the Manciple's learning . . . is easily explained by his steady association with lawyers, as is his glib familiarity with the phrase "noght textueel." . . . A man shrewd enough to keep his financial dealings hidden from more than thirty lawyers could easily pick up such matters as these without any studying at all. . . . At other points in the tale we find touches perfectly suited to the "lewed" Manciple.

Donner (1955:245-49) has a brief but useful note remarking certain themes that, he argues, indicate a fairly close connection between *The Manciple's Tale* and *The Manciple's Prologue,* particularly the concern with lewd speech that moves the Host to cancel his request for another (?) tale from the Cook and the Manciple's sensitiveness to lewd speech in his *Tale* that follows. This sort of thing, Donner observes, is similar to linking themes and allusions that are found between other prologues and tales.

The relation of teller to tale has also occupied Birney (1963), who sees *The Manciple's Tale* as a perfect illustration of the lewd, selfish, shifty nature of the Manciple. Birney draws an interesting parallel between the Manciple and his performance and the Pardoner and his. The Manciple, as Birney observes, crudely abuses the Cook in a display of jangling and then, after contemptuously making amends, delivers a sermon against jangling. Just such a contradiction between the Pardoner's performance in his *Prologue* and his *Tale* is found. Further (Birney 1963:261):

There is irony within irony here, for Chaucer is not only highlighting the Manciple's rascality by pretending, through his Pilgrim double, to admire it; he is also presenting a figure who fancies himself to be an ironist, albeit a crude and mocking one. For who other than the Manciple could have revealed his dishonesty, since he remains undetected by his victims? It is *his* voice and *his* sardonic phrasing we hear in the *General*

Prologue, echoed by Pilgrim Chaucer's. . . . we can hear, behind the amused pretence of wonder and approval by Chaucer, the irrepressible savoring of his own slyness by the talkative Manciple.

Of the effect of *The Manciple's Tale,* Birney remarks (pp. 264, 265): "It has . . . all the earmarks of an unsuccessful attempt at a 'gentil' tale by a fundamentally 'lewd' man" and ". . . the morals extracted from it are oily with the sort of worldly wisdom and utterly selfish expediency we find in the Manciple."

A very extensive and ambitious essay urging an essentially negative appreciation of the *Tale* was written by Hazelton (1963), who developed at length suggestions that he had earlier made (1960) and argued that the *Tale* is from beginning to end a parody on several levels. He says (1963:1-5):

> The *Manciple's Tale,* one of Chaucer's most subtly wrought parodic poems, has been little appreciated by the commentators, chiefly because they have failed to recognize its parody and have consequently misread the poem.
> Like all parodic art, Chaucer's can be understood only in the context of its "sources." . . . The tale the Manciple tells is firmly established in the tradition of the moral fable. . . . In each of these versions [the *Ovide,* the *Voir dit,* the *Confessio*] is found a medievalized account of Ovid's fable, . . . and attached to each, as preface or a pendant, is a harangue on the evils of a loose tongue. . . .
> So, superficially, is Chaucer's version. But Chaucer seems to have noted what escaped all the moralizers; namely, that this "moral" fable creates more problems than it solves. The fact that the well-meaning truth-teller is often rewarded with punishment rather than praise lends itself to paradoxical or ironic statement, but it is not a secure ground on which to build a serious moral argument for the wisdom of holding one's tongue. On the other hand, the moral issues raised by the sexual betrayal and the murder in the tale are completely ignored by the moralizers. To a critical intelligence like Chaucer's the mindless moralizing of the *Ovide moralisé* and the mechanical purveying of clichés by its imitators were evidently all too obvious.

In short, Chaucer, says Hazelton, has created a poem that is both mock romance and mock moral. In the stripping off of the romantic elements found in the French analogues, in the eliminating from the character of Phoebus all but elements that leave him open to ridicule, Chaucer has created a burlesque of romance in something of the vein of *The Tale of Sir Thopas.* For instance, Chaucer tells of the slaying of the serpent Phitoun but emphasizes that the serpent was asleep. Phoebus's long suit is the bow and arrow—hardly the weapons of a knight (here a parallel with *Sir Thopas*). The moral is a mock moral, too, as Chaucer parodies Gower's sententiousness and the whole literature of *sententiae.* The mélange of styles, the explosion of rhetorical devices, the burlesque all contribute to a practical joke on the pilgrims. And, in conclusion, Hazelton does not stop far short of identifying Chaucer the narrator with the Manciple, who, like him, was an intelligent man forced to serve masters rather less intelligent. Hazelton's account is complex, and a brief summary cannot do justice to it, but it appears to me generally unconvincing. That there are parodic elements in *The Manciple's Tale* is obvious (particularly the parody of sententiousness in Gower, if the chronology is right), but to conclude that Phoebus, because he is armed with his traditional bow and arrows is being ridiculed, that Chaucer expected his readers and us to recall Phoebus's less heroic exploits in connection with this particular story seems overly subtle. The reader is referred to the acute criticisms of Hazelton's essay in Knight (1973:163-64) and in the pertinent passages discussed in the Explanatory Notes.

Cadbury (1964) reminds us that particularly in *The Manciple's Tale* it is important for the reader to keep the teller and his nature in mind. Some tales, he argues (p. 538), like *The Knight's Tale* and *The Parson's Tale,* "simply support their tellers by reflecting what we would expect of their characters; but others establish an active tension between character of teller and 'character' of tale, an opposition which can only be resolved by an understanding including both." In *The Manciple's Tale* he finds just such a tension. This allows, he thinks, the "apparent discrepancy in pregeneric forms among the different aspects of the whole tale" (p. 538). These discrepancies create in part the irony on many levels that characterizes the tale. He emphasizes among the pregeneric forms the importance of Ovid and of the English *Seven Sages of Rome* to the *Tale.* The antifeminist tone of the *Seven Sages* and its sympathetic treatment of the bird, together with its contemptuous treatment of the young lover, make it a more useful parallel with Chaucer's poem than has been realized, Cadbury argues. He agrees with Stillwell (1940) that Chaucer's expansive moral is, however, more akin to those of the French poems than to Ovid. In his interpretation of the poem Cadbury writes that the moral actually contradicts the implication of the fable. The Manciple is, he feels, mocking the pilgrims (and us) for taking the story so seriously. For the Manciple, expediency is all, and, although he can tell a tale with serious implications, when all is done, nothing matters but the practical and expedient. Cadbury is unhappy with the switch from the romantic moral against constraining one's wife, against rash action, etc., to the simple moral against jangling. He sees the crow as a loyal creature who does not deserve his fate. Therefore, the Manciple (and certainly Chaucer) cannot really be serious in proposing such a simple and ruthless interpretation. He writes (pp. 547-48):

. . . we know that Chaucer, not the Manciple, is really telling the story, moral and all, and with the distance gained by this knowledge we see that the Manciple's moral redounds upon him. . . . We know that the ethical problem is not absurd or simple, and that Phoebus, in killing his wife and in his subsequent self-laceration, is the victim of two very natural and very human impulses, "rakel" though they be. In the same way, the affectionate crow, who cannot restrain his indignation despite the highly predictable consequences, acts as any of us might be forced to act. The last irony, then, is that the conviction carried by the story itself discredits the rule of expediency by which the Manciple's moral tried to discredit the story. . . . We laugh, we are pleased to toy with a rule of expediency, but we are not taken in. In the last analysis, it is not our cap but the Manciple's that is set. The "mood of holiday and festivity" is preserved with our sympathy, and the Manciple takes his place in the larger pattern. Achieving this end is not, as Severs claims, "painting in black and white," but rather using the whole range of Chaucer's art. Characterization from the Seven Sages, the end of the plot from Ovid, the moral from the Old French romancers, symbolic details from the *Ovidius moralizatus*— these strange bedfellows make a tale more complex than any source, and place it in its context in the Canterbury pilgrimage.

Although Cadbury's discussion of Chaucer's variation from "sources" and the resulting amalgam with its stresses in different directions is enlightening, one cannot help feeling that his conclusions are in some respects naïve. I cannot see Chaucer, the Manciple, pilgrims, or Chaucer's audience much involved one way or another with the crow, for example, and Cadbury leaves out of account that perhaps *all* the morals are valid: that one should not restrain one's wife, one should not commit rash action, *and* one should not jangle.

The Manciple is instructively compared by Corsa (1964:229-33) with the Canon's Yeoman:

However cynical he may have become about his craft, the anguished tone suggests that the Canon's Yeoman is not really cynical about life. The truth he is in search of cannot be reached, but that does not necessarily deny the existence of other truths. For the Manciple, all truth is so difficult to get at, so bitter in the search, that it is best not to try at all; any concept of its nature turns out to be illusory and what is "fals" and what is "trewe" becomes impossible to distinguish. . . . The Manciple repeats his mother's advice almost as if it were a litany, its renunciation of the possibility of any vital communication between human beings underscoring unmistakably his own wearied view of life.

Howard's (1964) brief discussion largely summarizes the plot of the *Tale* and comments upon the various bits and pieces that went into a poem that he clearly considers a failure. His conclusion, however, is interesting: "If Chaucer had translated or adapted it from a single work, we might not be curious about it. But when it is, in effect, an original composition by reason of its having been synthesized from many sources, we are privileged to speculate why Chaucer thought it worth his while to compose it" (p. 186).

Although not revealing an especial appreciation of *The Manciple's Tale,* Ruggiers (1965:247-48n.) does note the emphasis upon self-governance and the admonitory elements of the poem in general as having some bearing on other works in the group, particularly in the Manciple's comments on marriage suggesting *The Miller's Tale, The Wife of Bath's Prologue, The Merchant's Tale,* and, perhaps more dimly, *The Franklin's Tale.*

Something has been said earlier to indicate Coghill's later admiration for *The Manciple's Tale,* but there are few briefer and better discussions of what many see as the principal concerns of the *Tale* (1966:136-99). Coghill is particularly interested in that aspect of the Manciple in which the concerns of Chaucer may be arguably present (pp. 136-39):

But more dangerous than to utter harlotry was to venture on the criticism of his hearers, and there is no better expression of the danger than in *The Manciple's Tale.* This little masterpiece seems to issue from Chaucer's most sardonic maturity. He was never a Manciple himself (so far as we know), but he knew what it was to be in a position of considerable, though inferior, authority. So, perhaps by professional sympathy, he chose a Manciple as his mask, and groomed him for the part by making him seem a coarse fellow of no account. . . . From behind this carefully constructed dummy Chaucer delivered a broadside of home-truths to his audience of courtiers. The advice he gives has its cynical side, in that it concludes with a heavy warning against exposing oneself to the "losengeours" and "totelere accusours," who, as we know from the BF version of the *Prologue* to *The Legend of Good Women* (352-4) infested the courts. . . . The Manciple's *end* is a story about moral ideas, and to the interest of these all other interests are sacrificed. Chaucer could use his pulpit for preaching as well as for entertainment, and if he could make a story of a sermon, . . . he could also make a sermon of a story, showing infinite play with the variations in distance and mode of address that were possible to him in confronting an audience of his friends and rulers. They made their effect on his narrative art, too, little though they knew it.

Whittock (1968:280-85) is not prepared to see any merit in the *Tale* itself; he thinks that the Manciple's self-revelation is interesting and successful; he is particularly concerned, as was Shumaker (1953) to see the relation between *The Manciple's Tale* and *The Parson's Tale* as one of deliberate contrast, that of the deviousness of the Manciple and the directness of the Parson, or duplicity opposed to self-examination. In other words, although the work may be of little merit, the unit of which it forms an important part is impressive.

In his interestingly titled essay "Polonius Among the Pilgrims" (1972:140-46), Campbell makes an entertaining case for the *Tale's* being ill-organized purposefully, as a continuing manifestation of the teller's true character. The Manciple is, according to Campbell, echoing Birney (1960), garrulous, gregarious, and eager to please, and thus he wanders through his tale with an intensely acute awareness of the audience's reaction and an eager anticipation to respond to possible displeasure by artful evasion or explanation. The principal difficulty with this charming examination is that its conclusions do not square very well with Chaucer's portrait of the Manciple, brief as it is, in *The General Prologue,* though in the Manciple's quick and clever reaction to the Cook's wrath one recognizes something of the portrait that Campbell draws.

Most of the later treatments of *The Manciple's Prologue* and *Tale* that will be discussed in this survey concern themselves with the problem of language in the Manciple's performance, a good illustration of Brewer's generalization (1966) referred to earlier. They are also concerned, to a greater or lesser degree, with the more serious implications of the language and its possible relation to that other kind of sermonizing which follows, in *The Parson's Tale.*

Harwood (1972) states flatly that "the subject of the tale is language" (p. 268). He does not mean, he says, to imply by this medieval rhetoric. "Rather, the tale is about the relationship between words and things. More precisely, it is a covert indictment in which the Manciple mocks at those who can be distracted from empirical reality by language which creates a bogus reality of its own" (p. 268). Harwood examines the differences between the *Tale* and Chaucer's possible sources and analogues, as we have seen in the previous discussion of that subject, emphasizing the way in which Chaucer has deliberately turned all these matters to account for his own purposes, assimilating all and differing from all, as the Manciple turns words to his own account. He insists upon the thingness in words. Harwood writes (p. 279):

Like the Manciple, the Parson tells us that he "wol nat glose (I 45) and that he is "nat textueel" (I 57); but in saying as much, he is, unlike the Manciple, both sincere and accurate. The Manciple's jeering tale at the expense of those who mistake the "word" for the "dede" nevertheless prepares the listener for the Parson by questioning, however satirically, the relationship between language and reality. Those who listen to the word rather than see the thing are gullible; yet the satiric capital which the Manciple makes of them serves as a curtain-raiser—a kind of satyr play—before the Parson leads the pilgrims from "ernest" into a "game" that is other than the sleep of fools. The Manciple's performance is a moment of verbal Misrule, as the Host's apostrophe to Bacchus and talismanic use of liquor are Misrule of the usual kind. Intoxicating language reconciles the Cook to the Manciple and Phebus to his wife. By language the Parson will reconcile the pilgrims to God. Acting out his own destiny, the Manciple, ridiculing words which become reality, prepares the pilgrims in his way for the Word become flesh.

The Manciple is, according to Harwood, a hard-headed realist who has nothing but contempt for those, like the proud possessors of "gentilesse," who delude themselves by confusing words with the things, by creating a false reality that has its home only in a world of words. The directness of the Parson, his refusal to confuse words with the real things of this world, is prepared for by the Manciple.

The famous phrase that the word must be cousin to the deed serves as the center of Gruber's interesting examination (1973:43-50). The word, according to Gruber, is usually quite *un*related to the deed, but is rather hostile and antithetical; there is a radical disjunction between the two, and language is fatally infected with error. Thus, Gruber observes, the series of ironic contradictions in the events of the brief tale, following a series in *The Manciple's Prologue:* the

32

compounding of the quarrel between the Cook and the Manciple by compounding the drunkenness of the Cook (but it is now described as an act blessed by Bacchus himself instead of the swinish act that it was before), and Phoebus himself teaching the bird to sing and to counterfeit the language of others and then being undone by the very language that he has set in motion. Language, in short, is uncontrollable, hence the moral of the Manciple's mother, and perhaps of the poet as well.

By far the most instructive treatment of *The Manciple's Prologue* and *Tale* since those of Severs and Hazelton is Knight's (1973:161-83). Its subject, too, is language, but approached from the point of view of the medieval rhetoricians rather than from the point of view of modern theorists. Knight very usefully examines in detail the rhetorical structure of the *Tale* (actually it is done here for the first time, since Plessow's elaborate marking of rhetorical figures [1929] did not in fact examine how they worked but only observed that they were present). Knight's deprecation of much current, highly laudatory criticism of the *Tale* is based upon the argument that it is praised for the wrong reasons, praised for being a "modern" rather than a medieval performance. He urges, in contradiction of Hazelton, that the *Tale* is a quite serious rhetorical performance, whatever its other implications, and that it is developed straightforwardly according to rhetorical principles, and is in no sense a pastiche. Although Knight praises the *Tale,* he argues that the style, tone, and structure of the *Prologue* and the *Tale,* though each is excellent in its kind, "draw away" from one another, and that the *Tale* sheds no light upon the character of the Manciple as presented in the *Prologue.* In this he develops much further a brief insight of Speirs (1951:200).

Scattergood (1974:124-46), on the other hand, argues that *The Manciple's Prologue* and *Tale* must stand or fall together. There is a coherence, he urges, that derives from the consequences of the lack of self-control, a coherence remarked by previous critics. Scattergood emphasizes that, although the theme is of the unfortunate consequences of the lack of self-control in speech, the *Tale* itself is an object lesson on how language can be used to escape the penalties of language, how by verbal dexterity one can escape the implications of what one says. This the Manciple does by feigning imperfect control over his speech, both in the *Prologue* in the altercation with the Cook and in the false "mistakes" in the *Tale,* such as the "lemman" references (line 205). He means what he says but escapes by pretending that he does not. Scattergood observes that Chaucer seems interested in the Manciple partly because the Manciple's handling of language bears some relation to the strategies of the poet. This interest, however, is not to be confused with endorsement, because, as Scattergood argues, the Manciple's ability with language lacks a moral dimension. Thus, like many other later critics, Scattergood assumes a thematic link between fragments H and I, moving toward the moral culmination of *The Parson's Tale:* "The Manciple is made to invoke criteria against which his own way of seeing self-restraint in speech appears inadequate. The Manciple has verbal ability; he has style; but Chaucer shows that in themselves they are not enough" (p. 144). Scattergood (pp. 141-43) also remarks upon the element of class conflict implicit in the tale—the servant who tells the truth, for whatever motive, and is punished, *in* a tale told by a servant, the Manciple, and of course, in a larger frame told by one, Chaucer, who was in varying capacities a servant—thus emphasizing Coghill's remarks (1966:176) about both Chaucer and the Manciple, and Whittock's (1968:284) about the "class bitterness." See also Tupper (1915:264).

In no criticism are *The Manciple's Prologue* and *Tale* valued more highly than in Howard's book (1976:298-306), which is concerned with the controlling ideas of *The Canterbury Tales.* He sums up much previous criticism and states his own point of departure in the following words (pp. 299-300):

The tale is almost always treated as a throwaway. The prologue is admired for its realistic byplay, but the tale is left out of selections and regarded by most commentators as a slender effort. It is amusing that it suits the Manciple's character and circumstances, that its jeering tone suits his easy-going cynicism, and that his advice might well apply to himself. But it is usually viewed as mechanical and ineffective—a tale written in Chaucer's earlier days and stuck in here for want of something better. I want to argue that it is a perfect choice for the last tale: its effect is astonishing, and it prepares perfectly for the Parson's Prologue and Tale which follow.

Though fair enough to criticism until the mid-1950s, as we have seen, this summation does less than justice to most interpretation and comment since. Howard goes on to describe, but in less technical terms than had Knight (1973), the way in which *The Manciple's Tale* is built: "The tale is neatly structured on principles of medieval rhetoric; it is another instance of unimpersonated artistry. The Manciple tells it in four economical narrative steps, each followed by a digression or 'amplification'" (p. 300). Howard sees its function in *The Canterbury Tales* as preparatory (p. 304):

I hope I have managed to show that the last three tales [before *The Parson's Tale*] are not leftovers stuck on at the end but a sequence meant to recapture themes interlaced throughout the work. The movement of this sequence, like that of Fragment I, is degenerative: the Second Nun's Tale enunciates an ideal; the Canon's Yeoman's Tale is about a failed or impossible ideal; the Manciple's Tale fastens upon fallen nature and makes all ideals—of thought, word and deed—seem impossible.

Howard goes on to remark that "the three tales have the effect of an ironical *De contemptu mundi*—they let us see the vanity of earthly pursuits, the mutability of human deeds, the disappointing uselessness of human striving, the corruptness of human nature" (p. 304).

Again Howard emphasizes the importance of language in the *Tale*. What earlier critics had condemned as mere repetitious moralizing Howard sees as the necessary demonstration of the confusion of language and morality, the endless talking and explaining of the *Tale* that never arrives at a point (the ostensible point, that one's mouth should be kept shut, being contradicted by the Manciple's blathering) that must precede the Parson's sermon, which is an unvarnished answer to the questions about language, speakers, morality, and their relations to one another. In a sense, of course, Howard, like Hazelton and many later critics, is seeing the *Tale* not as a high achievement *as a tale* but as a representation of something else: Howard sees it as an object lesson of what all the talking in *The Canterbury Tales* amounts to: finally only "words, words, words" (p. 306). This Howard argues, as Shumaker, Ruggiers, Scattergood, and others argued before him, is anticipatory of the *Retraction* as well as of the demonstration of words put to *use* in *The Parson's Tale.*

Trask (1977) takes quite a different tack in his approach to the Manciple and his performance. He agrees with Campbell (1972) that the Manciple is a witless bore. He argues that the Manciple shows a lack of perception (p. 111), that he is a "tipsy sort" (p. 112), though not under the influence of drink, and that he lacks humor (p. 113). He is competent in a mechanical sort of way, but has become a moral simpleton. His vision is "blinded to color" (p. 109), and he can see only in terms of black and white. In short, Trask argues, the Manciple is an example of a man who has mother trouble. He tells a "tale of utter moral blindness, vapidity and self-delusion" (p. 115). The Manciple "doesn't mean any serious harm, and he couldn't help who his mother was" (p. 116). He cannot even speak for himself at the end but must rely upon his mother to solve his problems (pp. 113-14). Trask's essay is interesting as being the first to extend to the Manciple a psychological analysis of the sort that has long been popular in treating some of the other pilgrims, notably the Pardoner, the Merchant, the Franklin, and the Wife of Bath.

Davidson (1979) takes quite a different approach from those of Trask and Campbell (1972). He examines the confusions in the *Tale* discussed by Severs (1952), Hazelton (1963), and others and comes to the conclusion that they are intended by the Manciple, in keeping with his character drawn by Chaucer in *The General Prologue* as well as with his character in *The Manciple's Prologue.* Davidson writes (p. 8):

The Manciple, recounting his turbid tale and concluding with a lengthy reiteration of his mother's repetitious injunctions enjoining discretion and silence, presents himself as merely the simple son of a simple parent. One is tempted to laugh at both him and his dame. But I would here argue that such laughter is precisely what the Manciple desires. Those who see him as comic, as a mere source of easy amusement, have been manipulated by the Manciple into overlooking the actual roguery that seeming simplemindedness can effectively mask. The real joke is on them. The Manciple, with the contradictions and confusion which pervade his whole performance, plays the fool but does so to make fools of those who take him for a fool.

In keeping with the common appreciation of the relationship of fragments H and I, Davidson concludes by arguing that the character of *The Manciple's Tale* must be contrasted with the one that appropriately follows it, *The Parson's Tale* (pp. 11-12): ". . . by so effectively portraying a protagonist who deliberately deceives his immediate audience while remaining himself self-deceived, Chaucer achieves, with the Manciple and his tale, the subtly ironic Christian comedy that characterizes his best work in the Canterbury Tales."

R. D. Fulk (1979) spurns much of the philosophical tendency of recent interpretation and returns to a view of *The Manciple's Tale* that sees its function as primarily within the drama of *The Canterbury Tales.* The tale, well organized, focuses its three themes (that "heigh degree" is negligible, that anger is dangerous, and that a wanton tongue is foolish) on a single purpose: a warning against the Cook should he be tempted to do mischief against the Manciple. This is a more elaborate restatement of the argument of Elliot (1954) and except for its emphasis upon organization is not concerned with the tale aesthetically. Fulk argues that the Crow corresponds not to the Manciple, as usually assumed, but to the Cook (in private correspondence Fulk has advised me that he now thinks that the reiterated moral, though dull, is caused by the Manciple's awareness of the drunkenness of the Cook and his determination that his message shall get home).

In their books, both published in 1979, Fyler and McCall treat the effects of classical material on Chaucer's art. McCall, in a brief analysis, sees Phoebus in *The Manciple's Tale* as a comic divinity, building in a sense upon Hazelton's thesis (1963). He argues that the Manciple is oblivious to what he has done to Phoebus: "As nearly as *he* can tell the god is a complete gentleman" (p. 130). But the complete gentleman's world comes tumbling down when confronted with ordinary human problems: "What Osgood sensed Chaucer proves, for his gods and goddesses consistently depend upon some kind of clearly identifiable naturalness" (p. 131):

There is nothing esoteric in the classical mythology which Chaucer gives us, nothing foreign to the traditions which he knew, and nothing secret in the meanings of the myths he used. Problems there certainly are, but they invariably come from where we should expect them—from the manipulating hands of a playful writer who liked to puzzle and surprise his audience with his contrary ways and multiple effects.

Fyler is concerned, as have been many other modern commentators, with the relationship of *The Manciple's Tale* and *The Parson's Tale.* He interestingly treats both as sermons, emphasizing the elements of language (p. 155):

As a sermon, the *Manciple's Tale* ironically prefaces the *Parson's*. . . . Even when dressed up in fictions to sweeten its message, wisdom apparently cannot be transmitted—

at least not with the ease possible in the miraculous days of the early church, when Cecilia could provoke mass conversions by verbal argument and saintly example. The Parson's modern saintliness makes possible his candor and utter indifference to the worldly distinctions of class and polite language . . . and his efficacy as a spiritual guide. Yet though he opposes the Manciple in these respects, his no-nonsense attitude toward language is the same, and it prepares us for Chaucer's Retraction. The Manciple in fact nearly recreates the concluding scene of the *House of Fame* when his mother implicitly attacks the whole enterprise of Chaucer's poetry: "'My sone, be war, and be noon auctour newe/Of tidynges, wheither they been false or trewe.'" . . . The rest is silence. The end of the *Canterbury Tales* thus transcends words and a delight in poetic artifice by moving beyond them—first by an ironic disintegration, then with utter seriousness—to the absolute simplicity of supernatural truth, where no words are necessary and human language cannot follow.

Conclusions

One is finally left, after reading and surveying modern criticism of *The Manciple's Prologue* and *Tale,* with something of the feeling that Knight expressed (1973:164-65): that there is some basic contradiction among the assumptions of those who would assert that they are fine performances. Only Knight still seems to maintain that there is a real, unbridgeable difference in tone and characterization between the *Prologue* and the *Tale,* and he argues from an analysis of the rhetorical and stylistic structure of the two. Most of the rest urge a close relationship, but for differing reasons, usually thematic. And the assessment of the *Tale* itself as a fine poem is urged for reasons that range from Hazelton's assertion (1963) that it is a fine work because it parodies poor stuff so well and Campbell's argument (1972) that the meandering, shambling gait of the *Tale* is successful because it perfectly characterizes the Manciple, on the one hand, to Scattergood's insistence (1974) that the *Prologue* and the *Tale* are both coherent, finely wrought works by any standard, on the other.

The probability is that the current wave of enthusiasm for the performance of the Manciple (called by Chute [1947:308] a "gabby little meddler") will not be maintained at its present crest and that a somewhat less strained appreciation will soon be generally accepted. We shall not likely go back to the sort of dismissal that was common in the first half of the century, but examination in the future will most probably be based upon a realistic assessment of the rhetorical performance of the Manciple. As judicious an examination as Knight's is, he does not seem to see that, although the genres and rhetorical developments of the *Prologue* and the *Tale* may well "draw away" from one another, as he acutely phrases it (1913:182), they do not necessarily suggest different characters for the Manciple in the *Prologue* and the Manciple in the *Tale.* A better suggestion might be that the two sides of the character are met in *The General Prologue:* the sly, circumspect man who is yet scarcely unacquainted with the behavior of his masters and their students, mixing in immemorial fashion morality and debauchery. But such a suggestion necessarily brings us again to the still greater, and as yet unanswered, questions of the generation and the controlling ideas of *The Canterbury Tales.*

TEXTUAL COMMENTARY

The Textual Tradition of The Manciple's Prologue *and* Tale

Manly and Rickert (MR 1940) describe the textual affiliations of *The Manciple's Prologue* and *Tale* in 2.445-53. They conclude that the *Prologue* and the *Tale* appear to have been derived from different textual traditions. As they put it (2.445; see also 1.140-41):

The omission of McP [*ManP*] from several MSS, the large number of differences in affiliation between McP and McT [*ManT*], the disappearance of several clear-cut small groups in McT, and the instability of McP of the large group, usually headed by Ha^4, suggest the possibility that the prologue was lacking in the ancestor of many of the MSS.

MR go on to point out that this "large group" of manuscripts, usually headed by Ha^4, lacked the Prologue in Bo^2 Dl Ni Ry^2 To, though Ha^4, of course, has it. Several manuscripts do not contain the *Prologue* because of missing leaves (including Dd of our base-ten manuscripts of *The Canterbury Tales*—it also does not have the *Tale*), and of these—seven in all (Ad^2 Dd En^2 Ha^5 Ld^2 Ph^3 S1^1)—En^2 clearly never contained it, "since the missing folio could not have held more than the missing part of NPT (B 4577-4636) and H 104-119" (2.443). Fi has only the first two lines of the *Prologue,* followed by six spurious lines (see Textual Notes). As MR observe, the scribe of Ha^2 must have received the *Prologue* late, for he did not leave enough space and had to write part of it on an extra leaf added to the quire.

MR assert that several other manuscripts "usually affiliated with the large Ha^4 group" (2.445) seem to have picked up the *Prologue* from other sources: Ht, which is important in the large group headed by Ha^4 for the text of the *Tale,* is affiliated with Pw in the text of the *Prologue;* Ra^2, with the large group in the *Tale,* cannot be placed by MR in the textual affiliations of the *Prologue.* MR go on to point out that in the *Prologue* the *b* and *c* groups and Bw are derived from a common exemplar but that this relation does not persist in the text of the *Tale.* Py, which is not affiliated to the "large group," also has different textual affiliations for the *Prologue* and the *Tale.*

Very interesting in the light of these remarks is what MR see as the relatively steady nature of the textual affiliations of *The Manciple's Tale.* To quote MR again (2.450): "In spite of the shortness of the tale, there is clear evidence that all MSS are derived in two independent lines from O (the archetype of all extant copies): 1) Ha^4-Ld^1 Ra^3-Gl-Ra^2 Mc-Tc^1 Ht *b* cd** Bo^2 Nl To, and on the same line

the edited and corrected Hk-*En³*; 2) Hg-Ps-Py-Ad³-Ch El-Gg-Ha³ *a*-Ln-Ry¹-Se."
The Manciple's Tale is present in all relatively complete manuscripts except Ad²
Dd Ha⁵ Ld² Ph³ Sl¹. It is missing from Dd Sl¹ by loss of leaves, and He lacks
lines 48–255 of the *Tale.*

MR then conclude (2.449) that *The Manciple's Prologue* was received by the
scribes in different ways and frequently from different sources from those in
and from which *The Manciple's Tale* was received. MR make much of this,
arguing Manly's oft-reiterated interpretation of the relation of the *Prologue* to
the *Tale,* i.e., that the *Tale* was very early, with a well-established text, whereas
the *Prologue* was written late, was hurriedly affixed to the *Tale,* and subsequently
was not picked up by the "large group" consistently, and in some cases not at
all. The several textual affiliations would therefore indicate that the text of the
Prologue was still in something of a flux so that the MR O is very difficult to
determine.

Textual statistics, like other varieties of statistics, can often be interpreted in
different ways. To look at the larger picture first: the manuscripts that lack the
Prologue while *containing* the *Tale* are only five (Bo² Dl Nl Ry² En²). This
proportion of coexistence stands comparison well with that of the prologues and
links to several other tales as MR signal them in their charts (vol. 2, between
pp. 494 and 495). The *Squire-Franklin Link* is missing from fifteen manuscripts;
the *Reeve-Cook Link* is missing from nine relatively complete manuscripts; the
Physician-Pardoner Link is missing from eight manuscripts; even *The Wife of
Bath's Prologue* is missing from two (one of them, Ha³, nearly complete). I am
not deprecating the textual evidence that the tradition for *The Manciple's Prologue*
is somewhat different from that of *The Manciple's Tale.* I am merely urging that
in the nature of the composition and transmission of such a work as *The Canter-
bury Tales*—a nature only very imperfectly understood in spite of the labors of
MR—this small difference in manuscript affiliation is not overly surprising (one
assumes that normally a tale was written first and then provided with introductory
and linking material) and exists in more than half the cases (see the charts referred
to above) and that the difference may not necessarily signify the lapse of a long
period between the composition of a tale and that of its link or prologue. In
fact, there is relative stability in the textual tradition of *The Manciple's Prologue*
(especially compared with that of *The Wife of Bath's Prologue*). In spite of MR's
detailed discussion of the different groups of textual affiliation for *The Manciple's
Prologue,* the evidence for the existence of some of the groups is very slight, as
might be expected for a passage of only 104 lines. The evidence for the "small
groups" (2.446) is very sketchy indeed, as is revealed in such a statement as
"Group *c* does not appear alone, but there is some slight evidence that *b**-*c*-Bw
have an exclusive ancestor" (2.446). This is a fair representation of much of the
evidence, a great deal of which MR admit is probably variation by editing and
scribal confusion, and which is confirmed by referring to the evidence presented

by MR in their *Corpus of Variants.* We find (2.447) this statement about *c* Bw *d**, *b* c* Bw *d**, and Ra³ Gl *b* c* Bw *d**: "The readings combining these manuscripts into a large group are few and of doubtful value." MR are more assertive about Ha⁴ Ld¹, *a* Ln Ry¹ Se, remarking (2.447) that they are "from a common ancestor derived independently from O. MR's Ha⁴, we will remember, is the usual head of the "large group" some of whose manuscripts lacked *The Manciple's Prologue:* Ha⁴, however, the head and one of the earliest extant manuscripts, grouped by MR (1.220) with Hg El Ad⁴ Me as 1400-10, had it. It might be remarked in passing that MR do not go quite far enough in describing two manuscripts of this group, Ha⁴ Ld¹, which are clearly sister manuscripts for the text of *The Manciple's Prologue,* agreeing time and again against others of the "large group" (Ld¹ is, however, missing the first 33 lines of the *Prologue* by loss of leaves).

The examination of the evidence of the base-ten manuscripts would seem to confirm the existence of the following affiliations: Hg El Ad³ and frequently Gg (its notorious eccentricities conceal some affiliations, which are discussed in the Textual Notes, and in Parkes and Beadle [1980:3.1-57]), which, as the table reveals, have 3, 12, 13, and 30 variants, respectively, from the present edition; Cp La, which, as one would expect, are closely allied as the chief representatives of *c,* and which have 47 and 78 variants, respectively, 32 of which they share (there would undoubtedly have been more congruence except that La's scribe created 15 unique variants, nearly all of which are the result of careless copying—in only 104 lines); a consistent association of more distant kind between Cp La Pw, and these with He *(b)* and CX¹; a clear affiliation of Ha⁴ and En¹ (our substitute for Dd, which is Out for *The Manciple's Prologue* and *Tale,* representing the *a* grouping of MR). The last two groups of associations confirm MR's conclusions to some extent, for Ha⁴ En¹ share 26 variants, and there is a remarkably consistent pairing of He CX¹, which share 60 variants from the present edition in 104 lines. There seem to be no cases of clear switching of manuscript affiliations for passages of any length, and, of course, for such a short passage there would have to be very clear evidence indeed. The data are presented in the Textual Notes and in the Table of Correspondences for the manuscripts. To summarize: there would appear to have existed three broad textual traditions of affiliation: Hg El Ad³ Gg, Cp La Pw He CX¹, and Ha⁴ En¹, the last steering its own course but in several instances of "hard readings" and other critical tests throwing its lot with Cp La Pw He CX¹. There is little evidence for a multitude of textual traditions for *The Manciple's Prologue.*

Let us now repeat MR's statement about the text of *The Manciple's Tale* (2.450): "In spite of the shortness of the tale, there is clear evidence that all MSS are derived in two independent lines from O: 1) Ha⁴-Ld¹ Ra³-Gl-Ra² *Mc-Tc¹* Ht *b* Cd** Bo² Nl To, and on the same line the edited and corrected Hk-*En³*; 2) Hg-Ps-Py-Ad³-Ch El-Gg-Ha³ *a*-Ln-Ry¹-Se." MR are clearly right in implying a switch of affiliation between Ha[4] and *a* (represented in our base-ten manuscripts by En[1]), for whereas they share 26 variants in the 104 lines of *The Manciple's Prologue,* they share only 15 in the 258 lines of *The Manciple's Tale.* Such large groupings must always seem misleading in the case of a short poem; for instance, Ha[4], which MR place heading the first large group, shares with He and CX[1] only 26 variants in *The Manciple's Tale;* but in very general terms, on the basis of the evidence of the base-ten manuscripts, as well as a review of the material in MR's *Corpus of Variants,* this broad two-tiered grouping would seem to be sound if one had to class the textual tradition in such a blunt way. There is a similar grouping in the first class of Cp La, with somewhat stronger affiliation with Pw than was the case in *The Manciple's Prologue;* He CX[1] are in very much greater agreement with one another than are any other groups (it must be remembered that He is Out for lines 48-255, and we have used Ne, the remainder of the *b* grouping, or Tc[2] as a single representative where useful, but this variation would not seem to alter the overall consistency of the He CX[1] affiliation). In short, the proportion of the shared variations among the affiliated manuscripts from the base-ten for *The Manciple's Tale* is approximately the same as for *The Manciple's Prologue,* except for the remarkable shift of Ha[4] and En[1] from close partners in the *Prologue* to distant friends in the *Tale.* Except for this switch, I would suggest that, instead of the great variety that MR find between the textual traditions of the *Prologue* and the *Tale,* there seem really to be only two traditions of each, the traditions being the same except for the switch in affiliation of *a* (here En[1]) and its associated group Ln Ry[1] Se from their alliance with Ha[4] in the *Prologue* to an alliance with the Hg-headed groups in the *Tale.*

After a review of the evidence in the *Corpus of Variants,* and in particular on the evidence of the base-ten manuscripts, one must conclude that the Hg El Ad[3] Gg and Cp La Pw He CX[1] branches of affiliation in the *Prologue* also remain the basic branches in the *Tale.* The almost independent affiliation of Ha[4] *a*(En[1]) in the *Prologue* becomes resolved in the *Tale* by Ha[4] joining the latter groups and *a* (En[1]) the former. The difficulty, of course, is that, as MR observe, the 362 lines overall are too few for the fine discrimination possible among the affiliations of the longer tales. But this very fact should seem to suggest that MR discriminate much too finely on much too little evidence for the textual affiliations of the *Prologue.* We feel bound to assert that MR seem less than objective in assessing the evidence, particularly in view of their summation (2.449):

Nowhere else in CT is the contrast between a tale and its prologue so remarkable as here. In matter, in style, and in its indebtedness to the *Roman de la Rose* the tale obviously belongs to Chaucer's 'prentice period, whereas the prologue, with its involvement of three *personae* in the action, shows a very highly developed technique. The comparative simplicity of the MS relations in the tale indicates that, although copies of the text were easily accessible to the organizers of the commercial exemplar, the piece had not been widely circulated; the recently written prologue seems to have been difficult to procure.

The only variant that suggests a late retouching of the early tale is "rude" for "wilde" in 170.

This is, of course, a restatement of Manly's attack upon *The Manciple's Tale* in his "Chaucer and the Rhetoricians" (1926a:16-17). I do not wish to deny, and indeed have clearly stated, that there is *some* evidence for a slightly more complex textual tradition of affiliation for the *Prologue* than for the *Tale* but would suggest that when it is examined it does not amount to a great deal, as MR in their actual comments upon the evidence would seem to concede (2.445-49). It would appear, I hope, to most judgments that the particular interpretation placed by MR upon the evidence is—one must use the word—prejudiced and out of place in a purely textual analysis and that their point of departure is perhaps not that of textual analysis but the aesthetic conviction that the *Tale,* because of its alleged rhetorical padding, indebtedness to the *Roman de la Rose,* etc. (heaven help *The Wife of Bath's Prologue!*) is early, "'prentice work," and that the *Prologue,* because of its "lively realism," is late. Therefore, the argument goes, the text of the *Prologue* was written late and was difficult to obtain, whereas that of the *Tale* was stable, being long established, and that this state of affairs accounts for the complexity of the textual tradition of the first and the simplicity of that of the second.

I must conclude, in opposition to the opinion of two giants of Chaucerian scholarship, and partly indeed on the basis of the evidence that they present in perhaps the greatest edition of any English writer, that, with the single though important exception of the Ha[4] En[1] relationships, the textual traditions of the *Prologue* and the *Tale* are in fact quite similar. Manly's opinion on the time lapse in the composition of the two, while subsequently very influential and being voiced even today (see Critical Commentary), had by no means been universally held. Skeat (1894: 5.436), taking his cue from Tyrwhitt (1775:1.88), had been content to conclude that the *Prologue* had been in fact written before *The Cook's Tale.* And TR himself, no mean critic of Chaucer, had urged, in one of his infrequent emphatic judgments (1.111) that "[Chaucer's] skill in new dressing an old story was never, perhaps, more successfully exerted." But this, like much of Manly's commentary on the *Tale,* is more appropriate to the Critical Commentary than to the Textual Commentary.

To return to matters of textual tradition, I would further suggest that the logic upon which MR's conclusions are based is open to question. They observe that copies of *The Manciple's Tale* were easily accessible to the organizers of the commercial exemplar (such as Ha[4] or its predecessor) but, because of the simplicity of the textual affiliations of this tale, it had not been widely circulated. They do not mention in this summary that apparently the earliest scribe whose work survives, that of Hg, did not have access to the *Tale* initially (1.270). They do not admit that their conclusion that the *Tale* was early does not fit easily with their assumption that it had not been widely circulated; this does not necessarily contradict their assumption, but it certainly does not follow it. Other acknowledgedly early (and short) tales show signs of fairly wide circulation (in MR's terms, for they assume in many cases for the tales lines of descent from copies in circulation before any attempt was made to create a coherent set of *Canterbury* groups; see Dempster 1946:387-92, who questions this assumption). *The Physician's Tale* (which has one very large group of manuscripts but also Hg El Bo² Gg and *a* and Ch of independent descent), and *The Second Nun's Tale* are only two examples. About the latter MR say: "As the tale of St. Cecilia had been in circulation for fifteen or twenty years before Chaucer's death, the copies accessible to the scribes who were assembling the tales for the CT collection may have suffered a good deal of corruption and mixture of textual variation, which sometimes obscures the evidence for particular readings" (2.424).

One need only remark that MR assume likewise a career of at least fifteen years for *The Manciple's Tale* before Chaucer's death (the "'prentice period"—2.449). From the same kind of textual affiliation evidence that MR apply to other pieces, one might derive the reverse conclusion from theirs, that is, that the *Tale* could have been quite late, though this is not certain. As I observed, the evidence of textual affiliation is not vast and certainly not conclusive if one approaches it objectively, and I am not trying to base an argument for late composition of the *Tale* upon an inside-out interpretation of that evidence; I maintain only that MR's evidence is insufficient to support an argument of early composition (see discussion in the Critical Commentary, "The Date of the Manciple's Tale" above).

Evidence of the Glosses

The glosses of the manuscripts are not very helpful in establishing textual affiliation. Hg has an interesting and unique gloss at line 147, a long quotation from Jerome *Epistola contra Jovinianum* 1.47. El and Ad³ have a set of identical simple glosses of "location": line 163, "Exemplum de volucre"; line 175, "Exemplum de Murelego"; and line 183, "Exemplum de lupo"; and the very interesting "gloss" to the notorious "swyve" of line 257, "Nota malum quid," the last also being present in Tc² at line 247. Other manuscripts not in the base-ten share some of these short "spotting" glosses: shorter or differently worded versions of El Ad³ at line 163 are found in *Cn En³ Ln*, whereas Se has simply "Exemplum"; line 175, *Cn En³ Ln*, whereas Se has simply "Exemplum"; line 175, *Cn En³ Ln*, with Se again simply "Exemplum"; line 183, *Cn En³ Ln Tc²* and, again, Se, "Exemplum." Of the base-ten manuscripts only Gg contributes another gloss, for line 337, "In multiloquio non deest peccatum" (Prov. 10.19). Why Hg's long gloss of Jerome was not picked up by manuscripts that stay so close to it, El Ad³ in particular, one can only guess. The El Ad³ "locating" glosses were probably simply part of the larger finishing job of the scribe (see Parkes 1976:115-41; Doyle and Parkes 1978:163-203, on the processes of finishing manuscripts in Chaucer's time and later).

For convenience, the base-ten glosses are as follows:

147　Verum quid prodest diligens custodia cum uxor impudica servari non possit pudica non debet feda enim custos est castitatis necessitas pulcra [cito?] adamatur feda facile concupiscit difficile custoditur quod plures amant Hg
163　Exemplum de volucre El Ad³
175　Exemplum de Murelego El Ad³
183　Exemplum de lupo El Ad
223　sine titulo Hg
257　Nota malum quid El Ad³
337　In multiloquio non deest peccatum Gg

MR observed (3.523) that the glosses of *The Manciple's Tale* which occur in El Ad³ and in *Cn En³* Ln Se, though similar and frequently occurring in the same places, are of independent origin. Whether their conclusion is in fact accurate, there is not enough evidence, as I have observed, for any close affiliation among the manuscripts.

The Question of Authentic Lines

Although spurious lines occur with some frequency in manuscripts for both the *Prologue* and the *Tale,* none occurs in the base-ten manuscripts, and none of the lines in the base-ten is open to question. There is also no question of including in the authentic textual tradition any of the spurious lines at one time or another added to the text or substituted for other lines in any of the manuscripts of *The Canterbury Tales.* All such spurious lines are given in the Textual Notes and, of course, are to be found in the *Corpus of Variants* of MR.

Order Among The Canterbury Tales

I must emphasize at the beginning of this section that the discussion of the order of *The Canterbury Tales* as it involves *The Manciple's Tale* is severely limited to the textual evidence; questions of Chaucer's theme and ultimate intentions appear in the Critical Commentary. There can be little question that the evidence of the manuscripts, in spite of certain internal inconsistencies, strongly suggests that the earliest scribes interpreted the evidence before them as requiring that *The Manciple's Prologue* and *Tale* (fragment H) should immediately precede *The Parson's Prologue* and *Tale* (fragment I). To use the fragment labels, H and I are in that order at the end of *The Canterbury Tales* in all complete manuscripts and in all but five manuscripts in which both fragments occur: Gl Ra³, which have *marchaunt* in line 1 of *The Parson's Prologue* where other manuscripts have *manciple*—though neither has *The Merchant's Tale* preceding; Tc¹, which has *frankeleyn,* and indeed *The Franklin's Tale* precedes; Ch, which has *yeoman* in line 1 and indeed has *The Canon's Yeoman's Tale* preceding *The Parson's Prologue* and *Tale,* and, of course, Hg, the order of which has presented many problems. (The importance of Hg should not blind us to the fact that it is incomplete, though for an argument that it is complete, and one that rejects the authenticity of *The Canon's Yeoman's Tale* because it is not included in Hg, see Blake (1979:13-14). Although I believe Hg to be the superior text for nearly all the *Tales,* as MR concluded, I cannot agree with Blake's argument. The very absence of *The Canon's Yeoman's Tale,* together with the presence of the incomplete form of *The Nun's Priest's Prologue,* and Hg's lack of the formal *ordinatio* and *compilatio* of El, are probably what have kept Hg from receiving its just appreciation for so long. For the moment what must be emphasized is simply the overwhelming evidence of the manuscripts for the H-I order; recognition of this fact does not argue that Chaucer intended this relationship as his final aim, though one must certainly take into account the state in which Chaucer's unfinished work was left, a state for which we have only the evidence of the manuscripts. The H-I relation was followed by the printed editions until TH[3], which inserted *The Plowman's Tale* between *The Manciple's Tale* and *The Parson's Prologue* and *Tale.* This practice continued through UR and was ended by TR's omission of *The Plowman's Tale* altogether when he concluded correctly that it was non-Chaucerian.

The internal evidence linking H to I is not as impressive as the physical evidence of the manuscripts themselves. The internal evidence is chiefly the appearance of the word *Maunciple* in line 1 of *The Parson's Prologue.* In what is probably the earliest extant manuscript, Hg, the linking word *Maunciple* appears to have been written over an erasure. In view of the disturbed order in Hg, it is perhaps significant that *Manciple* should have been written in over another name; perhaps the scribe did receive the *Tale* late as MR conjecture (1.270) and substituted the name for an earlier guess. In any case, it *is* written in the scribe's hand (MR imply this [1.276] and Parkes and Doyle positively assert it in Ruggiers 1979:xxxii). MR come to the conclusion (1.276-77) that the name the scribe had erased had been *Frankeleyn,* though, as Parkes and Doyle observe (p. xxxii), this would require a form of abbreviation that is unparalleled elsewhere in the manuscript. In Ch the Yeoman is named logically, since *The Canon's Yeoman's Tale* preceded *The Parson's Prologue* and *Tale* in the manuscript. Ch Gl Ra[3] (the latter two naming the "marchaunt") are, according to MR, in the same line of descent as Hg for *The Parson's Prologue* (4.360).

If this is the case, it is possible that all three scribes, using Hg's exemplar or a related manuscript with the same error or guess that Hg's scribe had made, interpreted the confusion before them as best they could. It might seem that the initial letter, however obscured, had a descender (as appears upon close examination in the facsimile of Hg) that might be taken for the descender of a capital *M,* or for part of the descender of an initial *Y* (though MR assert that *Frankeleyn* is the only possible original name for Hg itself; Parkes and Doyle do not speculate on this). Since neither Gl nor Ra[3] had *The Merchant's Tale* preceding, theirs is a flimsy guess. But Ch does have *The Canon's Yeoman Tale* preceding, so that if the initial confused or erased letter did have the suggestion of a *Y* descender, it would have suited the inclination of Ch. A somewhat similar confused picture with the suggestion of two loops above and perhaps a descender below might have led to *Frankeleyn* in Tc[1] (though Tc[1] is, of course, with *b* in a different line of descent in *The Parson's Prologue* and elsewhere from Hg). At any rate, such speculation is perhaps not worth the "montaunce of a gnat"; one can only observe that the *Manciple* reading is nearly universal, however puzzling, and the H-I order must prevail on this account as well as on the prevailing relationship in the manuscripts themselves.

The other aspect of the evidence of the texts must be dealt with narrowly, because to do otherwise would intrude into another field of discussion: not only the order of the tales generally, their thematic relationships to one another, but the question of whether the tales were finally designed for a one-way journey or a round trip, etc. These questions have been discussed in the Critical Commentary but must be touched on here in the barest outline. The second point of "internal" textual evidence is the matter of the time reference in line 5 of *The Parson's Prologue,* where Hg and most other manuscripts have "ten" and Ch and En[3] have "four." "Ten" makes excellent sense, because of the shortness of *The Manciple's Tale,* but the trouble is caused by the reference in the following line to the length of the poet's shadow "ellevene foot or litel moore or lesse" and in the preceding line to the fact that the sun had descended "Degrees nyne and twenty as of highte." The latter two facts clearly correspond to "four" rather than "ten" (Eisner 1976:20-21 demonstrated conclusively that Chaucer's original intention was to name the time as 4:00 P.M., and that this information was derived from the calendar of Nicholas of Lynn). Assuming that "ten" is wrong, MR assert that Chaucer himself could not have been "guilty of the absurdity of making a tale of 258 lines, begun early in the morning (H 15[*sic*—correctly H 16]), last until four in the afternoon" (2.455).

This argument, though cogent within narrow limits, leaves aside other possibilities, among them that Chaucer may have altered his original intention concerning the time sequence (if in fact he had intended H to precede I) but never got around to changing the actual time reference in *The Parson's Prologue.* Or the other way round. MR's argument (following Skeat 1909) about this strangely seems to presume what they usually do not presume, that we have a finished text in *The Canterbury Tales,* in which Chaucer's intentions are, if not realized by him, realizable by us. Further, the question of time reference in line 5 of *The Parson's Prologue* is not perhaps as simple as MR would have it (2.455): "5. 'Ten'; so read all MSS except Ht La Ra[2] 'Than,' Ii 'Thre,' and Ch En[3] correctly (probably by emendation), 'Foure.' The error originated, not in any learned reflection that 4 P.M. was "the tenth hour of the day reckoning from 6 A.M., but in the simple fact that the 15c form of the arabic numeral 4 so much resembles the roman x for 10 that they are sometimes confused in the MSS" (2.455). Exactly. But MR do not consider the possibility that Chaucer, as revealed in O or O[1], had originally intended *The Parson's Prologue* to begin at four in the afternoon (hence the references to long shadows, etc.), but had, with the later idea of linking *The Manciple's Tale* directly to *The Parson's Prologue* and *Tale*—for whatever reason—changed the time to "x," intending later (as so frequently must have been the case with Chaucer) to revise *The Parson's Prologue* and *Tale;* the alteration, though picked up correctly by most manuscripts, nevertheless naturally caused confusion, so that a handful of manuscripts, even the good Ch, have got the original, now wrong, reading (some have just wrong readings). I argue not that such a thing occurred but that it could have (particularly in view of Chaucer's many alterations elsewhere and failure to make the subsequent necessary changes, viz., the *Shipman's* and the *Second Nun's* peculiarities) and that such an explanation has nearly as much probability on its side as MR's analysis of what happened.

The confusion about *Manciple* in line 1 of *The Parson's Prologue* and the confusion about the time word or figure in line 5 leave room for speculation in a number of directions about the relation of fragments H and I, on Chaucer's intention for the final form of *The Canterbury Tales.* Something of the same problem surrounds the much-vexed questions of the order of the tales in view of conflicting geographical references, and clearly there seems as well no satisfactory —that is, generally accepted—view of these. See Pratt (1951:1141-67) as the starting point for such speculation, going back to Furnivall's and Bradshaw's speculations in the pages of the Chaucer Society's publications to TR and beyond. Skeat argued, persuasively (1909:43):

It seems a pity to trouble about the fact that the Manciple's Prologue hints at early morning (H 16), while the Manciple's Tale, when prefixed to the Parson's, belongs to the afternoon. The solution is extremely easy, as the Hengwrt MS. shows us. The Manciple's Tale there precedes the Man of Law; and that is why the Man of Law is so emphatic about the progress of the day, and laments that it is already ten o'clock. But in his very first arrangement of the Tales, Chaucer moved the Tale down so as to precede the Parson's, without troubling to remove the inconsistency, because he could easily do that when he rearranged the Tales again *finally.* And that day never came.

We do not have to accept Skeat's assumption that Hg represents any arrangement of Chaucer's to grasp his point about the triviality of the objection to the arrangement H-I.

At any rate, MR opposed the view that the H-I sequence was in any sense "Chaucerian" (2.493-94). Tatlock (1935a:122-25, 138-39) defended it as Chaucerian; Dempster (1946:394), though allowing weight to MR's view, clearly leaned toward Tatlock. Benson (1981) has made anew the argument, from a reexamination of the manuscript classifications, that the El order (and hence H-I) may be regarded as Chaucerian. Textually, from the evidence of the manuscripts there can be no doubt of the H-I sequence; the question of Chaucer's final intention cannot be determined solely on textual evidence. For thematic, aesthetic, moral, theological, and other interpretations that have their beginnings in the question of order or bear upon it, see Critical Commentary above.

There is a problem of a minor nature involving the text of *The Manciple's Prologue* with whatever tale preceded it. The *a* order requires in general that *The Canon's Yeoman's Tale* precede *The Manciple's Tale* (all manuscripts described by MR as "Type *a*, Pure and Mixed" [2.494, chart 1], and reasonably complete have this arrangement); a group of incomplete *a* manuscripts, Bo² Ha⁵ Ad², lack one or both *Manciple's* and *Canon's Yeoman's Prologue* and *Tale*, whereas Ad³ Bo¹ and Ph² of *a* have *The Nun's Priest's Tale* preceding *The Manciple's Prologue*. The *b* group, on the other hand, has as the standard order *The Nun's Priest's Tale* preceding *The Manciple's Prologue* (excepting four disordered and incomplete manuscripts); this is usual also for the manuscripts of type *c* and of type *d* with some exceptions.

Now *The Nun's Priest's Tale* in nine manuscripts, including Dd En¹ of the manuscripts that have played so large a part in the creation of the Variorum Edition text as well as the good Ch, has an epilogue, the Words of the Host to the Nun's Priest, of sixteen lines (Chaucer Society and our numbering lines 4637-52). MR discuss the question of the authenticity of the lines and their probable history (2.422-23) and conclude that most of them are certainly authentic. The lines are printed by MR (4.280-81) and in other modern editions; they are printed in the present edition in the Textual Notes as a matter of historical interest because their significance for *The Manciple's Prologue* and *Tale* is only in that all printed editions after CX¹ until TR printed them *as a part of The Manciple's Prologue,* the lead-in to line 1 of the *Prologue* and following "Heere bigynneth the Prologe of the Maunciple" or a similar rubric. That they are Chaucerian is in my opinion beyond doubt; that they have nothing to do intrinsically with *The Manciple's Prologue* seems almost equally beyond doubt. They may bear latent witness to some stage in the development of *The Canterbury Tales* when *The Nun's Priest's Tale* preceded and led into *The Manciple's Prologue,* but this is doubtful. On the questions surrounding the *Nun's Priest's Endlink,* see SK (5.259), Hinckley (1907:156), Lawrence (1913:254; 1950: 106), Brusendorff (1925:88-89), Tatlock (1935*a*:115) and RB² (1957:896) for the matter of authenticity—on which all are inclined to agree—and Dempster (1953:1147-51) for an argument, supporting MR, that the *Endlink* was canceled by Chaucer. Tatlock (1935*a*:113-14), Lumiansky (1955:109-12), Owen (1958: 472-73), and Pearcy (1968:43-45) reject the view that the *Endlink* was canceled by Chaucer, the argument for cancellation being principally the small number of manuscripts in which it is found. Another six lines added after line 4652 in Ad¹ Gn En³ Ma are printed by MR (4:516); these are very much open to question and have been generally rejected, but here I must refer the reader to that part of the Variorum Edition dealing with *The Nun's Priest's Tale* for the reason that the lines never got into the textual tradition of *The Manciple's Prologue* even in so marginal a way as the sixteen of the *Endlink*.

Table of Correspondences

The following table records, for each manuscript of the base-group (and also for CX[1], the only printed edition with manuscript status in MR):

1. The total number of recorded variants for that manuscript, readings in the MR *Corpus of Variants* and a few readings missed by MR and caught by examination of the manuscripts themselves (either in the original or in photographs) that substantially vary from the readings adopted in the present edition (presumed to represent the nearest approach to Chaucer's original text available through the evidence of the manuscripts).

2. The number of recorded variants that are unique to that manuscript, i.e., unattested in any other manuscript collated by MR.

3. The number of recorded variants from the manuscript that are unattested in any other manuscript of the base-group.

4. The number of recorded variants in which that manuscript agrees with one or more other manuscripts of the base-group, listed in the standard order of collation.

In the case of *The Manciple's Prologue* and *Tale*, Dd, one of the base-group of manuscripts, is Out completely and is replaced by En[1], which in any case is considered by MR to be in some respects superior to Dd in the subgroup *Dd*, the earlier branch of *a* (1.131-32). In the case of He, that manuscript is Out for lines 48-255, the omission being accounted for by substituting the remainder of *b*, particularly Ne but on occasion Tc[2] as well, in an effort to account as thoroughly as possible for the text of CX[1], the first printed edition. Also Out for briefer passages are Pw, lines 47-52; Gg, lines 215-16; and CX[1], line 316. These defects are not supplied from other manuscripts, for they would not seriously affect the numbers of variants: those of Pw and CX[1] in particular are sufficiently large in any case so that there is no danger of misrepresentation.

The table is presented in three parts. The first part is for the *Prologue:* the second is for the *Tale*. This may be putting too fine a point on the matter, but the problem raised by MR of the complexity of the textual affiliations of the *Prologue* as compared with those of the *Tale* has seemed to make this distinction worth making.

The third part shows the correspondences among the printed editions, from CX[1] through Wright (WR). Generally, the same categories of information are there presented, with the notes elucidating what is peculiar to the printed edition. The principal point to observe is that the data for *The Manciple's Prologue* and

Tale are there given together, there being, except for WR's dependence upon Ha⁴, no significant textual variation in the traditions of the two, depending as both do so heavily upon the *b*-manuscript tradition. The history of the printed editions is of particular significance for the later study and criticism of Chaucer; it has no immediate importance for our present text, for no printed-edition readings are adopted into it.

Table 1. Table of Correspondences
A. *The Manciple's Prologue**

Manu-script	Total No. of Recorded Variants	Unique Variants	Variants Unattested in Other Base-Group Manuscripts	Agreements with Other Base-Group Manuscripts										
				Hg	El	Ad³	Cp	En¹	Gg	Ha⁴	He *(b)*	La	Pw	CX¹
Hg†	3‡	1§	1	..	..	..	..	..	..	..	..	1	1	..
El	12	..	5	..	..	1	1	2	4	1	2	2	2	2
Ad³	13	1	2	..	1	..	1	..	2	1	3	2	..	3
Cp	47	4	1	..	1	1	..	12	4	7	30	32	16	34
En¹	53	..	18	..	2	..	12	..	2	26	18	10	15	17
Gg	30	4	8	..	4	2	4	2	..	2	7	4	6	7
Ha⁴	34	4	3	..	1	1	7	26	2	..	11	9	7	11
He *(b)*	76	4	5	..	2	3	30	18	7	11	..	27	21	60
La	78	15	17	1	2	2	32	10	4	9	27	..	21	31
Pw	85	5	41	1	2	..	16	15	6	7	21	21	..	18
CX¹	72	1	3	..	2	3	34	17	7	11	60	31	18	..

*Lines of *ManP* with *no* variants among base-MSS:20.

†Omissions resulting from torn leaves are not counted as variants here and in *ManP* when the missing word is clear from context and supplied from El.

‡MR list as a unique Hg variant *As* for *And* in line 87; in fact, this is wrong. The Hg reading is clearly *And* with the first part of the word torn.

§MR miss in their Corpus of Variants Hg's unique error of *a* for *and* in line 98.

Table 1. Table of Correspondences (continued)
B. *The Manciple's Tale**

Manu-script	Total No. of Recorded Variants	Unique Variants	Variants Unattested in Other Base-Group Manuscripts	Agreements with Other Base-Group Manuscripts										
				Hg	El	Ad³	Cp	En¹	Gg	Ha⁴	He *(b)*	La	Pw	CX¹
Hg†	3	2	1	..	..	..	..	..	..	..	..	..	..	..
El	21	3	3	..	..	3	7	6	10	8	8	6	6	8
Ad³	18	4	6	..	3	..	4	3	1	6	6	2	3	6
Cp	56	2	..	..	7	4	..	13	12	29	30	49	43	35
En¹	43	1	22	..	6	3	13	..	9	15	9	11	9	11
Gg	41	2	22	..	10	1	12	9	..	9	11	12	8	15
Ha⁴	89	2	47	..	8	6	29	15	9	..	26	26	25	26
He *(b)*	120	7	3	..	8	6	30	9	11	26	..	30	23	115
La	83	20	8	..	6	2	49	11	12	26	30	..	40	34
Pw	81	6	23	..	6	3	43	9	8	25	23	40	..	28
CX¹	118	1	..	..	8	6	35	11	15	26	115	34	28	..

*Lines of *ManT* with no variants among base-MSS: 69. Lines of *ManT* with no variants in MR's *Corpus of Variants:* 1 (line 144).

†Omissions resulting from a torn leaf are not counted as variants if the word or part of a word is clear in context and can be supplied from El; similarly, roman numerals, e.g., *.xx.* in line 269, are not counted as variants.

Table 1. Table of Correspondences (continued)

C. Correspondences in Printed Editions to WR*

Printed Edition	Total No. of Variants from Present Text	Unique Variants	Variants Without Manuscript Authority	Variants Not Attested by Other Printed Editions	Agreements with Other Printed Editions														
					CX¹	CX²	PN¹	WN	PN²	TH¹	TH²	TH³	ST	SP¹	SP²	SP³	UR	TR	WR
CX¹	190	1	2	25	...	153	149	155	149	130	130	130	130	131	126	127	95	64	26
CX²	164	..	3	..	153	...	153	153	155	139	139	139	136	137	131	132	96	65	28
PN¹	173	6	6	6	149	153	...	155	154	144	145	145	141	143	146	141	102	67	29
WN	176	1	12	2	155	153	155	...	163	154	155	155	154	155	151	146	108	69	30
PN²	171	2	7	2	149	155	154	163	...	142	142	142	141	142	138	143	98	66	30
TH¹	178	..	17	..	130	139	144	154	142	...	178	178	178	178	165	166	125	70	31
TH²	179	1	18	1	130	139	145	155	142	178	...	179	179	179	168	167	125	70	31
TH³	179	..	17	..	130	139	145	155	142	178	179	...	179	179	166	166	124	69	30
ST	182	2	19	2	130	136	141	154	141	178	179	179	...	182	167	167	121	71	30
SP¹	183	1	19	1	131	137	143	155	142	178	179	179	182	...	167	167	120	72	30
SP²	191	1	30	1	126	131	146	151	138	165	168	166	167	167	...	191	123	74	31
SP³	194	2	32	2	127	132	141	146	143	166	167	166	167	167	191	...	124	74	31
UR	180	24	41	38	95	96	102	108	98	125	125	124	121	120	123	124	...	73	36
TR	114	6	12	15	64	65	67	69	66	70	70	69	71	72	74	74	73	...	37
WR	103	1	1	49	26	28	29	30	30	31	31	30	30	30	31	31	36	37	...

*Much of the information in the table is, of course, overlapping, unique variants naturally being also variants without MS authority and without attestation in other printed editions. The figures here represent *ManP* and *ManT* combined. The printed-edition tradition, based upon the *b* group of MSS, does not show sufficient variation between *ManP ManT* to warrant two tables, unlike the base-group MSS. An exception is the dependence of WR upon Ha⁴, which does reflect considerable difference between the two; but since Ha⁴ has already been given for *ManP* and *ManT*, there seems to be no reason to repeat that information.

Descriptions of the Manuscripts

Hengwrt (Hg)

Hg is fully described in MR (1.266-83), by Manly and Rickert (1939:59-75), and most recently and completely by Doyle and Parkes (Ruggiers 1979:xix-xlix). Valuable discussion of Hg is found in Tatlock (1935:128-29, 133-39) and Dempster (1946:392-95; 1949:1131-32, 1139-40). MR describe the deficiencies of Hg caused by vermin damage (1.269-70), which has cost the manuscript many top corners of leaves (the reader can see this for himself in Ruggiers 1979). In the present edition, which uses Hg as its base-manuscript, such losses (lines 7, 165, 245, 326) are made good from El for reasons that will become apparent. MR conclude that, in spite of these deficiencies, "because of its freedom from accidental errors and its entire freedom from editorial variants, Hg is a MS of the highest importance" (1.276). It is worth noting that after producing his own great edition, not based on Hg, Skeat was to write (1909:55) ". . . MS Hengwrt (to which I now always look *first*)."

Doyle and Parkes (Ruggiers 1979:xix) are much more specific in their assessment of Hg:

The importance of the Hengwrt manuscript of *The Canterbury Tales* is that it is probably the earliest surviving copy of that unfinished work, that it shows, through its makeup and various deficiencies, the lack of an established sequence of the whole collection, alterations in the relative arrangement and personal assignment of particular tales and their links, and delays in receiving them, yet that it reproduces with remarkable fidelity sources better than those used by most other known copies and subjected to less adaptation and amendment.

Dempster (1951) complained that inattentive scholars had assumed that MR had used Hg as a base-text, whereas they had used the recension method; she added, however, that MR arrived largely at a text so close to Hg that it was understandable that some should assume Hg as a base-text. Hg has come to be realized and recognized over the past forty years to be the best text in general for *The Canterbury Tales* (see "Modern Editions" below). The movement has gone so far that Blake (1979) has even urged the importance of Hg to the extent that he dismisses anything not in Hg (even *The Canon's Yeoman's Tale*) as non-Chaucerian. It has often been urged that "Hg" as a sigil be dismissed as a sigil in favor of the manuscript's now correct title "Peniarth 392"; this would be a bibliographic nonsense, however, in view of the fact that MR's sigils are nearly universally used (and are used in the present edition)—we would be changing sigils as often as manuscripts have changed hands (why not "Huntington El.26.C.9" for Ellesmere?).

In the 362 lines of *The Manciple's Prologue* and *Tale* the present edition introduces only six emendations of the text as found in Hg. Of these, one is of a reading that is not normally considered a variant (i.e., *.xx.* for *twenty* in line 269) and is therefore not found in the Table of Correspondences. The other five are as follows (the emended form constituting the lemma):

    82   **wite ye]** wite
    98   **and many a]** a many a [MR miss this in the *Corpus of Variants*]
   103   **thy tale]** thy
   205   **this is a]** this a
   256   **sey hym swyve]** sey hym etc.

Of these five emendations required, four are simply scribal slips, two unique (lines 98 and 205), and duly emended from El. The other, line 256, is an interesting variant because clearly *swyve* is intended, yet the scribe avoids it, and the same scribe, in El, goes only so far as *swy etc.* The proper reading is supplied from Ad³, though clearly almost any manuscript would have served.

Other readings in Hg are accepted in the present edition that have by no means been accepted by all, many, or, in one instance, any editors and scholars, usually because of the presumed metrical or syntactical superiority of another reading or because traditionally the readings of such a manuscript as El or Ha⁴ have been considered to be superior. One can almost never claim certainty in the complicated matter of adopting readings, unless one has the self-assurance of a Housman; and it is to be expected that some of the Hg readings adopted in this edition against the judgment of some, most, or, in one case, all editors, and against the evidence of many good manuscripts (and, in two instances, nearly all manuscripts) will stir discussion. For ease of reference, they are listed here, the Hg reading constituting the lemma and the variant adopted by one or more printed editions being taken from the manuscript that is highest in the standard order of the Collations. The Collations and Textual Notes provide full information on the variant readings in the other base manuscripts, and MR's *Corpus of Variants* provides, of course, the full body of variants in all manuscripts.

All the Hg readings listed below have been adopted for the present edition:

    47   **bigan he nodde faste]** he gan n. f. El
    49   **men up hym took]** m. h. u. t. Cp
    89   **What neded it]** W. n. hym El
    96   **good drynke we with us carye]** g. d. with u. c. Cp
   102   **ye gete namoore for me]** y. g. n. of m. El
   143   **that the sothe if I shal sayn]** if t. s. that I s. s. Cp
   147   **for naught]** in ydel El
   148   **in werk]** of w. El
   157   **wenynge for swich]** w. by s. Cp
   170   **rude]** wylde Cp
   185   **And leest]** Or l. El
   188   **but no thyng]** and n. t. El
   254   **in comparisoun]** as i. c. Cp
   263   **And thoughte]** Hym t. Cp

266 **ther nys namoore**] t. is n. El
268 **and gyterne**] g. Cp
280 **smytest**] smyteth El
290 **Fully fordoon or**] F. f. and El
310 **what I seye**] w. ye s. Ad³
316 **I nam nat**] I am n. El
356 **leef or**] never so Cp
360 **wher**] wheither El

The grounds for the acceptance of the Hg readings above, together with the chief manuscript and printed editions on either side of the evidence and arguments, are to be found in detail in the Collations and in the Textual Notes. However, it may be convenient for the reader to have described under their headings the general considerations, other than mere reverence for Hg, that have led to their adoption:

1. Superior sense: lines 185, 188, 263, 280.

2. Equally acceptable sense: lines 89, 102, 147, 157, 170, 254, 266, 290, 310, 356. In these cases, of course, the belief that Hg, as probably the earliest extant manuscript of *The Canterbury Tales* and as the now-recognized best of all manuscripts *textually,* has had some effect on my judgment. But even here some consideration is being given to differing textual tradition because a few instances of "equally acceptable" sense could be argued in Hg's favor, particularly lines 102, 157, 170, 290, 310.

3. More difficult but arguable sense or syntax (the test of the "hard reading"): lines 47, 49, 96, 143, 268. These examples show no evidence of having been edited or "smoothed out" but make excellent sense, and are in my opinion more effective rhetorically than the readings that have replaced them in many editions, in spite of apparently awkward pauses and emphases. Analyses will be found in the Textual Notes.

4. More authentic metrical practice. This consideration does not play a large part in the adoption of the "maverick" readings of Hg in the case of *The Manciple's Prologue* and *Tale.* Metrical considerations have been subordinated to sense and syntax, but in lines 47 (where an extra foot is involved), 96 (an extra syllable), 254, 310 (loss of a syllable) there is no doubt that I have felt that the rougher meter has seemed more "Chaucerian." The theories of Chaucer's versification that dominated the creation of the printed editions until very recently (see the Textual and Explanatory Notes for specific discussions) are now recognized, however grudgingly, as the products of the study of previous printed editions that had been smoothed by editors (improving still further upon the smoothing by scribes and their supervisors). Study of the earliest manuscripts has begun to suggest that the metrical practice in Hg, unedited, is more likely to have been "Chaucerian," though, of course, certainty will never be attained in such a matter (see Doyle and Parkes, in Ruggiers 1979: xix-xxi, for general statements from

which one can infer the value of Hg as a witness, and, of course MR's great edition of *The Canterbury Tales,* while not specifically adopting Hg as a model, is nevertheless conspicuously closer to Hg in metrics as well as spelling than previous printed editions and away from the edited though excellent El). In Hg, as Doyle and Parkes observe (p. xix), the scribe was clearly not in full control of his work, receiving some pieces late and others not at all; yet the quality of his work is now almost universally recognized to have been superb under difficult circumstances. Since he could not hope to achieve a smooth production, he was likely inclined to copy what was before him. The same scribe in his almost certainly later, finished, polished, production of El, was apparently given to smoothing the rough edges a bit (see Donaldson, Southworth, Baum, and Ian Robinson in the Bibliographical Index, as well as the earlier work of UR, TR, Ten Brink, RB, and others on the general subject of Chaucer's metrics. A special section of a volume of the *Variorum Chaucer* will be devoted to this subject, which cannot be considered in reference to each work in the series). At any rate, there is nothing in the Hg text of *The Manciple's Prologue* and *Tale* (except for the four scribal slips noted above) of which one could say with confidence, "Chaucer could not have written this." Even in so short a piece, there is no other manuscript of which one could make this statement responsibly.

In spite of the disordered physical nature of Hg, the superb textual qualities of the manuscript have caused the editors of the *Variorum Chaucer* to adopt it as the base-text of *The Canterbury Tales* wherever possible.

On the question of the order of the tales in Hg as it may affect the reputation of the Hg text of *The Manciple's Prologue* and *Tale,* MR argued (1.270) that there could be no doubt that section 3 of Hg had been simply disarranged and should logically have come between sections 4 and 5 (*The Manciple's Prologue* and *Tale* end section 3, and section 5 is *The Parson's Prologue and Tale*); Doyle and Parkes (in Ruggiers 1979:xxiii) agree.

Ellesmere (El)

El is fully described in MR (1.148-59). It is an extremely important manuscript that has shaped the textual tradition of *The Canterbury Tales* for the past 120 years; it is a careful, beautifully finished job, probably the work of the same scribe who wrote Hg (see Doyle and Parkes, in Ruggiers 1979:xxiv-xxv, but see Ramsey 1982, Samuels 1983) and inferior only to Hg in textual authority. In the present edition El is normally used to supply missing words where Hg is defective because of loss of parts of leaves. El is very, very close to Hg, sharing among other interesting readings an aversion to *swyve* in *The Manciple's Tale,* line 256, *swy etc.* instead of Hg's simple *etc.* It shows, however, just a bit more carelessness than Hg and a distinct tendency to editing and smoothing. There can be no argument from the Table of Correspondences for *The Manciple's*

Prologue and *Tale* for an association of El with any of the base-manuscripts. In spite of the textual closeness of Hg and El, they were clearly not, in the case of *The Manciple's Prologue* and *Tale,* copied from a common exemplar. The readings listed under debatable variants in the discussion of Hg make this clear, particularly in lines 89, 102, 147, 148, 185, 188. These are not likely scribal errors of copying, though some may conceivably be so. There are in addition variants in El that were not picked up by subsequent scribes and editors and that may in some particulars indicate a different exemplar: lines 46, 47, 59, 64, 85, 96, 251, 266, 284, 290, 316. El is especially important for the strong support that it gives Hg elsewhere in view of the independence of the two manuscripts. But finally El must be relegated to second importance for the text of *The Manciple's Prologue* and *Tale* because of the following kinds of errors and variants:

1. Scribal slips: lines 29, 40, 64, 79, 133, 157, 251, 300 (105 may be a scribal slip, but it may also be evidence of a different exemplar: it is supported by a number of secondary manuscripts and was adopted by Koch; there is no difference in meaning, though Hg and the larger tradition seem preferable).

2. Variants arguably inferior in sense: lines 46, 284, 290.

3. Variants that indicate an editor's attention to smoothing and eliminating apparent awkwardnesses: lines 47, 59, 96, 143, 180, 256, 266, 316. Both of Hg's double negatives with contracted forms are eliminated (lines 266, 316), and in passages of more difficult syntax El invariably prefers the smooth or "natural" order of subject and verb: lines 47, 59, 96, 180. See Textual Notes for full discussion.

4. Some of these variants are little, if at all, inferior to Hg, and several— lines 46, 47, 256, 266, 284, 290, 316—have been adopted by many or all major editions. All of them, however, attest to editorial smoothing rather than to authenticity, and one, line 180, though a typical bit of smoothing in order of subject and verb, has never been adopted by any edition.

In view of the beauty of the manuscript, its relative completeness, and the editorial work that had made the lines so frequently of that regularity which pleased nineteenth- and early-twentieth century editors, one cannot be surprised that El has been the base-manuscript for nearly all editions, except, of course, for MR, which was constructed upon a different principle, and for PR, which shows a remarked tendency away from RB's dependence upon El and toward Hg (Donaldson likewise shows a marked preference for Hg).

Additional 35286 (Ad³)

Ad³ is described fully in MR (1.41–47). It is a relatively complete manuscript, though of a disturbed order, and has no "clear signs of supervision but many corrections by erasure and rewriting" (1.42). It was originally affiliated, say MR, with Ha[5], but between *MerT* 1691 and 2137 became affiliated with a manuscript of the Hg type: "From whatever sources derived, its text was originally near the archetype but in its descendants was much contaminated and altered" MR (1.43). Whatever the contamination elsewhere, Ad[3] offers for *The Manciple's Prologue* and *Tale* an excellent text, inferior only to Hg and El. It has played almost no role in determining the present text for the reason that, except for line 256 (which could have been supplied from most manuscripts), for the few emendations I have deemed necessary, Ad[3] follows El in sequence and authority in the MSS collations.

Corpus Christi 198 (Cp)

Cp is described in MR (1.92-99). They consider it to be the best representative of the *c* manuscripts (1.95). It is very closely associated with La, another *c* text, and with Pw, a member of the *d* group in a number of the tales. Cp is indeed with La in the text of *The Manciple's Prologue,* sharing 32 variants with it, and in *The Manciple's Tale,* sharing 49. It would undoubtedly have shared even more variants had not the scribe of La given way to a spate of creations of unique variants, all by poor copying: 15 in the *Prologue* and 20 in the *Tale.* Cp's affinities with Pw in both *Prologue* and *Tale* are strong, sharing 16 variants in the *Prologue* and 43 in the *Tale.* Cp has very strong affinities with He *(b)* CX[1] also, sharing 30 variants with He *(b)* and 35 variants with CX[1] in the *Prologue* and 30 variants with He *(b)* and 35 variants with CX[1] in the *Tale.* No readings from *c* manuscripts are accepted into the present text. Cp is heavily editorialized and supervised, even if the supervision was incomplete (see MR, 1.93), and the desire to smooth seems rampant: some examples of this work can be found in lines 2, 9, 24, 41, 57, 74, 80, etc. Unfortunately, this care was not matched in the actual copying, for there are many omissions. Cp is, in addition, not complete (MR 1.92), though these imperfections do not affect the text of *The Manciple's Prologue* and *Tale.* MR note (1.96) that Cp and Ha[4] may have been from the same shop, and Doyle and Parkes (1978:192-94) conclude that the two manuscripts are by the same scribe; perhaps so, but in the text of *The Manciple's Prologue* and *Tale,* Ha[4] is superior, in addition to sharing almost no textual affiliation with Cp, a point that is not, of course, in question here. Cp has earned its place in the base-ten manuscripts on the strength of its having been among the Chaucer Society's Six Texts, and hence of considerable influence upon the printed editions, particularly SK.

Egerton 2726 (En[1])

Dd, of the base-ten manuscripts, is Out entirely for *The Manciple's Prologue* and *Tale.* Therefore, En[1] has been chosen as the representative of MR's group *a.*

En[1] is described by MR (1.130-35), who say that it is derived from the same exemplar as Dd (1.131) and, furthermore, that it is the most constant member of subgroup *Dd*. En[1] is described as a careful copy, very little edited, and this seems to be the case on the basis of the text of *The Manciple's Prologue* and *Tale*. MR say that "*Dd* is with El to c. A 1880, then with Hg" (1.132). This would not seem to be true in the text of *The Manciple's Prologue* and *Tale*, for, as we have seen in the discussion of the relation of *Prologue* to *Tale*, there is a marked affiliation of En[1] with Ha[4] in the text of the former (sharing 26 variants in 104 lines), whereas the affiliation falls off somewhat in the *Tale* (sharing 15 variants—not the proportion that one would expect in view of the *Prologue*, but in fact En[1] shares more variants with Ha[4] there than with any other of the base-ten manuscripts). The present edition, then, profits by having in its principal collations a manuscript somewhat superior to the base-manuscript Dd, though, of course, without the historical significance of the latter for the study of Chaucer's work (Dd was also one of the Chaucer Society's Six Texts and strongly influenced SK).

Cambridge Gg.4.27 (Gg)

Gg is described in MR (1.170-82), and is now available in a facsimile edition (1979-80) with a full description by Parkes and Beadle. It is in many ways the most interesting and challenging of all the Chaucer manuscripts, for it mixes nearly everywhere an almost pedantic accuracy to a text in the Hg-El tradition on the one hand, and a wild, almost comic habit of misreading or miswriting on the other. For speculations on the scribal reasons for the manuscript's peculiarities, see MR (1.177-78), Caldwell (1944), and Parkes and Beadle; the last reject the speculations of Caldwell that the principal scribe may have been a Fleming (1980:3.47-49). In the text of *The Manciple's Prologue* and *Tale* the variants of Gg are seldom important, whereas its authority for the authenticity in general of the Hg-El text is quite important, far more so than the 71 recorded variants for *Prologue* and *Tale* would indicate. But one must in fairness give a sample of the kind of egregious errors of omission and commission of the Gg scribe: lines 7, 21, 55, 75, 79, 88, 134, 152, 159, 163, 183, 192, 203, 204, 238, 245, 247, 251, 254, 299, 306, 328, 334, 337, 339. These are all clearly miswritings, and a few even suggest an exemplar of a totally different tradition from that which has determined the present text. The MR judgment, then, that Gg is "a MS of the highest importance, [representing], in the main, the El tradition without the El editing" (1.176) must be allowed to stand without challenge, though one is moved to wonder at the number of niggling errors ("without the El editing," indeed!). MR's explanation of the peculiar nature of Gg, its scribes, etc., can be read there and need not detain us here. What may be noted in passing, however, is that in addition to the 14 shared variants with El in *The Manciple's Prologue* and *Tale,* which are to be expected, there are 16 with Cp and La, 18 with He *(b),* and the largest number of all—22—with CX[1]. MR postulate an affiliation with Ha[3] in the *Prologue* and *Tale* (1.176) but do not mention the possibility of an affiliation here with an ancestor of *b*. The variants shared with the *b* tradition through CX[1] are scattered through the *Prologue* and *Tale,* and in any case an attempt to discover just where the manuscripts came into affiliation upon a basis of 22 shared variants in just 362 lines would seem a futile enterprise. The shared variants are usually shared with other manuscripts as well, but interesting examples of Gg *b* (and CX[1]) congruences are lines 82, 89, 102, 134, 198, 212, 251, 256, 266, 284, 289, 306. It is the total that is somewhat impressive, finally, not isolated instances. What is ironic here is that MR (1.211) consider Ha[3] a *b*-affiliated manuscript for much of *The Canterbury Tales* but that in *The Manciple's Prologue* and *Tale* Ha[3] is associated with the Hg Ps Py Ad[3] Ch, El Gg Ha[3], *a* En Ry[1] Se groups of affiliation, and the evidence (2.453) would indeed seem to bear this out. Since Gg is an earlier manuscript than any surviving *b*-group manuscripts, we must assume some contact with an ancestor of He throughout the text of *Prologue* and *Tale* in Gg.

Gg also has 30 variants unattested in the base-ten manuscripts, a rather high number, but not in the same class with Pw.

Harley 7334 (Ha[4])

Ha[4] is described by MR (1.219), and its scribe is argued by Doyle and Parkes (1978:192-94) to have been that of Cp as well. Its great age (MR [1.220] date it ca. 1410, and this has not been seriously disputed) and its historical significance in the effort to establish a text of Chaucer give it an importance that its actual text does not perhaps deserve, at least, and certainly does not with reference to *The Manciple's Prologue* and *Tale*. Its many peculiarities gave rise to the idea that Ha[4] represented in some respects a text revised by Chaucer (Pollard 1901: 631; SK 3.viii; SK 5.471; Hammond 1908:178). Tatlock (1907 for 1904) assembles the evidence and, after judicious examination, dismisses the case for Chaucerian revision. There has been general agreement with Tatlock's opinion, though Skeat (1909) argued that it is the most important manuscript as regards evidence for the order of the tales (p. 35). Ha[4], as MR suggest, has probably the widest range of affiliations: "In general, Ha[4] is associated with the large composite groups of MSS, forming with some member or members of this an independent subgroup, usually apart from the main line of tradition" (1.221). By the "main line of tradition" MR presumably mean Hg El Gg. Ha[4], however, is associated at times with this "main line," as well as, particularly, with *a* and *b*. The explanation for this is that "Ha[4] is the earliest example of the commercial type of MS picked up from many sources and edited with great freedom by some one other than Chaucer" (1.222). For the text of *The Manciple's Prologue* and *Tale,* Ha[4], "never authoritative," as MR say (1.222), is not of great interest except for the way in which it is closely affiliated with En[1] in *The Manciple's Prologue* and only moderately so with other manuscripts; in the *Tale,* however, as we have seen, it loses this remarkable affiliation and moves to a closer relation to *c* and *b,* though in both these cases the similarities are not enough to suggest close association—merely that sort of similarity which highly edited manuscripts are likely to have. Its importance in the tradition in the text of *The Canterbury Tales* may be merely fortuitous: its appearance, which is good; its accessibility; and its high degree of editing, which created a good deal of smoothness. WR used it as his base-text, from which in *The Manciple's Prologue* and *Tale* he seldom wandered except to emend from La; this was slightly corrected and respelled by Morris, and, through WR, and the importance given to it by the Chaucer Society, Ha[4] remained very influential with SK, though he considered it overrated textually (5.442). For our purposes it need only be remarked that Ha[4] at no point supports a disputed Hg reading, nor is its weight heavy against a Hg reading; it is of no consequence in determining the text, in spite of the light that its association with En[1] *(a)* in *The Manciple's Prologue* may or may not throw on the history of the transmission of the *Prologue.*

Helmingham (He)

He is described in MR (1.254–65). *The Manciple's Prologue* and *Tale* appear in the older, vellum portion of the manuscript (MR 1.12). He is a heavily edited text, carelessly copied, and claims our interest because it is, as MR say (1.258), "always the highest member of the *b* group." Since it is from the ancestor of the *b* group of manuscripts from which CX[1] derived its exemplar, and since the *b* group therefore thus dominated the printed edition tradition for two centuries, and since He is, according to MR, the highest member of the *b* group, it is quite properly one of the base-ten group. It is, however, Out for lines 48–255 of *The Manciple's Prologue* and *Tale;* for this passage it is replaced in the Collations by Ne (described by MR [1.381–86]).

MR say that "it [Ne] is chiefly valuable for establishing the [ancestor of the] *b* reading when He and *Cx*[1] [Cx[1] + Tc[2]] disagree" (1.382). In the Collations, when *b* readings are uniform, we simply give that sigil— *(b);* CX[1] as a separate manuscript-printed edition is also noted in its place. When neither He nor Ne can attest to *Cx*[1] (other than CX[1] itself), I have occasionally had recourse to Tc[2] in the Collations (I should perhaps note, to avoid confusion, that in quotations of MR the sigil Cx[1] is used, for that is their habit, and quotations require accuracy; in our own collations we use CX[1] for consistency because our printed editions are cited in double capitals; because of its dual role, CX[1]-Cx[1] [and *Cx*[1]] is the only inconsistency in the use of sigils). He *(b)* and CX[1] are consistently together in *The Manciple's Prologue* and *Tale,* sharing 60 variants in the *Prologue* and 115 in the *Tale.* There is no reason to believe that the relationship between He and CX^1 is misrepresented by substituting Ne or Tc^2 for He, though in some respects Ne is closer to CX^1 than He in *The Manciple's Prologue* and *Tale,* from the evidence of the collations; about Ne, MR say (1.382), ". . . at times it seems to be from the same exemplar as He." That Tc^2 is, in MR's sigils, included in the group Cx^1 seems adequately to suggest its closeness to CX^1 for our purposes. At any rate, the pattern of correspondence with *b* seems roughly the same whether He is In or Out of the text. There is also the expected high degree of correspondence between He and *c* (30 variants shared with both Cp and La in the *Tale* and 30 with Cp and 27 with La in the *Prologue.* There are nearly as many with Pw (21 in the *Prologue* and 23 in the *Tale*), as one would expect with the tradition of highly edited and contaminated manuscripts.

Lansdowne 851 (La)

La is described in MR (1.304-308). It forms with Cp the basis of *c* and shares the expected high number of variants (32 in *The Manciple's Prologue* and 49 in *The Manciple's Tale).* It is also clearly affiliated with Pw in *Prologue* and *Tale,* sharing 21 variants in the former and 40 in the latter. This is a consistency representative of La for much of *The Canterbury Tales.* MR describe La, comparing it with Cp, as "slightly later and independently edited by the scribe" (1.95). La's scribe is easily the most incompetent of all the scribes of the base manuscripts; he commits 35 unique errors in the 362 lines of *The Manciple's Prologue* and *Tale.* La's importance in the tradition of the text of *The Canterbury Tales* derives in large measure from the significance given to it by the Chaucer Society and by the fact that WR had emended his basically Ha^4 text from it. This in turn had more influence on SK than the actual textual authority of La should have required. It is, however, a beautiful manuscript, and perhaps this fact in itself had some influence on the nineteenth-century response to it.

Petworth (Pw)

Pw is described in MR (1.410-14). It is a prominent member of the group *d,* which is a rather loosely affiliated group. The ancestor of *d* in *The Manciple's Prologue* and *Tale* is, with the text of several other tales, closely associated with the exemplar of the ancestor of *c* (MR 1.96; 2.414). This is reflected in the association of Cp La with Pw in the *Prologue* and *Tale,* though the shared variants are not as numerous here proportionately as in some other pieces. Cp shares 32 variants with La and 16 with Pw in the *Prologue* and 49 with La and 43 with Pw in the *Tale.* One reason that the figures are not even higher may be that Pw has the largest total number of variants for *Prologue* and *Tale* of the base-ten manuscripts, and also the largest number of variants unattested in other base-ten manuscripts: 41 and 85 in *Prologue* and *Tale,* respectively. Pw is not a dependable manuscript by any means; it is a bit more careful than La in respect of unique readings (11 in all), and it is a bit less careful than Cp. La and Pw do share one variant with Hg (line 82), a scribal slip that should not be given much textual weight. Pw, like Cp and La, was one of the Chaucer Society's Six-Text manuscripts and so, like them, influenced SK, as well as RB[1-2].

Summary

These manuscripts have been chosen as representing, for *The Manciple's Prologue* and *Tale,* and for most of the *Tales* (1) the two best texts (Hg and El) and (2) the principal representatives of the families of manuscripts as delineated by MR, which determined the course that Chaucer's text was to take. For *The Manciple's Prologue* and *Tale* Hg and El, though independent, strongly reinforce one another, supported generally by Ad[3] and Gg. The broad descriptions of the manuscripts above will be much more fully detailed in the Textual Notes.

Descriptions of the Printed Editions

The Printed Editions have been chosen for a number of reasons, not all of them bearing upon *The Manciple's Prologue* and *Tale.* They have been judged to be those which have chiefly determined Chaucer's text. Caxton and his followers in the fifteenth and sixteenth centuries printed a text of *The Canterbury Tales* largely drawn from the *b* manuscript tradition, a bad text, but nonetheless the Chaucer that the early commentators knew. This was the period in which Chaucer's canon was being determined, and most of these printings, however feeble as editions, had some contribution to make. Urry was the first attempt at a "modern" Chaucer and, though probably the worst of all the editions textually, deserves inclusion for historical reasons. Tyrwhitt's great effort was a landmark, and, although Wright's edition is poor, it nevertheless made a contribution by being specifically based upon two manuscripts which the editor thought the best. Skeat's monumental edition of the works is still considered by many scholars to be the best full edition, though for most it was replaced by the labors of Robinson. The Manly-Rickert text of *The Canterbury Tales,* whatever its faults, provides us with the best data that we have for that work and, most now believe, the best text of the work as well. Pratt and Fisher are included in the Collations because I recognize that both have reedited *The Manciple's Prologue* and *Tale* in useful ways that deserve to be recorded. Fisher is not collated in some of the fascicles of the *Variorum Chaucer* but is noted by all editors in the series.

Caxton 1478 (CX[1])

CX[1] is discussed in MR (1.79-81), where it is designated Cx[1]. The first Caxton is, they say, derived from the same exemplar as that of Tc[2] (the two being classed as *Cx[1]*), the latter manuscript having been copied from the exclusive common ancestor after the printing of CX[1] (2.57). MR observe that the exemplar of CX[1] has been extensively edited, and this is proved, if proof is needed, by the appearance of this editing in Tc². Further, MR state (1.80) that Ne and the manuscript used by Caxton (the sister manuscript of CX¹) are so "close in dialect and spelling that the language is evidently that of their common ancestor." The group *b* in MR therefore normally includes He as the head and oldest manuscript of the group, Ne and *Cx¹*. It is for this reason that *b* is represented in the Collations, for it both accounts for and includes CX¹, which established the printed tradition of *The Canterbury Tales*.

As I observed, He is Out for lines 48-255, and is replaced by Ne or occasionally Tc². The close correspondence with He and Ne for the whole, thus amalgamated, text is indicated by the 60 shared variants of *The Manciple's Prologue* and the 115 of the *Tale*. It might be interesting to break down these variants within certain limits. Of the shared variants in the 48 lines of the *Prologue*, He is with CX¹ in 23 (out of the 60 shared by He Ne CX¹); Ne is with CX¹ for 34 shared variants in the remaining 55 lines. For the 107 lines of the *Tale* that He contains, CX¹ and He share 34 variants (out of 115). For the 255 lines of the *Tale* in which He is Out, the *b* group, i.e., Ne and Tc², share 53 variants with CX¹. In addition, Tc² shares 16 variants with CX¹ that are not shared by Ne (though the figures are too small to be significant for the incomplete He). CX¹ would seem to be a bit closer, therefore, to Ne than to He and closer still, as one would expect, to Tc². These distinctions cannot be reflected in the Table of Correspondences, and in the Collations the *b* group, if together and He is Out, is simply given in its order, so that it is difficult to see the relationship between Ne and CX¹ and Tc² and CX¹ (though Tc² is given alone in parentheses when it is the only representative of *b* other than CX¹ itself.

CX¹ reveals its position at the end of a long, popular, widespread, and heavily editorialized tradition, by having only 3 variants unattested in other base-ten manuscripts (both in *The Manciple's Prologue*) and only two variants not found at all in other extant manuscripts, one each in the *Prologue*—line 94—and the *Tale*—line 196. It has, however, 25 variants unattested in later printed editions (including line 94). This has clearly to do, as we shall see, with the hasty revisions in CX² and the introduction, however imperfectly, of a new manuscript into the editorial procedure. It may also reflect some of Caxton's own handiwork in CX¹ that may have formed some of the imperfections against which readers protested, in spite of Caxton's disclaimers in his preface to CX² (for further discussion of these matters see Dunn 1940: passim; Blake 1967: 101-108; and Boyd 1973: 131-37). CX¹ is out for line 316 and shows 190 variants from the present text.

Caxton 1484 (CX²)

CX² is briefly discussed in MR (1.81), but is excluded from their collations, as are all subsequent printed editions. They have this to say about the origin of CX²: "Caxton collated his first edition with a MS lent him by a patron, but his collation was so hasty and imperfect that the readings of CX^2, though interesting, are of no textual authority." That the collation was hasty is obvious, but perhaps MR are too dismissive in their denial of textual authority for CX^2, for 32 faulty CX^1 readings have been removed from *The Manciple's Prologue* and *Tale,* one must suppose as a result of the collation, though some may have been typographical errors introduced in the new setting: lines 25, 32, 36, 39, 40, 44, 82, 86 (2), 94, 111, 121, 143, 149, 150, 183, 200 (2), 206, 223, 232, 236 (2), 243, 251, 254, 263, 266, 281, 284, 314, 331. CX^2 has introduced 5 new readings of its own: lines 92, 263, 267 (these 3 without extant manuscript authority), 274, 316. CX^2 shares with CX^1 a total of 153 variants from the present edition. It restores line 316 and shows a total of 164 variants from the present edition. In view of the large number of variants shared, CX^2 remains CX^1 with considerable touching up. Although doubtless there was some consultation with a new manuscript, Caxton's claims for a new edition can largely be dismissed (Greg 1924:738-40; Blake 1967: 23-25; Blake 1969: 104–106). It is generally agreed by the above authorities and by Dunn (1940) that Caxton used a manuscript of the *a* group (chiefly on the grounds that the *a* order was used for CX^2 as opposed to the *b* order for CX^1, though this does not affect *The Manciple's Prologue* and *Tale*). The one new reading of CX^2 in the *Prologue* and *Tale* that has extant manuscript authority (I do not count the restoration of line 316 here) shares that reading with El Ad³ Cp Ha⁴ La Pw of the base-ten manuscripts. A large woodcut of the Manciple on horseback, facing left, is added with a narrow border. This and the other woodcuts added to CX^2 were presumably derived from the manuscript that Caxton consulted for his second edition.

Pynson 1492 (PN¹)

Greg (1924:755) is of the opinion that a manuscript of unknown affiliation was consulted in the preparation of PN^1, but his argument is based upon insufficient evidence and is certainly unsupported in the form of *The Manciple's Prologue and Tale.* PN^1 shares with CX^2 a total of 153 of the latter's 164 variants from the present edition. It follows the rejection by CX^2 of all the CX^1 readings in *The Manciple's Prologue* and *Tale* eliminated from CX^2 except lines 25, 143, where PN^1 agrees with CX^1. PN^1 follows CX^2 in its new contributions at lines 263, 267, 274 (for the first two CX^2 has no extant manuscript authority) and in the CX^2 text of line 316. It does not follow CX^2 at lines 26, 27 (2), 28, 122, 133, 143, 192, 196, 209, 228, 283, 294, 298, 308, 309, 350 (for line 26, one of the variants in line 27, and for lines 28, 122, 133, 228, 350 there is no extant manuscript authority), where PN^1 introduces its own variants from the present text. The fact that for PN^1's 15 original variants there is no extant manuscript authority for 7 would perhaps suggest that PN^1 did not have in *The Manciple's Prologue* and *Tale* the support of additional manuscripts (in spite of Greg's argument). That PN^1 follows CX^2 in its departures (except two) from CX^1 would seem to indicate that, on the scanty evidence of *The Manciple's Prologue* and *Tale,* PN^1 was set up from CX^2, the additional variants and the two agreements with CX^1 being probably the accidentals of printing or the result of editorialization. A new woodcut of the Manciple, facing right, is added, with a thick, broken border. This woodcut is not later repeated. PN^1 has altogether 173 variants from the present edition.

Wynkyn de Worde 1498 (WN)

WN appears to have been set up from CX^2 (Greg 1924:756), though in *The Manciple's Prologue* and *Tale* it does share 2 original PN^1 variants, lines 27, 209, and agrees with CX^1 in 251. It introduces its own variants at lines 1, 2, 32, 52, 62, 132, 138, 170, 230, 234, 273, 279, 341 (there being no extant manuscript authority for the variants in lines 132, 273). The manuscripts that support the other readings are minor, none being in the base-ten manuscripts or a prominent member of any other group. WN shares with CX^2 a total of 153 variants from the present edition and shows 176 variants in all. A manuscript was consulted in preparing WN (Garbáty 1978), for WN's copy of CX^2 was defective in parts, but there is no evidence from *The Manciple's Prologue* and *Tale* to substantiate this because the *Prologue* and *Tale* were in the CX^2 used by WN. The woodcut of the Manciple, facing left, found in CX^2 is here repeated.

Pynson 1526 (PN²)

PN^2 introduces in *The Manciple's Prologue* and *Tale* 5 variants of its own unique to the printed editions: lines 23, 45, 49, 74, 104, 122, all but line 45 also lacking extant manuscript authority. It would seem overall to be a further resetting of CX^2, printing its additions to and corrections of CX^1 (see discussions above). PN^2 rejects 10 of PN^1's original variants (one of those at line 27 and lines 85, 122, 133, 192, 209, 228, 308, 309, 350). Greg (1924:756) believes that PN^2 may have drawn occasional readings from a manuscript of the *Pw* group; in the small number of lines of *The Manciple's Prologue* and *Tale* there is apparently no evidence of this. PN^2 shares with CX^2 a total of 155 of the latter's 164 variants and shows 171 of its own in total. Of some interest, undoubtedly, is that PN^2 shares 163 variants with WN, which would suggest that, to judge from *The Manciple's Prologue* and *Tale,* PN^2 profited from WN as well as from CX^2. PN^2 shares 154 variants with PN^1. The woodcut of the Manciple, facing left, found in CX^2 and in WN replaces in PN^2 that from PN^1 and here has a moderately thick border.

Thynne 1532 (TH¹)

TH^1 shows agreement with CX^2 in 139 of the 164 CX^2 variants from the present edition and altogether shows 178. It introduces 19 variants that lack either manuscript or printed-edition precedent, some lacking both: lines 8, 21, 23 (2), 48,

53, 61, 62, 72, 133, 143, 168, 169, 183, 217, 218, 219, 220, 346. It shares with WN the 12 variants from CX^2, including lines 132 and 234, for which there is no extant manuscript authority. It also shares with WN the two PN^1 variants from CX^2, lines 27, 209, and with WN a CX^1 reading at line 251 that was rejected by CX^2. In addition, TH^1 corrects an error at line 196 that all printed editions had continued from CX^1. All these TH^1 variants are of continuing textual importance because most of them remain in printed editions through SP^3 and many through UR, some continuing to TR. The total number of lines does not, as always, allow for very many generalizations; it might indeed appear, as Greg has concluded (1924:757), that TH^1 was set up from WN; the additional variants from WN lend support to this conclusion. There may also have been consultation with CX^2—it would be surprising if there was not—but on the evidence of *The Manciple's Prologue* and *Tale* one can only surmise that, if there was, it was not constant. The introduction of a relatively large number of new variants in such a short poem seems to indicate some reference to a source outside the printed editions, as Koch suggested (1898:xix-xx), but it would be foolish to speculate on the basis of the evidence (7 of the new TH^1 variants have no extant manuscript authority). TH^1 is a vital text in any case because it determines in a more specific way than before the reading text of Chaucer for two hundred years (see Hetherington 1964; Brewer 1969; Alderson 1970). A woodcut of the Manciple, facing right, is added; it is quite different from that in PN^2, which is larger and has a border, and different also from the CX^2 and PN^1 woodcuts.

Thynne 1542 (TH²)

TH^2 is a fairly careful resetting of TH^1. There is a single variant from TH^1, a typographical error at line 72. The woodcut of the Manciple in TH^1 is retained. TH^2 shows 179 variants from the present edition.

Thynne 1545 (TH³)

TH^3 is, for *The Manciple's Prologue* and *Tale,* a resetting of TH^1. The misprint at line 72 in TH^2 is removed, and a new variant is introduced at line 246— almost certainly a misprint, though there is extant manuscript authority. There is no evidence in *The Manciple's Prologue* and *Tale* for revision or reference to outside authority, either manuscript or printed edition. There are 179 variants against the present edition. The woodcut of the Manciple in TH^{1-2} is not repeated. TH^3, for the first time in the printed editions, inserts the non-Chaucerian *The Plowman's Tale* between *The Manciple's Tale* and *The Parson's Prologue,* a practice that continued through UR.

Stow 1561 (ST)

ST is a resetting of TH^3 (without the paragraph markers of TH^3), carefully retaining the misprint at line 246. It contributes, for *The Manciple's Prologue* and

The Manciple's Tale

Tale, 3 variants: 2 simple errors, lines 105 and 257 (the printer had misread *þ* for *y* in line 105), and the other, line 301, a substitution of a present participle for an infinitive. for the accuracy of ST see Fletcher (1978). ST had access, of course, to manuscripts of *The Canterbury Tales* but apparently did not use them, at least for *The Manciple's Prologue* and *Tale.* There are 182 variants against the present edition. ST does not have the woodcut of the Manciple found in TH[1-2].

Speght 1598 (SP[1])

SP[1] was clearly set up from ST even to the paragraphing without use of paragraph markers, the format, and number of lines per page, at least as far as *The Manciple's Prologue* and *Tale* are concerned. The misreading of ST in line 301 is continued, and a unique typographical error is added at line 232. See Hetherington (1964) for a discussion of SP[1]. There are 183 variants against the present edition. The woodcut of the TH editions discontinued in ST also does not appear here or in SP[2-3]. The ST error of line 105 is corrected.

Speght 1602 (SP[2])

Whatever the exemplar from which SP[2] was set up, either ST or SP[1], SP[2] contributes 25 variants from SP[1]: lines 22, 45, 67, 72, 73, 98, 106, 119, 135, 153, 184, 187, 196, 215, 245, 258, 262, 285, 293, 301. The correction at line 262 is especially important (*prien* to *wrien*) and perhaps suggests consultation with a manuscript, for the wrong *prien* had appeared in every printed edition, but this may have been a lucky hit or an error. The others are variants also with some manuscript authority, 3 of interest: line 119 (Dl) and lines 98, 294, both with Ha[4] giving those readings among the manuscripts. Although SP[2] may have used TH in his revisions elsewhere (and took advantage of Francis Thynne's suggestions in his *Animadversions* [See Wright 1959: passim], there is no evidence of either action in these variants. As for *The Manciple's Prologue* and *Tale* as a whole, there is little evidence of "The whole worke by old Copies reformed," even though Pace (1968) makes a strong case that SP[2] took at least the text of *An ABC* directly from Gg. In our instance, if Speght used the text of Gg for *The Manciple's Prologue* and *Tale,* he used it very curiously, agreeing with Gg only in instances shared by the printed tradition and missing many opportunities to print Gg's peculiar readings. There are 191 variants against the present edition. SP[2] is Out for line 219, which is not counted in the variant total.

Speght 1687 (SP[3])

SP[3] is clearly for *The Manciple's Prologue* and *Tale* a resetting of SP[2]. For a discussion of SP[3] see Alderson (1970:40-52). It adds the dropped line 219, follows SP[2] in its variants, but contributes 3 variants of its own, one in line 8 and 2, unique, in lines 132, 183. SP[3] has 194 variants from the present edition.

Urry 1721 (UR)

It is most probable that for *The Manciple's Prologue* and *Tale* UR was based upon SP². It does not have the two curious errors of SP³ or the eccentricities of ST-SP¹. There is again, however, little evidence upon which to judge. The one obvious fact is that UR is the most eccentric edition of all, in spite of its editors' (Urry and the Thomas brothers) care in taking into consideration for the first time in nearly a century a variety of manuscripts of *The Canterbury Tales.* For a discussion of UR's use of manuscripts see the preface to UR and Alderson (1970). Although UR brings to an end a great number of variants, almost certainly errors, that had existed in printed editions since the Caxtons and the early-fifteenth-century editions (e.g., lines 2, 24, 27, 37, 39, 41, 60, 61, 80, 92, etc.), UR introduces 24 errors with no manuscript or printed-edition authority: lines 39, 44, 60, 81, 105, 107, 135, 172, 173, 185, 215, 224, 267, 274, 276, 279, 288, 294, 296, 321, 336, 338, 352, 358. Some are simple errors, but most seem to be examples of smoothing. For the variants introduced with MS authority, many seem to be from Dl, the Cholmondeley manuscript (which is Out for *The Manciple's Prologue*). Other manuscript uses are identified by the Thomases in the preface (sigs. K¹-K³ [see Hammond 1908:130; Alderson 1970:106–12 for a discussion of these manuscripts]). Of these manuscripts MR deal with Dl (1.115), Ds (1.121), En¹ (1.135), En² (1.141), Gg (1.182), Nl (1.389, 394), Ph² (1.424), Sl¹ (1.509), Sl² (1.514), Ra¹ (1.631). Only two of all these manuscripts, Gg and En¹, are of prime importance for the text of *The Canterbury Tales.* Although UR makes use of Gg in his edition, it is far from clear that Gg has had any influence on the UR text of *The Manciple's Prologue* and *Tale* (except perhaps for line 7). On the other hand, Dl can be fairly clearly traced in lines 119, 193, 198 (2), 274, 314, 332; Ry¹ is quite likely behind lines 60, 135; and Ha² may lie behind line 62. Two SP²⁻³ variants introduced without manuscript or printed-edition authority, lines 153, 184, are retained, and the hitherto unique ST error at line 105 is revived. There are many oddities, but two of UR's confusions stand out: line 262, in which, after SP²⁻³ had retrieved the correct reading *wryen,* UR returned to SP¹ (probably) for the old CX¹-SP¹ blunder *prien* attested to by the *b* manuscripts, of course; in line 185 all manuscripts and all early printed editions have either *that* or *him*—UR omitted to print either, and all important later printed editions except MR followed suit, though PR and FI have now restored *that.* The method of operation of Urry and the Thomases must have been to use SP² as the base- and copy-text and to rummage among other printed editions and manuscripts for ideas, all the while smoothing and "correcting" for their sophisticated audience. There are altogether 180 variants from the present edition. UR reintroduces the woodcut of the Manciple but, unlike the sixteenth-century cuts, this one is clearly designed after the miniature of the Manciple adorning Gg that shows him carrying what is apparently the gourd from which he gave wine to the

Cook instead of the purse shown in the Gg picture. On sig. K¹ of the UR preface is an appreciative mention of the quality of the miniatures of that great manuscript, which even then had lost most of them (see the reproductions in the Gg facsimile (Parkes and Beadle 1980. 3, fol. 472 in "Colour Plates" section).

Tyrwhitt 1775 (TR)

TR is the first of the printed editions to make extensive and systematic use of good manuscripts (though not yet Hg or El), but, as a glance at the Textual Notes of the present edition will reveal, he was still wedded to the printed edition that had formed the tradition of Chaucer's text. Of the 114 variants to be found between TR and the present edition, the vast majority are most probably derived from earlier printed editions, particulalry SP². Considering what is known of TR's methods, it could hardly be otherwise (Hench 1950:265-66). TR used SP² as a base-text and corrected it by manuscripts and other printed editions. Of the 114 variants to be found in *The Manciple's Prologue* and *Tale* between TR and the present edition, 42 can be found in SP²; 7, even—lines 24, 85, 145, 173, 185, 224, 265—are not in SP² but are to be found in the wretched UR. Most other variants can be traced to manuscripts that TR is known to have used, except for a few instances of what are probably typographical errors or editor's slips: lines 65, 99, 143, 168, 181, 215, 244, 349 (and perhaps an example of "smoothing" in 122). At line 224 there are 2 variants, one from UR, the other unique, representing the only textual difference between the first edition of TR of 1775 and the second of 1798; the first edition has the unique reading, and the second adopts the UR reading that TR in a note to the line in his first edition states that he prefers to his own, even though it is "only conjecture" and he cannot find it in any manuscripts but would have adopted it if it had come to his attention in time. TR lists the twenty-six manuscripts of *The Canterbury Tales* that he collated or consulted (1775:1.xxii-xxiii), of which he gives five most credit for their help: Ha⁵ Dd Ad¹ En³ En¹ (listed here, of course, by their MR sigils). Others that can be identified by their MR sigils are: Bo², Bw, Ha¹, Ha², Ha³, Ha⁴, Ht, Ii, La, Ld¹, Ld², Ne, Ry¹, Ry², Se, Sl¹, Sl², Tc¹, Tc² (see Hammond 1908: 205-11). Of manuscripts that can be said with some definiteness to have contributed to the text of TR's *Manciple's Prologue* and *Tale,* we can point to En¹ (lines 76, 168, 226), La (lines 10, 170, and probably 330), Tc¹ (lines 72, 227), En³ (lines 62, 99, 181), Ha⁴ (lines 310, 311, 327). Of this evidence perhaps the little clustering of probable Ha⁴ sources is the most interesting. Other variants are frequently shared by two or more of the manuscripts that TR used, together usually with one or more printed editions, so that no conclusions can be drawn. TR eliminates the non-Chaucerian *Plowman's Tale* and so restores the H-I order of the fragments. For all its many weaknesses, TR is the first modern edition of Chaucer, and one that commanded the respect of Henry Bradshaw (who finally persuaded Furnivall to consult it—at the founding of the Chaucer Society, Furnivall was unfamiliar with it; see Bradshaw Correspondence, Cambridge University Library, Add. 2591, box 3, letter to Furnivall, August 6, 1868).

Wright 1847 (WR)

WR is the first edition to be set from a manuscript, and should be accorded a certain respect for this. WR, however, blindly follows his manuscript, Ha⁴, an interesting and important but certainly not a dependable text for *The Manciple's Prologue* and *Tale,* and when Ha⁴ is Out or disappointing, WR emends from La, a beautiful manuscript but one far inferior generally to Ha⁴ and famous for its unique readings. WR's emendation is not consistent. A total of 36 eccentric readings by Ha⁴, alone of the base-ten manuscripts in these instances in all but two cases, account thus for a high percentage of WR's 103 variants from the present text. WR varies from Ha⁴ on 16 occasions when Ha⁴ cannot be countenanced; on at least 8 occasions he makes good from TR rather than from La. He clearly emends from La only once in *The Manciple's Prologue* and *Tale* (line 37), but such a short poem is not a good test. Besides, where the Ha⁴ reading is poor, La's is usually even worse, given the evidence of *The Manciple's Prologue* and *Tale.* As a result of WR's reliance upon Ha⁴, he prints 49 variants unattested in any printed edition. Overall, however, one must admit that WR's much lower total of variants from the present edition than that shown by other, earlier printed editions, even 11 fewer than TR, is the result of simply adhering to a manuscript of a generally solid tradition, however highly edited or contaminated, rather than relying upon the corrupted tradition of printed editions or upon the *b* family of manuscripts that gave rise to that corrupted tradition.

Modern Editions: Skeat 1894 (SK), Robinson 1933 (RB¹), Manly-Rickert 1940 (MR), Robinson 1957 (RB²), Pratt 1974 (PR), Fisher 1977 (FI)

The modern printed editions share among them a total of 39 variants from the present edition of *The Manciple's Prologue* and *Tale:* lines 7, 9, 10, 36, 46, 47, 49, 59, 64, 85, 89, 96, 99, 102, 110, 143, 147, 148, 157, 170, 185 (2), 188, 226, 254, 256, 263, 266, 268, 280, 284, 290, 310 (2), 316, 327, 330, 356, 360. As would be expected, SK has the largest number, 28, testifying to the malign continuing influence of Cp Ha⁴ La; the eccentricities of Gg; SK's justified enthusiasm for El, in those instances which I regard as examples of El's editorial and smoothing hand at work; and a justified though incautious reverence for TR. La is present disturbingly in SK behind lines 10, 36, 143, 157, 263, 330, and Ha⁴ behind lines 99, 226, 254, 327 (it supports La in line 330 as well). SK's impact upon the study of Chaucer's text, deriving cumulatively from the labors of the Chaucer Society as well as from his own acumen as an editor, has had a continuing effect upon all subsequent editions, as can be seen in the Collations and Textual Notes in the present edition.

The steady growth of the influence of the El-Hg tradition can be seen in RB[1], which, though relying heavily upon SK, shows a fall in variants compared with the present edition from 28 to 23, one of the latter being a typographical error corrected in RB[2] (line 110). And all subsequent editions collated except MR have used El as their copy-text (and usually base-text as well).

Even so, the rise of Hg as an even more authentic source of Chaucer's text than El for most of *The Canterbury Tales* was clearly signaled by MR (who used SK as their copy-text); their great edition arrived by the recension method at a text consistently closer to Hg than to El, including the incidentals of spelling, and shows only 19 variants from the present text of *The Manciple's Tale.* Even MR are occasionally led astray by careless though smooth readings from inferior manuscripts, particularly Cp La Pw and occasionally Ha[4] (cf. lines 49, 96, 143, 157, 170—Cp La's *wilde* for *rude,* which no other modern edition prints—254, 263, 268, 310, 356). In most but not all of these cases SK preceded MR in the readings.

RB[2] is a somewhat revised text, still based upon El-SK, but giving MR and hence Hg considerable weight; it has 22 variants from the present edition, the typographical error of RB[1] having been removed.

PR, ostensibly a revision of RB[2], adheres generally more closely to MR than to RB[2], and PR's total number of variants from the present edition is only 19.

FI is a rather eclectic edition, based upon El, but arrives at the same number of variants as MR and PR from the present edition, 19. One of these is certainly a typographical error, FI's unique reading at line 85. FI depends more than previous editions upon the authority of Bo[2], to judge by his text of *The Manciple's Tale,* e. g., lines 143, 263 (and it is possible that the error in line 85 may have resulted from a miscopying of Bo[2]'s reading); these are the instances in which dependence is clear, and in other cases Bo[2] may have decided the issue rather than El, Gg, Hg or others used for previous editions. It is interesting to observe that in at least one instance the malevolent influence of UR continued to affect modern editions: a variant in line 185, unattested by any manuscript, clearly an example of UR's smoothing, which was adopted not only by TR but also by SK and RB[1-2]. It seems now, however, to have died of natural causes.

To summarize, the modern editions have consistently drawn away from the manuscripts that determined early editions (Cp Ha[4] La and the *b* group) and toward the El-Hg tradition, with Hg itself becoming in the middle of this century the dominant text (Donaldson, although he printed only *The Manciple's Prologue,* perhaps is most indicative of this new adherence, considering that MR arrived at an "Hg text" not by choice but as the end of a process).

In the case of *The Manciple's Prologue* and *Tale,* the reasons to depart from Hg have been few indeed. Hg is clearly superior to any other manuscript for them, even the excellent El. I certainly do not assume or argue that a demonstrably inferior manuscript may not occasionally have a reading superior to that of a better manuscript; an inferior manuscript may even by error arrive at a "correct" or superior reading (see Donaldson 1970:102-33). And it may be true, as Donaldson argues (1970:115) that "a MS's authority extends no farther than any line in which it is known to be right." But this argument skirts, by a larger sophistry, the fact that certain manuscripts are demonstrably, time after time, better than others. And very often the temptation to yield to an unusual reading in a demonstrably bad manuscript derives not from editorial perspicacity but from a previously held critical judgment or instinct about what the author intended, and when the editor finds a manuscript that supports this opinion, the result may derive more from a "Chaucer and I" syndrome than from sound editorial practice. No Hg reading has been adopted merely from the fear of taking chances or making judgments. As the Textual Notes indicate, the opposite has on occasion been the case.

The Present Edition

The present edition is based upon Hg. The Collations record such variants as are are recorded in MR, though the forms of the lemmata are frequently different from those in MR owing both to the smaller number of manuscripts dealt with here and to the introduction into the Collations of the variants in the printed editions. There are, in addition, a few occasions in which variants not recorded by MR as standard practice must be recorded here because of their special importance in the tradition of the printed editions or for other reasons. These always receive comment in the Textual Notes; examples are lines 31, 80, 187. All variants recorded by MR in their *Corpus of Variants* for the base-ten manuscripts are included in the Collations for *The Manciple's Prologue* and *Tale* except for lines 5, 35, 36. Variants for the base-ten manuscripts missed by MR in their *Corpus of Variants* are dealt with in the Textual Notes: lines 30, 60, 74, 75, 87, 125, 132, 168, 187, 190, 194, 216, 222, 230, 245, 251, 263, 299, 334, 358 (2).

The variants are recorded in a standard order in the Collations, with Hg first (if its reading is not adopted for the text), followed by El; the remaining base-ten manuscripts then follow in alphabetical order based upon the MR sigil: Ad^3 Cp Dd Gg Ha^4 He La Pw CX^1. CX^1 as the only printed edition with manuscript authority is at the end of the manuscript sigils and at the beginning of the printed-edition series in the Collations. CX^1 is followed by the printed editions in chronological order: CX^2 PN^1 WN PN^2 TH^1 TH^2 TH^3 ST SP^1 SP^2 SP^3 UR TR WR SK RB^1 MR RB^2 PR FI. Where Hg has lost parts of words by damage to the manuscript, the deficiency is made good from El, as has already been indicated. Numerals in Hg are expanded as words according to the forms in El and are not listed as variants. Where Dd is Out, the deficiency is made good from the highest manuscript in the *a* group, En^1; as has been explained, En^1 is used throughout for *The Manciple's Prologue* and *Tale* because Dd is missing them—as it happens, this does not disturb the alphabetical order of the sigils. Where He is Out (lines 48-255), the deficiency is made good from Ne or, in some cases, Tc^2. On occasion the symbol *(b)* is used, meaning that the whole family except He, which is Out on these occasions, i.e., Ne and Cx^1 ($CX^1 + Tc^2$), is in agreement. The presence of a plus sign after a sigil means that according to MR the variant is attested in additional manuscripts. The citation of a nonmember of the base-ten manuscripts in the Collations is in parentheses, and this should be taken to mean that manuscript precedent exists for a printed-edition reading not attested in the base-ten manuscripts; if the precedent exists in more than one manuscript, that manuscript sigil is followed by $+$. Normally the non–base-ten manuscript is cited that is first in alphabetical order in MR's *Corpus of Variants* for that lemma or that part of the lemma which is germane. Occasionally, however, when a non–base-ten manuscript is clearly the authority for a printed-edition reading (as in known cases for UR and TR, for instance), that manuscript is singled out, and, in addition, attention is called to this relationship in the Textual Notes. The presence of a tilde ($\sim$) before a printed-edition collation means that there is no extant manuscript authority for the reading. Corrections in manuscript readings are recorded in the Collations as in MR's *Corpus of Variants,* with subscript (e.g., La_1) used to indicate corrections in the hand of the main scribe.

A number of manuscripts have marginal glosses, and these are the subjects of commentary in the Textual Notes, and, on occasion, in the Explanatory Notes as well.

The base-ten manuscripts have been collated afresh for this edition. All of them have been consulted on microfilm, and Hg Cp Gg Ha^4 La in the original. In addition Hg El Gg have been consulted in facsimile. CX^{1-2} have been consulted in the standard STC microfilm copies, and in the originals in the British Library. PN^1 WN PN^2 TH^1 TH^2 TH^3 ST have been consulted in the standard STC microfilm series, and SP^{1-3} UR TR WR SK in my own copies of these texts. As is well known, many changes often took place during the printing runs of incunabula and sixteenth-century books. Some care has been taken to ensure that the inevitable variation to be found in those books is of no textual importance; occasional spelling and punctuation differences exist in the texts of *The Manciple's Prologue* and *Tale* in the early printed editions, but nothing that could be described as a "variant": change of spelling sufficient to suggest either a different form of the same work or perhaps even a different word, for example.

The Textual Notes frequently cite readings from manuscripts and printed editions not found in the Collations regularly or at all. The sigils for the manuscripts are those of MR: Ad^1 Bo^{1-2} Ch Cn Dl En^3 Gl $Ha^{2-3,5}$ Ht Lc Ld^1 Ll^1 Ln Ma Mc Mg Ps Ra^{1-3} Ry^1 Se Tc^1. For readings of these manuscripts, I have depended upon MR's *Corpus of Variants.* Readings of the other manuscripts that are not in the base-ten group but from time to time figure in the Collations are drawn from MR's *Corpus of Variants;* they are discussed in the special cases under the general descriptions of the manuscripts in the Textual Commentary. An exception to this is En[1], which has been collated from a microfilm of the manuscript. The printed editions are those of Pollard (Globe edition, 1898), Manly (1928), Donaldson (1958), and Baugh (1963). Manly and Donaldson print only *The Manciple's Prologue.* These editions are never collated but are referred to in the Textual Notes, where they are signaled by the editor's name. A special case is the edition of Plessow (1929), which, though valuable for its printing of a reduced fascimile with facing transcription of La, a transcription of Ha[4], and a transcription, facing German translation, phonetic transcription, and metrical analyses of El, for its rhetorical analyses, and for its informative notes, is nevertheless not really an edition even in the limited sense in which WR is an edition, and so is not collated, though it is frequently cited in the Explanatory Notes.

The Textual Notes follow the Collations. The Explanatory Notes follow the Textual Notes, separated by the symbol §. The Explanatory Notes comment on individual words or phrases and particular passages and themes. They are brief commentaries, not extended essays. Every effort has been made to bring to bear all significant commentary that has been published. For simple explanations of words that need no further elaboration, no citations have been made: the reader need not go beyond *MED, OED,* or *A Chaucer Glossary* (Davis et al. 1979). When an explanation or comment carries no citation to the Bibliographical Index, the reader can assume that I am responsible. There is inevitable overlapping in the Critical Commentary, the Textual Notes, and the Explanatory Notes, but I have taken considerable pains to keep this to an acceptable minimum. When a similar comment has been made by a number of scholars, I have not sought to assemble references to everyone who made the observation. Generally, I have cited the first, historically, to offer commentary on particular points.

Part Ten
The Manciple's Tale

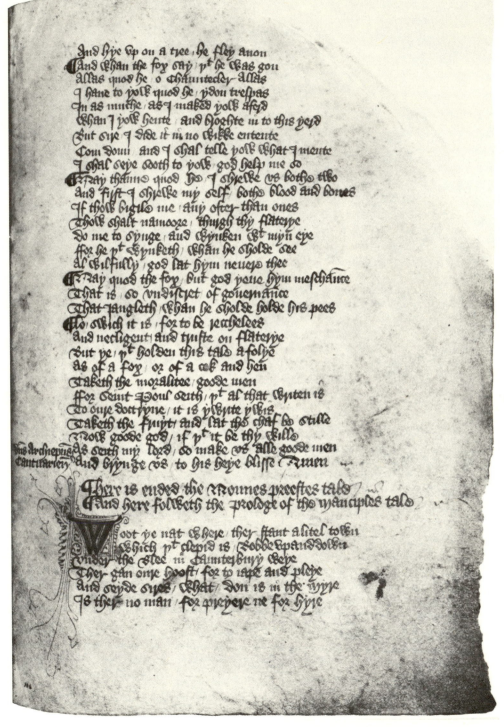

And hye vp on a tree / he fley anon
And whan the fox say / þt he was gon
Allas quod he / o chauntecleer allas
I haue to yow quod he / ydon trespas
In as muche / as I maked yow afeyd
whan I yow hente / and broghte in to this yerd
But sire / I dide it in no wikke entente
Com doun / and I shal telle yow what I mente
I shal seye sooth to yow / god help me so
Nay thanne quod he / I shrewe vs bothe two
And first I shrewe my self / bothe blood and bones
If thow bigile me / any ofter than ones
Thow shalt namoore / thurgh thy flaterye
Do me to synge / and wynken with myn eye
For he þt wynketh / whan he sholde see
Al wilfully / god lat hym neuere thee
Nay quod the fox / but god yeue hym meschaunce
That is so vndiscreet of gouernaunce
That iangleth / whan he sholde holde his pees
Lo swich it is / for to be recchelees
And necligent / and truste on flaterye
But ye / þt holden this tale a folye
As of a fox / or of a cok and hen
Taketh the moralitee / goode men
For seint Poul seith / þt al that writen is
To oure doctrine / it is ywrite ywis
Taketh the fruyt / and lat the chaf be stille
Now goode god / if þt it be thy wille
As seith my lord / so make vs alle goode men
And brynge vs / to his heye blisse Amen

Heere is ended the nonnes preestes tale
And here folweth the prologe of the maunciples tale

Woot ye nat where / ther stant a litel town
Which þt clepid is / Bobbe vp and down
Vnder the Blee / in Caunterbury weye
Ther gan oure hooste / for to iape and pleye
And seyde sires / what Dun is in the myre
Is ther no man / for preyere ne for hyre

Hengwrt Manuscript, folio 107r, National Library of Wales, Aberystwyth

And here folweth the Prologe of the Manciples tale   on 107r

Woot ye nat where ther stant a litel town
Which that clepid is Bobbe up and down,
Under the Blee, in Caunterbury weye?

Out: Dd (*lines 1-362*) He (*lines 48-255*) Pw (*lines 47-52*) CX¹ (*line* 316) SP² (*line* 219)

1   **ther]** *om.* Pw+ WN TH¹-TR   **stant]** stondith He+ CX¹-TR
2   **clepid is]** i. c. Cp He Pw+ CX¹-PN²; i. called (Cn+) WN-SP³
3   **Blee]** blene La

Note: NPE, found in nine MSS, was, after CX¹, printed in all editions until TR as a part of *ManP*. Although it can be stated with definiteness that, as they stand, they are not a part of *ManP*, the sixteen lines of the endlink are reprinted here, the text taken from Dd (Out for the *ManPT*) as the best text, and not collated. For a brief discussion of the matter, see the Textual Commentary in the Introduction and that part of the Variorum Edition dealing with *NPT*. It is printed here simply because for two hundred years the endlink was apparently read as part of *ManP*.

[*The Nun's Priest's Epilogue*, or *Endlink*]

"Sire Nonnes Preest," oure hoost seide a noon,   195r
"I blissed be thy breche and every ston!
This was a murie tale of Chauntecleer.
But by my trouthe if thou were seculer   4640
Thow woldest ben a tredfoul a right,
For if thou have corage as thou hast myght
The were nede of hennes, as I wene,
ʒa, moo than sevene tymes seventeen!
Se which braunes hath this gentil preest,   195v   4645
So gret a nekke and swich a large breest!
He loketh as a sperhauke with hise eyen.
Him nedeth nat his colour for to dyghen
With brasile ne with greyn of Portyngale.
Now sire, faire falle ʒow for ʒoure tale."   4650
And after that he with ful merie chere
Seide un to another as ʒe shuln heere.

1   **Woot ye:** As SK long ago pointed out (5.435), the form *woot* is singular, not plural, and to be perfectly grammatical, the opening words should be *Wite ye*, to which SK emends, following TR. SK admits, however, that Chaucer used the *woot* form in the plural, as in *GP* 740. In keeping with their view of Chaucer's practice MR do not treat this as a variant in their *Corpus of Variants;* nor do I in the Collations to the present edition. See Davis 1979:173.

2-3   **Bobbe up and down / Under the Blee:** Perhaps the most puzzling geographical reference in *CT*. TR says that he cannot find it on his map (1.111). It is usually identified (SK 5.435) as Harbledown, which is about two miles from Canterbury, between Boughton-under-Blean (*CYP* 556) and the cathedral city. The matter was discussed at great length by Furnivall (1868:31,124,127,131) and briefly by most editors since. Although variously spelled (Herbaldoun, Helbadonne; see Furnivall), Harbledown is nowhere else in contemporary reference called "Bobbe up and down," though the location suggested in *ManP* would certainly suit it. In any case, "the Blee" is Blean Forest. The suggestion of Cowper (1868:886), reprinted by Furnivall (1868:32), that "Bobbe up and down" may refer to a place called Up-and-down Field, in the parish of Thannington, has not been generally accepted. It would presume a more southerly route than is usually supposed for the London-to-Canterbury Way in the fourteenth century, though it is not impossible. The reference by Chaucer would seem clearly to be to a town of some kind, however, and it is doubtful that the reference would be confused with the name of a field or, at best, a farm. A tiny village may have existed there, but there is no archeological evidence for it. Another possible candidate was proposed by "S" (1932), who dismissed Thannington as about a mile and a half southwest of Canterbury (surely requiring a circuitous Pilgrims' Way) and suggested Bobbing, about two miles west of Sittingbourne, and hence west, presumably, of the medieval Pilgrims' Way, and about a mile north of Canterbury. But this suggestion, attractive as it is, does not contain the second part of the common name, whereas Harbledown does contain both ("Harble" could easily have degenerated into "Bob"). If the reference is to Harbledown, some difficulty is caused in the linking of fragments H and I, for in *ManP* the time is "by the morwe" (line 16), and after a short prologue and tale, *ParsP,* which follows, cites a time of four in the afternoon (line 5). This problem is discussed in the Textual Commentary. Clearly it is difficult to imagine the pilgrims, even if all were in the condition of the Cook, taking about seven hours to travel less than two miles and then having time for *ParsPT* before arriving at Canterbury. It has, therefore, been long suggested (see the discussion in the Critical Commentary) that the discrepancy could be explained if *ManPT* were the first prologue and tale of the homeward journey, beginning in the morning an hour or so on their way. SK (5.435), following Bradshaw (Baker 1981:2–6) and Furnivall (1868:31), remarks that the break between *CYT* and *ManPT* corresponds to the break between the first and second parts of Lydgate's *Siege of Thebes:* "At the end of Part I, Lydgate mentions the descent down the hill (i.e. Boughton hill), and at the beginning of Part II, he says that the pilgrims, on their *return* from Canterbury, had 'passed the thorp of Boughton-on-the-blee.'" The linking of *ParsP* to the *ManT* in line 1 of the former would be explained by a scribe's attempt to make sense of the *Tales* as he found them, assuming all to belong to the outward journey. For contrary views, see the discussion in the Critical Commentary. I permit myself the observation that the name "Bobbe up and down" may well have been merely a popular one, used particularly by pilgrims, because in walking to Canterbury from the London Way, as I have done, one discovers that a series of hillocks of varying heights that carries the path does indeed make Harbledown "bob up and down" to the approaching traveler, in turns revealing the village to his view and then hiding it. Norton-Smith (1974:151) also suggests this.

    2 **clepid:** This edition follows Hg's *clepid* rather than emend to the more popular (among editors) form of the participle prefixed by *y.* The prefixed form is more common in the MSS, and is the lemma form for MR. In the Collations *Yclepid* is not listed as a variant, nor is it in MR. The retention of the Hg reading would seem justified rhythmically if not metrically, for the prefixed participle would give the line three light accents in a row initially. The use of the prefixed participle would seem, in the case of El, to have been part of the scribe's (or supervisor's—we can have no idea which) smoothing operations, in an effort to get the syllables into a line at the expense of colloquial roughness.

    3 *Spurious lines following line 2:* There our oste spake now lete se with þe best / Who schal tell as meryly as hath þe preste / Come ner mauncypull and tell a tale her / Alle

80

Ther gan oure Hoost for to jape and pleye,
And seyde, "Sires, what! Don is in the myre! 5
Is ther no man, for preyere ne for hyre
[Th]at wole awake oure felawe al bihynde? 107v

---

4   **for to**] t. He Pw+ CX¹-TR   **pleye**] to p. He+ CX¹-TR
5   **what**] ywisse La; *om.* Pw+
6   **Is ther**] I. Cp; T. Is. En¹+
7   **That**] at Hg *(leaf torn)*   **felawe**] felawes En¹ Ha⁴+   **al**] arn En¹+; here Gg+ UR SK; *om.* Cp He La Pw+ CX¹-SP³

---

redy oste quothe he with gode cher / But hawe me excused ful sympully y kan / And with a glad cher his tale he bygan Fi *(lacks lines* 3-104). These lines were printed for the first time by Brusendorff (1925:70) and reprinted by MR (8.142), from which the above lines are taken. As a matter of practice, spurious lines are printed from the best sources, but are not punctuated.

5   **Don is in the myre:** The meaning of the sentence in context is, of course, that things are at a standstill and must be got moving again, i.e., that the tales should continue. The reference is probably to a rural, primarily children's, game, in which "Don" (a dun horse, or horse in general, like "Bayard"—see Rowland 1971:115) was said to be stuck in the mire; the horse was represented by a log or any large or unwieldy object. The purpose of the game was a test of strength as a team of first two, then three, or finally any number required attempted to pull it out. The game began with the cry, "Dun is in the mire!" SK (5.435-36) cites many references to the game. The allusion of the Host is apparently also to the Cook as the company's "Dun," for he is so unwieldy that, once he falls, as he appears likely to, the task of getting him up and on his horse again will be the equivalent of the game, and this is, of course, what happens. Therefore, the Host gives the cry that traditionally began the game, calling for a new tale, perhaps with the hope of waking the Cook before he tumbles off. See Rowland (1971:115), who cites Capgrave's *Life of Saint Katherine.* Brusendorff argues (1925:484) that there is no allusion here to the game, that the phrase is only the equivalent of "The fat's in the fire," a proverbial saying, and he instances the Towneley *Judgement,* line 205, where the phrase seems to bear the meaning that he assigns to it. See also Whiting (1938, D434) for the proverbial use. Manly (1928:654) also argues that the game is not in question. But the subsequent events in *ManP,* in which the phrase is a prophecy of an action very like the game ("Ther was gret showvyng bothe to and fro"—line 53) as the Cook is lifted out of the mire and put back on his horse, tell strongly against Brusendorff and Manly. Rowland (p. 115) also makes this point.

    Don: MR in their *Corpus of Variants* (8.142) list *Downe* in Pw as a variant of *Don.* We do not always agree with MR in their concept of a variant, and indeed they are inconsistent, as is inevitable. A variant must be a different word or words, a significantly different form of the same word (different person, number, tense, etc.), or a spelling so different as to give rise *in context* to a different interpretation of significance. *Dun, Don, Down,* etc., could give rise to different interpretations of meaning, but not, I judge here, *in context.* Although one or two scribes may have been confused, the printed editions were not.

6   **preyere:** Request (to perform an act as a favor).

7   **al:** UR reads *here,* thus agreeing with the reading of Gg; although we have the testi-

A theef myghte hym ful lightly robbe and bynde.
Se how he nappeth! Se how, for Cokkes bones,
That he wol falle from his hors atones!   10
Is that a Cook of Londoun with meschaunce?

---

8   **myghte hym ful lightly**] m. f. l. En[1] Ha[4]+ WR; m. f. l. h. Gg+; m. h. both l. He; m. h. l. La+; m. h. Pw+; h. m. f. l. ~ TH[1]-SP[2] UR TR; he m. f. l. ~ SP[3]

9   **Se how for**] se for Cp En[1] Ha[4]+ CX[1]-SK; se h. f. for Gg (for *erased* Gg[1]); for La Pw+   **Cokkes**] goddes Cp En[1] Ha[4] Pw+ WR

10   **That**] What He+; As La+ TR SK; A waite Pw+; How (Tc[2]+) CX[1]-UR   **wol**] wald La+

11   **Is that**] I. þat þat La; This i. Pw+

---

mony of the Thomases that Gg was known and used in the preparation of UR (fol. k[1]), Gg's influence is negligible in *ManPT*. The reading could have come from Ha[3], the only other MS that has *here;* the "Student of Christ Church" (Timothy Thomas) who prepared UR for the press reports in his preface (fol. l[1]) that he himself used a "Harley 3" MS for the glossary, but this could not have been MR's Ha[3], for it was not acquired by the Earl of Oxford until 1733 (MR 1.217-18). Perhaps, therefore, this reading is the only direct influence of Gg in the UR text of *ManPT*.

8   **theef:** The Host's reference to a thief is usually taken to suggest the dangers of the pilgrims' passing through Blean Forest, where thieves lurked. It may be, however, simply that the drunken Cook is lagging so far behind the other pilgrims that he could be bound and robbed, whether or not in a forest, before his companions could come back to his aid. Trask (1977:115) suggests that there is symbolic significance in the Cook's falling behind: "He is not eschatalogically vigilant, like the wise virgins." The "theef" may be the devil who will bind and rob the Cook, but the Cook is rescued through the help of "friends." Chaucer's own experience of being robbed twice on the same day by highwaymen in 1390 (Crow and Olson 1966:477-89) may possibly be reflected.

    myghte hym ful lightly: There is no extant MS containing the reading from which TH[1] may have drawn *hym myght ful lightly;* evidently the reading arose from a compositorial error or an editorialization, picked up by subsequent editions through SP[2] and by UR and TR as well. TR's printing is one of many pieces of evidence showing clearly TR's use of SP[2] as a copy-text (see Textual Commentary).

9   **Se how:** MR (4.525) speculate that the repetition of *Se how* was in O[1] and dropped by Ha[4]+ for smoothing.

    for Cokkes bones: A "minced oath" or corruption of the common oath "for Goddes bones," which appears in several MSS.

10   **That:** Manly (1928) follows TR, SK, and Pollard (1898) in printing *As* for Hg's *That; As* is found only in La of our base-ten MSS; MR adopted the Hg El reading found in nearly all MSS. Furnivall prints *As* for *That* in his transcription of El in the Six-Text edition.

11   **with meschaunce:** A mild oath, "unluckily," "to make matters worse." The preposition *with* here carries a common adverbial sense. Perhaps, as Lawrence suggests (1950:148), the Host is implying that the Cook is scarcely to be recognized.

Do hym come forth, he knoweth his penaunce,
For he shal telle a tale, by my fey,
Althogh it be nat worth a botel hey.
Awake thow Cook," quod he, "God yeve the sorwe!   15
What eyleth thee to slepe by the morwe?
Hastow had fleen al nyght, or artow dronke?
Or hastow with som quene al nyght yswonke
So that thow mayst nat holden up thyn heed?"
    This Cook, that was ful pale and no thyng reed,   20
Seyde to oure Hoost, "So God my soule blesse,

---

12   **come forth**] comford La; comforth (Ne+) CX¹-UR
14   **hey**] of h. Pw+ WN-UR
15   **quod he**] sit up En¹ Ha⁴+ WR; *om.* Pw+
16   **slepe**] s. so La Pw
17   **al**] to Pw+   **artow**] þou a. Pw+
18   **with som quene al nyght**] a. n. w. s. q. He Pw+ CX¹-UR
20   **Cook**] *om.* La+ (Koc *added by* La₁)   **ful**] *om.* En¹ Ha⁴ Pw+
21   **to**] *om.* Cp He La+ CX¹-UR   **oure Hoost**] sir h. ~ TH¹-UR   **so**] as En¹+
my soule] me Gg Pw+   **blesse**] saue and b. He; yblesse ~ SP²-UR

---

12   **Do hym come forth**: I.e., "make him come forth."
    penaunce: The telling of his tale, perhaps an implied play on words with the telling of the beads, the usual penance. Cf. *Ven,* in which a difficult literary composition is described as a "penaunce" (line 79).
    14   **botel hey**: A small bundle of hay (here a symbol of worthlessness). Whiting (1968, D470) cites CX¹ as providing the earliest example. Cf. *galoun wyn* (line 24) for a similar construction.
    16   **by the morwe**: A phrase meaning not necessarily that the Cook has slept through the morning but that he is sleeping *in* the morning, as SK observed (5.436). TR had suggested (1798:2.507) that the phrase indicated that the time was then afternoon, but SK quite rightly rejects the inference. TR also remarked that the Host's address to the Cook could be taken as an indication that *ManP* was written before the abortive *CkT* in fragment A, and SK accepts this possibility; there seems to be no reason, however, to surmise this.
    17   **fleen**: The bedding in medieval pilgrims' hostels usually consisted of seldom-changed straw spread upon a stone or earthen floor, and thus fleas were at least as great a nuisance to pilgrims as were robbers.
    18   **quene**: Here a prostitute, though elsewhere it is roughly equivalent to "wench," or woman of the lower classes; see the Manciple's discussion of "lemman" and "lady," lines 205-22; see also Davis (1979:115) and Ross (1972:174-75).
    20   **reed**: Furnivall's Six-Text edition mistranscribes *rede* for *reed.*
    21   **oure Hoost**: The origin of the variant *sir hoost* is obscure, there being no extant MS authority; it appeared in all the sixteenth-century editions after PN², and is found for the

As ther is falle on me swich hevynesse,
Noot I nat why, that me were levere slepe
Than the beste galoun wyn in Chepe."
    "Wel," quod the Manciple, "if it may don ese   25
To thee, sir Cook, and to no wight displese
Which that here rideth in this compaignye,
And that oure Hoost wole, of his curteisye,
I wole as now excuse thee of thy tale.

---

22 **As**] *om.* He+ CX¹-PN¹   **falle**] holden Pw+   **swich**] s. an La+; greet He+ CX¹-UR

23 **Noot I**] I n. La+; That I n. Pw+; But I n. ~ TH¹-UR   **nat**] *om.* La Pw+ TH¹-UR   **why**] wheder Pw+   **that**] but En¹+; *om.* Cp He La Pw+ CX¹-UR   **me**] me m. ~ PN²   **slepe**] to s. Cp He+ CX¹-TR

24 **than**] Þat La   **wyn**] of w. Cp He+ (of *added by* He₁) CX¹-SP³   **in**] that is i. En¹+ UR-WR

25 **the**] this Ad³   **if**] i. þat Ha⁴ He+ WR; *om.* Pw+   **it may**] i. pe m. Cp; i. wil Pw; I m. En¹ Ha⁴+ WR   **don**] d. the (Ne+) CX¹ PN¹

26 **to**] *om.* En¹+   **wight**] wight w. ~ PN¹   **displese**] mysplese Pw+

27 **here**] *om.* Pw+   **rideth**] riden He Pw+ CX¹˒² PN²; ride ~ PN¹ WN-SP³

28 **And that oure Hoost**] A. o. h. En¹ Ha⁴+ WR; A. if o. h. ~ PN¹; Þat so o. h. Pw+   **wole**] wolde En¹ Ha⁴ WR

29 **wole**] wolde En¹+   **as**] *om.* El+

---

last time in UR. TH¹ may have inserted *sir* as a compositor's misreading of *oure,* the *to* having already been omitted in all editions (with MS authority); or it may have been an anticipation of *sir* from *sir Cook,* five lines later.

23-24 **me were levere slepe:** I.e., "I would rather slepe [infinitive] than [have] the best gallon of wine in Chepe"—the common dative-reflexive construction in Chaucer's English (see SK 5.436). The Cook is saying simply that, having given up sleep for wine the night before, he will willingly reverse the values today.

24 **Than:** Another hand than that of the scribe has written *Ye* before *Than* in the left margin of Hg; it is curious to note that Ra² has *Ya than* here, the only MS to have it.

    in: In printing *That is in,* WR is following TR and the *a* tradition (En¹ probably here) rather than that of Ha⁴ and La, from which with few exceptions he takes his text.

    Chepe: Cheapside, an area of London long famous for its taverns.

25 **don:** CX¹ and PN¹, following the tradition of Ne Tc², read *don the;* CX², followed by WN and all subsequent editions, omits *the* and is in the general MS tradition, this being one of many CX² corrections by another MS, probably of the *a* type (see Textual Commentary). It is easy to see how the error arose in the MS, through the anticipation of *thee* in the following line; it is even possible that the error arose independently in Ne and CX¹.

26 **to no wight displese:** To no person *be* displeasing.

28 **And that:** PN¹ reads *And if,* and this is most probably a simple typographical error, there being no MS authority; the nearest MS equivalent is Ht's *That if.*

For, in good feith, thy visage is ful pale, 30
Thyne eyen daswen eek, as that me thynketh,
And wel I woot thy breth ful soure stynketh—
That sheweth wel thow art nat wel disposed.
Of me, certeyn, thow shalt nat ben yglosed.
Se how he ganeth, lo, this dronken wight, 35
As though he wolde swolwe us anon right!

---

30 **feith**] fey Gg Pw+   **ful**] riȝt Pw+
31 **daswen**] dasowepe La   **eek**] soply Cp He La+ CX¹-TR; *om.* Pw+   **as that**]
a. Cp En¹ He La Pw+ CX¹-WR; also Ha⁴ WR
32 **ful**] *om.* La Pw+   **soure**] foule En¹ Ha⁴ He La+ CX¹ WR; sore Pw+ WN
33 **wel**] eek Ha⁴ WR; *om.* Pw+   **art**] nart Pw+   **nat**] *om.* He+
35 **Se**] Lo He   **he**] *om.* La+   **ganeth**] galpith He+ CX¹-TR; gope La+; golep
Pw+; yaneth En¹+   **lo**] l. how He+; se En¹+; *om.* La Pw+
36 **swolwe us**] u. s. Cp La+ CX²-SK; swelle He+ CX¹; swoune Pw

---

30 **feith:** MR do not treat *fey* as a variant of *feith,* for which there is justification;
I regard the spelling range as too great to ignore on principle, for, although here the words
are identical in meaning and derivation, the morpheme *fey* also exists as an entirely different
word.

31 **daswen:** MR do not deal with La's *dasowepe* as a variant.

32 **soure:** CX¹ follows the *a* and *b* MSS groups in reading *foule,* but CX² corrects
and all editions except WN until WR (following Ha⁴) print *soure,* as have all editions since.
WN's *sore* may be derived from a Pw-type MS, or may be simply a typograpical error. The
soure-foule is likely not, as are many variations in the *CT* text, a result of Chaucer's re-
vising; the confusion of initial *s* and *f* is so common as to be the obvious explanation.
Chaucer's wrote *soure,* a precise word associated with vinous breath, rather than *foule,* a
much more general word. *Sore* is, of course, simply the result of a scribe's missing the *u.*

33 **nat wel disposed:** Not in good health, obviously, but there may be a more literal
implication here as the Manciple observes the Cook's unsteady physical disposition on his
mount.

34 **yglosed:** Flattered; this is a figure based upon the practice of glossing, or giving
interpretative and explanatory commentary upon texts and thus, in common parlance, placing
a more sophisticated and perhaps extenuating meaning upon fact; the glosses were usually
in the margins, frequently actually surrounding the text and almost concealing it from the
reader. In the later centuries the glossators were almost as well known as the authors upon
whom they were commenting. The Cook is therefore remarking that he will not only not
provide an excuse for the Cook's condition but lay bare for all the company to see the naked
"text," as it were. This is the first figure of many in *ManPT* that are derived from text
and interpretation as the Manciple first uses the Cook for his "text" and then, in a turn-
about, uses his own rashness as a text for "glossing" in *ManT.*

35 **ganeth:** MR in their *Corpus of Variants* treat En¹'s *yaneth* as a variant of *ganeth.*

36 **swolwe:** In printing *swolwe us* (Hg El) instead of *us swolwe* (Cp La), Pollard (1898)

85

Hoold cloos thy mouth, man, by thy fader kyn!
The devel of helle sette his foot ther yn!
Thy cursed breeth infecte wol us alle.
Fy, stynkynge swyn, fy! Foule mote thee falle!   40
A, taketh hede, sires of this lusty man.
Now, swete sire, wol ye justen atte fan?

---

37   **man**] *om.* En¹ Ha⁴ He+ CX¹-SP³   **by**] for En¹+ PN¹
39   **Thy**] This Cp La+   **infecte wol us**] w. i. v. Ad³ Cp Gg La+ CX²-SP³; w. now
enfecte u. ~ UR; enfectith v. He+ CX¹; effecte w. v. En¹ Ha⁴+ WR; w. affecte v. Pw
40   **swyn**] hogge Pw+   **fy**] *om.* En¹ Ha⁴ He Pw+ CX¹   **thee**] thou El+   **falle**]
befalle Gg He Pw+ CX¹-TR
41   **A**] Now Pw+; *om.* Cp He La+ CX¹-SP³   **sires**] sire La+
42   **sire**] sires Gg+

---

went against all previous printed editions, including SK; all editions since have followed
him. MR list in their *Corpus of Variants* a correction in Ad³, *sw* over an erasure, but this
has no proper place in the Collations.

37   **by**: In its reading *for,* PN¹ was probably "corrected" from one of the En³ group;
PN² restored *by.*

38   **The . . . yn**: Usually explained (RB², p. 763) as an imprecation based upon the
superstition that the open mouth left a person vulnerable to evil spirits, who might take pos-
session of the body through this entryway. Pearcy (1974) suggests that the expression here
probably means that the devil entered the Cook through the beer or wine that made him
drunk and quotes Gower and *Le Ménagier de Paris* to the effect that sobriety or temperance
guards the mouth (the gate of the body's castle) so that the devil may not enter a man's
body in this way. In the Cook's case gluttony has taken over the guardian's role, and the
devil can easily enter. One might add that in *ManT* a similar role is seen for the lips and
teeth, which guard against unwise *exit.* Pearcy goes on to suggest that Chaucer may have
drawn the figure from contemporary dramatic and other representations of hell's mouth.
This latter suggestion is also briefly made by Norton-Smith (1974:151).

39   **infecte wol us**: UR's addition of *now* to the version *wol now enfecte us* has no
MS authority or printed-edition precedent; it is clearly an emendation for meter's sake.

     infecte: Infection was thought to be carried through the air.

41   **A, taketh hede**: The Manciple is calling the pilgrims' attention not to the Cook,
whose condition was obvious enough, but to himself, since he wants an audience for his
baiting of the Cook.

     lusty: A whole complex of meanings is possible here (see *OED;* Ross 1972:141–44,
216), all of them ironic. The Cook is not at all merry (he is sullen and drunk), vigorous
(he is apathetic), or sexually adventurous (that the latter is implicit is perhaps suggested by
the Manciple's question "Or hastow with som quene al nyght yswonk?" [line 18], which might
refer not only to his drunken, sleepy condition but also to the probability that he would
not be able to undertake a second such bout—if indeed the Manciple has hit upon the truth).

42   **justen atte fan**: A reference to a popular game demanding considerable agility.

Ther to me thynketh ye ben wel yshape.
I trowe that ye dronken han wyn ape,

---

43   wel] right w. En[1] Ha[4] WR; ful w. He+
44   that] *om.* En[1] He Pw+   dronken han] haue d. Cp He La Pw+ CX[1]-TR   ape]
of a. En[1] He+ CX[1] TR WR; you a. ~ UR; grape Pw

The "fan" was the fan, or vane, of the quintain, a crossbar pivoting atop a post. At one end of the crossbar was the fan, or vane, a board at which the player was to ride or run, like a jousting knight, and strike with a spear or stick in such a way and with such speed that he would be able to dodge the other end of the crossbar swinging around behind his head. To the other end of the crossbar was usually attached some heavy object, a club, a wooden sword, or a bag of sand, to encourage the agility of the player. Of course, the drunken Cook, far from agile, would have been laid flat by the wrong end of the crossbar had he been able to strike the vane of the quintain in the first place. Although Chaucer does not mention the Cook's carrying a staff (the El miniaturist provides him with a fleshhook, which, however, like the Physician's urinal, is to be taken symbolically), horseback pilgrims usually did carry a staff for walking after arrival at the shrine and for defense along the way, and it adds point to the Manciple's taunt if we are allowed to imagine the Cook with some sort of staff or crop, which he is now waving drunkenly like a bizarre player jousting at the vane. This would also fit with the Manciple's ironic reference to men who have drunk "wyn ape" and thus "pleyen with a straw" (lines 44-45). At any rate, the game of jousting at the fan was a common one to which there are many references (interestingly, SP[1-3] seems not to have understood the allusion, for in the glossary he treats the fan as something that one would strike with—see his definition of *win ape;* TR (2.507-508) gives a fine brief description). Strutt (1867:3.112-13), cited by SK (5.436), discusses and illustrates the development of the game from a military exercise in which the quintain was dressed as a Saracen (the crossbar being his arms with a shield on the fan end and wooden sword on the other) to a children's game in London in which the quintain was no more elaborate than that described at the beginning of this note. Donaldson states (1958:416) that the phrase means merely "to joust against a winnowing fan," but this seems highly unlikely.

44   **wyn ape:** There seems to be no textual explanation for UR's curious *you ape;* UR probably took *ape* to be an insulting name and prefaced it with *you* to make this clear. WR deserts Ha[4] and La, which record simply *ape,* and follows TR, who apparently took his *of ape* from Ha[3] and Ha[5] (which he labels [1798:2.508] "HA" and "E"), as well as perhaps from Ry[1]. § The expression *wyn ape* means either "wine of the ape or wine to degree of drunkenness that one behaves like an ape (Whiting 1968, A147). The difference in meaning is small, but two somewhat different traditions are involved. The second concept involves a reference to one of the degrees of drunkenness that one might successively attain, signified by the fabulous behavior of four animals: the lamb, the lion, the ape, and the swine. This medieval convention is illustrated in the 159th fable of the *Gesta Romanorum* and elsewhere. TR (2.508), scornfully dismissing SP (who had given perhaps a mock-serious definition—see Wright [1959:205]—of *win ape* as derived from the "wine of bees," which caused the drinker to see double), refers to the Talmudic tradition that when Noah planted the grape Satan poured about its roots the blood of a sheep, a lion, an ape, and a pig, with

And that is whan men pleyen with a straw." 45
And with his speche the Cook wax wroth and wraw,
And on the Manciple bigan he nodde faste 108r
For lakke of speche, and doun the hors hym caste,
Wher as he lay til that men up hym took.

---

45   is] *om.* Ha⁴   whan] w. as SP²,³   men] m. hem Pw+   with a] atte He+
CX¹-PN¹UR; at ~ WN-SP³

46   his] this El La Pw+ TR-RB¹ RB²-FI; that He   speche] speke La   wroth]
angry En¹ Ha⁴+ WR; *om.* Cp He La Pw+ CX¹-TR   and] al Cp He La Pw+ CX¹-TR

47   bigan he] h. gan El Ad³ Gg He+ CX¹-TR SK-FI; g. h. La+; g. En¹+ UR   nodde]
to n. En¹ He+ CX¹-UR   *Out:* Pw

48-255   *Out:* He

48   and doun] adoun He+ CX¹-PN²   the] his ~ TH¹-TR   *Out:* Pw

49   that] *om.* La+ PN²   men up hym] m. h. v. Cp Ha⁴ La+ CX¹-WR RB¹-PR;
h. m. v. En¹+; the h. v. Gg+   *Out:* Pw

---

the result that men who drank too much of the wine should come to resemble these animals
in turn. A somewhat different tradition, the first named, used the animal figures to indicate
the effects of drink upon persons of different humors, hence the phlegmatic man would have
drunk *vin de mouton;* the choleric man, *vin de lyon;* the sanguine man, *vin de cinge;* and
the melancholic man, *vin de porceau*—see *Kalendrier et compost des Bergiers* (1925:xli),
cited by SK (5.437). We have generally abandoned the particular animal descriptions in con-
temporary figures but usually adhere to the humor theory in such appellations as "a quiet
drunk," "a mean drunk," "a playful drunk," and "a sloppy drunk." SK (5.437-38) gives
many terms, including two (one from Lydgate's *Troy Book* and the other from "Colyn Blow-
boll's Testament") that describe the drunken person playing with straws. Norton-Smith (1974:
152) remarks that the Manciple's taunt is double-edged in that the Cook has already pro-
gressed beyond the ape and is "sow-drunk," quite beyond playfulness and in fact is called a
"swin" (line 40) by the Manciple. Rowland (1971:34-35) has a useful discussion.

45   **pleyen with a straw:** See notes to lines 42, 44; Whiting (1968, S821).

46   **his:** The ancestry of the reading *this* in TR and SK is clear: TR took it from La,
and SK from El. RB¹ and all subsequent editions except, curiously, MR, follow the El reading.
MR admit (4.525) that *his* was the reading of O¹ but prefer *this*.

47   **bigan he:** Hg has the support of only two "good" MSS, Cp and Ha⁴, in the *bigan
he* form and order, and only one printed edition, WR, which followed Ha⁴. La reads *gan he,*
and Donaldson (1958) adopted this form. But the Hg order seems right to me in rhythm,
and it is not emended. It is quite possible that *Manciple* could have been pronounced, at least
occasionally as a disyllable, with the middle syllable elided. UR's omission of *he* is derived
from Ry¹, the only MS listed among the MSS used for UR (fol. k²) that has it.

48   **the:** The reading *his* for *the* from TH¹ to TR attests to the tenacity of compositional
errors, there being no MS authority.

49   **that:** The omission of *that* from PN² is probably just a compositorial error. Although

This was a fair chyvachee of a Cook!   50
Allas, he nadde yholde hym by his ladel!
And er that he agayn were in his sadel
Ther was gret showvyng bothe to and fro
To lifte hym up, and muchel care and wo,
So unweldy was this sory palled goost.   55
And to the Manciple thanne spak oure Hoost,
    "By cause drynke hath domynacioun

---

50   a] þe La+   chyvachee] chiuacheef Cp; cheuesaunce *(b+)* CX¹-UR   *Out:* Pw
51   **Allas**] A. that *(b)* En¹ Ha⁴+ CX¹-WR   he] *om.* Gg   nadde] hade nat En¹+
Out: Pw
52   **his**] the (Gl+) WN TH¹-TR   *Out:* Pw
53   **Ther was gret**] T. w. a g. *(b)* Cp+ CX¹-UR   bothe] *om.* En¹ La Pw+ TH¹-UR
55   **unweldy**] vnwelde Ha⁴ La WR; vnwery Gg   this] þi La   sory] sely *(b)* Cp
La+ CX¹-TR; *om.* Pw   palled] appalled Pw+
57   **By cause**] B. c. that *(b)* En¹ Cp La+ CX¹-TR

---

the Hg reading *men up hym* is supported by El, the printed-edition tradition of *men hym up*
was so strong that only SK (and Pollard:1898) resisted it, all others of our collated editions
adopting the tradition based upon *a-, b-, and c-*group MSS. Manly (1928) printed the Hg El
reading but reverted to *men hym up* for MR. Donaldson and FI have adopted the Hg El
reading.

50   **chyvachee:** A chivalric exploit, feat of horsemanship (see *GP* 85 for a nonironic
use). The El miniaturist shows the Cook's horse looking around quizzically at his rider, as
though evaluating his horsemanship before casting him to the ground. On the possible
irony of the term if the Cook is indeed Chaucer's portrait of Roger Knight, see Rickert
(1932:761) and Brodie (1971:64).

51   **nadde:** The frequent *ne hadde* found in MSS and printed editions is not treated
as a variant, for the words would have been elided in pronunciation. Likewise, MR do not
treat such cases as variants.

    yholde hym by his ladel: A common figure, like "sticking to his last," implying
that the Cook should not have ventured out of his area of specialization, from the kitchen
to horseback (see SK 5.438).

52   **his:** Only G1 Mc and Ra¹ have the WN TH¹-TR reading *the;* the reading may
have come from one of these MSS or from another, no longer extant MS, or it may have
been an editorial "correction" in WN because of the repetition of *his* in lines 50-51.

55   **palled goost:** Although pale as a "goost," the Cook is far more substantial, as the
pilgrims will discover; on this description see Brodie (1971:66-68).

57-75   Pichaske and Sweetland (1977:193) treat this intervention of the Host in "be-
half" of the Cook as an indication of the Host's regeneration.

57   **domynacioun:** A joking allusion to the domination of man by the planets in as-
trology, or the spiritual domination of man by the gods (SK 5.438; RB², p. 764). By ex-
tension, Nature or virtue could be said to have "domynacioun" over man as in *KnT* 2758

Up on this man, by my savacioun,
I trowe he lewedly telle wolde his tale.
For were it wyn, or old or moisty ale   60
That he hath dronke, he speketh in his nose,
And fneseth faste, and eek he hath the pose.

---

59   **he lewedly telle wolde]** l. h. w. t. El Gg+ FI; h. l. w. t. Cp TR SK RB¹ RB²; l.
wil h. t. *(b+)* CX¹-UR; h. l. t. wol En¹ Ha⁴ WR; fill l. h. wolde t. La; h. wolde l. t. Pw+

60   **old or]** oold El Ad³ *(b)* Ha⁴+ CX¹-SP³; ellis Pw+; strong En¹+ strong old ~ UR
moisty] moiste Ad³ La+; moist Pw+; musty En¹+

61   **hath dronke]** dranke En¹+   **speketh]** s. so *(b)* Cp La+ CX¹-SP³   **his]** the
(Gl+) TH¹-UR

62   **And]** He En+   **fneseth]** snuffeth En¹+; galpep Pw+; snyueleth TH¹-UR; sne-
seth (En³) TR   **he]** *om.* Ad³+ WN TH¹-UR   **hath]** h. caught (Ha²+) UR

---

and *Sted* 16. The figure of wine as the Cook's dominating "spirit" rises again when the
Host ironically gives thanks to Bacchus (line 99) that the dispute between the Manciple and
the Cook is settled by the mediation of still more wine (cf. also line 181).

59   **he lewedly telle wolde:** Manly (1928) followed El and Gg in *lewedly he wolde
telle* but in MR adopted the Hg reading, which has been followed by Donaldson (1958)
and Baugh (1963). Robinson in both editions followed SK and TR in printing the Cp *he
lewedly wolde telle.* PR has adopted the Hg order, but FI returned to El.

old or moisty ale: "Old or new ale." The word *moisty* caused for many scribes
a confusion of "moist-e" with "musty" as the variant spellings cloud a double meaning of
"moist"—i.e., "damp" and "must" or new wine; *moisty* is the spelling of most MSS, but the
a group has *musty* generally (see below). Neither the *OED* nor the *MED* recognizes the
moisty spelling, though the *ManP* MSS amply attest to it; the *OED* does not recognize the
ManP appearance of the word somewhat earlier than the first citation. It is interesting that
one of the *MED* citations of *must* is a deliberate series of puns on *moist, most,* and *must.*
I do not suggest that Chaucer needed to draw such an obvious expression from a "source,"
but it is perhaps worth noting, in view of the alcoholic flavor of *ManP,* that the gloss in Hg
at line 147 is a quotation from Theophrastus, which Chaucer drew from Jerome's *Epistola
adversus Jovinianum* (1.47); a few hundred lines earlier (in Migne) Jerome quotes Acts
2:13: "Alii autem irridentes dicebant: Quia musto pleni iste" (Others, mocking, said, "These
men are full of new wine"). The point is, of course, that "musty," or new, wine was credited
with making a person drunk far more quickly than aged wine. See Brown (1980:11-12)
for the suggestion of a pun on "ape-ease" in this connection in line 98.

old or: Again, UR's reading, *strong old,* seems derived in part from Ry¹, though
there is no single MS authority.

moisty: MR's *Corpus of Variants* does not treat *musty* and *moisty* as variants,
though it does list *moist* as one; that there was confusion arising from the two words is
obvious, and on this basis the collations of the present edition treat both *musty* and *moist-e*
as variants.

61   **his:** If the reading *the* is not simply a compositorial error in TH¹, then TH¹ may
have been influenced by Gl or Ra³, the only extant MSS that have *the.* See note to line 48.

62   **fneseth:** It is difficult to account for the TH¹-UR reading *snyueleth;* there is no

He hath also to do moore than ynow
To kepen hym and his capil out of the slow.
And if he falle from his capil eft soone,   65
Than shal we alle have ynow to doone
In liftynge up his hevy dronken cors.
Telle on thy tale, of hym make I no fors.
But yet, Manciple, in feith thow art to nyce,
Thus openly repreve hym of his vice.   70
Another day he wole, par aventure,

---

63   **hath also]** a. Ha⁴ La; a. h. ~ WN TH¹-WR
64   **and]** in En¹+; on *(b+)* CX¹-TR   **capil]** sadyll En¹+   **the]** *om.* El+ SK
65   **from]** f. of ~ TR
67   **In liftynge]** To liftyn Gg+   **up]** v. of Pw+; v. againe ~ SP²-UR   **hevy dronken]** d. (Ii+) CX¹-UR; h. Pw+
68   **thy]** þin Cp
69   **yet]** now Pw+
70   **repreve]** to r. *(b)* Cp En¹ La Pw+ CX¹-TR

MS authority extant, and it seems a less probable typesetter's error or "correction" than many curiosities found in those editions. § Although *fneseth* is the origin of the modern word *sneeze, fnesen* did not mean "to sneeze" but rather "to breathe hard" or "to wheeze" (as if a person had an obstruction in the nose or throat) and was consistently in ME spelled *fnesen,* derived from OE *fneosung,* meaning "hard breathing" and related to *fnest,* meaning "snort." See *OED,* SK (5.438), *MED,* Davis et al (1979). The description by the Manciple of the Cook's wheezing and hard breathing is, of course, an accurate description of the effects of intoxication.

     pose: A cold in the head. SK (5.438) cites the explanation in *Batman uppon Bartholomew* 1.4, "Of the pose."

     hath: UR's *hath caught* seems probably derived from Ha², a MS that Thomas's preface (fol. k¹) indicates was used.

63   **hath also:** WN's compositorial error *also hath* (there is no MS authority) was picked up by TH¹, one of many pieces of evidence in *ManPT* for TH¹'s use of WN, and, like so many other errors of the sort, survived through UR and even TR; WR, which has the same reading, apparently relied on TR to make good Ha⁴'s missing *hath.*

65   **from:** TR's *from of* derives from no known MS, but he may have been influenced by En³ or Ad¹, which read simply *of.*

67   **up:** The clear compositorial addition of *againe* in SP² has no extant MS authority and survived only through SP³ and UR.

70   **repreve:** The reading *to repreve* is an interesting example of scribal editing unsupported by the oldest and best MSS; although emendations of this sort are usually made for metrical reasons, here an extra syllable is added to achieve a more acceptable syntax.

71-75   In this splendid figure of the Cook's potentially turning the tables on the Man-

Reclayme thee and brynge thee to lure;
I mene he speke wole of smale thynges,
As for to pynchen at thy rekenynges
That were nat honeste, if it cam to preef."   75
    "No," quod the Manciple, "that were a gret mescheef!
So myghte he lightly brynge me in the snare.
Yet hadde I levere payen for the mare
Which he rit on, than he sholde with me stryve.

---

    72 **brynge thee**] b. thy ~ TH²   **to**] t. the (Tc¹+) SP²,³ TR
    73 **he**] that h. ~ SP²,³   **wole**] wold Pw+
    74 **As**] And *(b)* Cp En¹ La+ CX¹-UR   **pynchen**] speke La   **thy**] pine Cp La+; the ~ PN²
    75 **if**] i. that Gg+; pouhe La   **preef**] the p. *(b)* CX¹-PN²
    76 **No**] Nowe Pw+; *om.* En¹ Ha⁴ TR WR   **a gret**] *om.* (Bo¹) UR
    77 **lightly**] *om. (b)* Cp La Pw+ CX¹-UR   **in**] into the *(b)* Cp La+ CX¹-UR
    78 **I**] me En¹+
    79 **Which**] W. that El En¹+   **rit**] rideth La+ CX¹-UR   **on**] vpon Pw+
stryve] styue Gg

---

ciple and, like a falconer, reclaiming him and bringing him to lure, i.e., to the falconer's wrist (thus bringing the bird "in hand"), by exposing the Manciple's dubious dealings, Chaucer seems to suggest through the Host that there is a relationship between the Cook and the Manciple not suggested elsewhere or otherwise in *CT.* Unless the Cook himself had had dealings with the Manciple in supplying victuals to the temple the Manciple served, or at least knew those who did, how would he be in a position to expose the Manciple? That he would be able to do so is clearly recognized by the Manciple (lines 76-79). But how would he have known? The Host clearly knows the Cook, as we know from *CkP.* But Chaucer probably did not intend to elaborate on this matter, and in pursuing it too far, we are likely to enter into the world of Lady Macbeth's children. Perhaps it is only a reflection, as RB² suggests (p. 763), of the traditional enmity between the two types; he cites Tupper (1926) as evidence (see also Tupper 1915:264). Lumiansky (1955:237) suggests that the Host, in warning the Manciple against railing upon the Cook, is perhaps recalling his own rashness in ridiculing the Cook (*CkP* 4345-55). At any rate, this is one of the finest figures in Chaucer, and one of the relatively few metaphors: the Manciple, who, like the falcon, has been flying free and "stooping" upon the helpless Cook, is to be "reclaimed" when the Cook sobers up and gathers his wits and his incriminating knowledge about him and is made once more a servant (see SK 5.439).

    72 **to:** TR's *to the* was perhaps derived from Tc¹ if not from his copy-text, SP².
    74 **thy:** MR's *Corpus of Variants* omits the Cp La+ variant *thine* for *thy.*
    75 **preef:** CX¹-PN² read *the preef,* but this is one of the rare occasions when a consensus reading of the earliest printed editions is not picked up by TH¹-UR.
    76 **a gret:** UR's omission of *a gret* has only one MS corroboration, Bo¹, and there is no evidence that it was consulted for UR.

I wol nat wrathe hym, also mote I thryve.   80
That that I spak, I seyde it in my bourde.
And wite [ye] what? I have here in a gourde
A draughte of wyn, ye, of a rype grape,
And right anon ye shul seen a good jape.
This Cook shal drynke ther of, if I may,   85
Up peyne of deeth he wol nat seye me nay."
[A]nd certeynly, to tellen as it was,   108v
Of this vessel the Cook drank faste, allas!
What neded it? He drank ynow biforn.

---

80   also] so *(b)* Cp La+ CX¹-SP³ TR; as En¹ Pw+
81   **That that**] What t. Pw+; T. Ad³ *(b+)* CX¹-SP³; T. at Ha⁴ La+; T. which ~ UR
spak] speke El+   it] *om.* Gg+   in my] but i. *(b)* Gg+ CX¹-UR
82   **wite ye**] w. Hg *(error)*   what] wel *(b)* Cp Gg+ CX¹; wel pat La   a] my *(b)* Cp
En¹+ CX¹-TR
83   ye] it is En¹+ UR; is Ha⁴ WR   a] *om.* Ad³+
85   if I] i. pat I El Pw+ PN¹ UR TR; i. I that ~ FI
86   **Up**] V. on *(b)* La+ CX¹   **peyne of**] *om. (b+)* CX¹   deeth] my lyf *(b)* Cp La+
CX¹-TR   nat seye me] n. s. *(b)* Cp La+ CX¹-TR
87   **And**] nd Hg *(leaf torn)*
88   the] this Gg+
89   **neded**] nedith *(b)* Cp En¹ Gg La Pw+ CX¹-TR   it] hym El̄ Gg+ SK RB¹
RB² FI   **biforn**] afforn Cp La+; toforne Pw+

---

80   **wrathe**: The form *wrathen* of El and most modern editions except MR and Donald-
son (1958) is not treated as a variant because *wrathe* could, of course, be pronounced as two
syllables; MR likewise do not treat it as a variant.

81   **bourde**: Jest. Norton-Smith (1974:151) thinks that *bourde* also has a certain re-
semblance to "bobbing," the cruel mockery of someone who is helpless (cf. *MED, bobben,* v.).

82   **gourde**: A gourde used as a drinking vessel or holder of drink, by extension a
general term for a vessel, a wine flask or skin. Norton-Smith (1974:150) says that it is also
a measure of about half a gallon. Manly (1926b:258) remarks that in offering the drink from
his "gourde" the Manciple exhibits his only "trait of humanity." Both the El and the Gg
miniaturists depict the Manciple with what might be a "gourde" (Manly 1928:665) but
which is rather more likely his symbolic purse.

83   **ye**: UR's *it is* again probably drew upon Ry¹.

85   **if I**: El's *if that I* is shared by several MSS, but of the early printed editions
only PN¹ accepted it (if it was not a compositorial error). UR printed it, but it is in none
of the MSS known to have been used by that edition, so that it was probably UR's "smooth-
ing." Pollard (1928) and Koch (1915) followed El, the latter naturally as he was printing
El. FI's *If I that* is probably a typographical error.

86   **Up**: The sense is "upon."

87   **And**: MR mistakenly have Hg as reading *As* in their *Corpus of Variants* (8.149);
actually Hg clearly has *And,* though the first letter is lost through damage to the leaf.

89   **it**: El Gg Ha³ are the only extant MSS reading *hym* for *it;* SK, much influenced

And whan he hadde powped in this horn,   90
To the Manciple he took the gourde agayn;
And of that drynke the Cook was wonder fayn,
And thanked hym in swich wise as he kowde.
Thanne gan oure Hoost to laughen wonder lowde
And seyde, "I se wel it is necessarie,   95
Where that we goon, good drynke we with us carye.
For that wol turne rancour and disese
T'acord and love, a[nd] many a wrong appese.

---

90   **this**] his *(b)* Cp En[1] Ha[4] La Pw+ CX[1]-WR
91   **To**] And t. La+   **gourde**] grounde Ad[3]
92   **that**] the *(b+)* CX[1]-UR   **drynke**] draught En[1] Ha[4] WR   **wonder**] ful *(b+)* CX[1]-SP[3]
94   **to**] *om.* La+   **laughen**] waxen La; lanwghe CX[1]
96   **good drynke we**] þat d. w. El+; w. g. d. Gg+; g. d. *(b)* Cp En[1] Ha[4] Pw+ CX[1]-WR MR-PR; d. La+   **carye**] to c. *(b)* Cp En[1] Ha[4] La Pw+ CX[1]-WR
98   **T'acord**] to pees Pw+   **and many a**] a m. a Hg *(error);* a. m. Ha[4] La+ **wrong**] word *(b)* Cp La+ CX[1]-UR; rancour En[1] Ha[4]+   **appese**] to pese *(b)* Cp La+ CX[1]-SP[1] UR; pese En[1] Ha[4] SP[2,3]; to sese Pw+

---

by El Gg, printed *hym* and was followed by Pollard (1898), Manly (1928), and RB[1]. MR, however, adopted the Hg *it;* RB[2] retained *hym,* as has FI, but PR accepted the Hg *it,* as Donaldson (1958) had done.

90   **powped in this horn:** Blown upon the horn, i.e., taken a drink from the horn-like mouth of the gourd. SK (5.439) calls our attention to the use of the word in *NPT* 4589, where it just means "puffed." In *ManP* we have almost certainly a play upon words (RB[2], p. 764) meaning "blew upon a wind instrument" and "took a drink"; that there is a further play can scarcely be open to doubt: "broke wind." See Baum (1958:168) for this observation and the recording of Hornstein's private suggestion of yet another play upon *powped,* "blew" and "gulped" (i.e., regurgitated). See also Ross (1972:110).

96   **good drynke we:** Only two MSS, Ad[3] and Ch, support Hg's reading; El has *we* but omits *good;* Gg has *we good drink.* All the rest have simply *good drink* or *drink.* All printed editions until SK omitted *we;* Manly (1928) followed SK, as had Pollard (1898), and so did RB[1]. MR emphasized the general weight of MS and printed-edition tradition and dropped *we,* RB[1] and PR following suit, but Donaldson (1958) and FI have kept the Hg reading. In spite of the paucity of support for Hg's reading, the present edition does not emend, preferring the extra, emphatic *we* to ten syllables in the line.

   carye: The introduction of *to* before *carye* in many MSS suggests that scribes or editors noticed the omission of the repeated subject and so created the formal infinitive.

97-98   Perhaps, as Norton-Smith (1974:151) suggests, a rough translation of Ovid's *Ars amatoria* (1.238): "Cura fugit multo diluiturque mero" ("Care flees, and is dissolved in much wine").

97   **disese:** The literal "dis-ease," or "lack of ease," rather than the modern "disease-sickness."

O Bacus, yblessed be thy name,
That so kanst turnen ernest in to game!   100
Worshipe and thank be to thy deitee!
Of that matere ye gete namoore for me.

---

99   **Bacus**] Ꝑou B. En¹ Ha⁴+ WR SK RB¹ RB²; Bacchus B. ~ TR   **name**] holy n.
~ CX²-UR
   101   **be to**] vn to En¹ Pw+   **thy deitee**] ꝑe Pw+
   102   **Of that**] For o. this Pw+   **ye gete**] g. y. La+; ne g. y. Cp+   **for**] of El
(b) Cp En¹ Gg Ha⁴ La Pw+ CX¹-FI

---

99   **Bacus:** Norton-Smith (1974:150) makes the suggestion that Chaucer may have had in mind, at the end of *ManP*, the scene on Naxos in Ovid's *Ars amatoria* (1:543-44) in which the drunken Silenus falls off his ass in a religious procession, behind which Bacchus rides in his chariot. Norton-Smith further speculates that, if this is true, an Ovidian bridge is provided between *ManP* and the Manciple's Ovidian tale. He compares the state of the Cook at the ending section of *CT* with the state of the Miller in the beginning section. Whether any of this is valid speculation, the invocation of Bacchus by the Host is appropriate, bringing attention to the god who has had "domynacioun" over the Cook and indeed *ManP*, and whose influence is contrary to reason and rational action: it is perhaps against the power of Bacchus that the Manciple, alarmed by his unaccustomed jocularity and lack of restraint in his dealings with the Cook, tells his tale of the dangers of losing control of emotions and of falling into glib responses. Harwood (1972:279) suggests that the Manciple's story which follows is a kind of "verbal Misrule," as the Host's apostrophe to Bacchus and use of liquor are "misrule of the usual kind."

100   **turnen ernest in to game:** Turn a serious matter into a playful one. Chaucer seems to have been much interested in the power of wine or poetry to transmute seriousness into play and the other way around; witness the many times these oppositions or versions of them appear in his poetry (Davis et al. 1979:48). The "game," or mocking of the Cook, has been turned by the Cook's anger into "ernest," the danger to the Manciple. He has then used wine, the cause of the "game" in the first place, to turn the Cook's anger into "game," though the mocking of the Cook, as the Manciple says in an aside to the Host (lines 84-86), continues in reality as the Manciple persuades the drunken Cook to accept more wine. *ManT* follows as an "ernest" fellow to the "game" of *ManP*, and hence the great difference of tone that many critics observe (see Critical Commentary). Although not addressing himself to the opposition in these terms, Norton-Smith (1974:149) relates *ManP* to *ManT* and *ManPT* as examples of paired opposites, a "juxtaposing of the spirit of free indulgence of animal appetite . . . and the doctrine of salvation through the penitential disciplines." See also Donner (1955) and Harwood (1972:274). Although he does not deal specifically with *ManT*, Owen (1977) makes the theme of "ernest and game" the underlying structure of his analysis of *CT*.

102   **for:** I have retained Hg's reading, supported only by Ad³ among the base-ten MSS (seven others in all), instead of emending to El's *of*, which is found in the rest of the MSS and in all printed editions. The Hg reading seems at least as good as the El in sense, and since it is of no importance for commentary, there seems no reason to alter Hg.

Telle on thy [tale], Manciple, I the preye."
"Wel sir," quod he, "now herkneth what I seye."

Here bigynneth the Manciples tale of the Crowe

Whan Phebus dwelled here in this erthe adoun,   105
As olde bokes maken mencioun,
He was the mooste lusty bachiler
In al this world, and eek the beste archer.
He slow Phitoun the serpent as he lay
Slepynge agayn the sonne up on a day,   110

---

103 **thy**] *om.* La Pw+   **tale**] *om.* Hg La Pw+   **Manciple**] pou M. Cp He La Pw+ CX[1]-UR
104 **Wel sir quod he now**] W. s. q. h. *(b)* Gg+ CX[1]-UR; Sires q. h. n. La   **herkneth**] herkyn En[1] Ha[4] PN[2] WR   **seye**] schal s. Gg+
105 **dwelled**] was dwellyng En[1]+   **here**] *om.* En[1]+   **in this erthe**] i. t. world El+; i.e. *(b)* En[1]+ CX[1]-TH[3] SP[1-3] TR; in pearth ~ ST; i. yearth ~ UR
106 **bokes**] b. to us ~ SP[2,3]
107 **was**] held w. ~ UR
108 **In**] Of *(b)* Cp Ha[4] La Pw+ CX[1]-WR   **this**] pe *(b)* Cp+ CX[1]-UR
109 **Phitoun the serpent**] anoon pe s. P. En[1]
110 **the**] *om.* La   **sonne**] soone ~ RB[2]   **a**] a mery En[1]+

---

103 **tale**: Hg omits, an obvious scribal slip, but one shared with La, Pw, and several others; that the object of the verb should be omitted in important MSS need not necessarily indicate a MS relation; although it is odd, it almost certainly occurred because three of the first four words in the line begin with *t,* and it is not surprising that one of the words should slip out (La Pw and others omit both *thy* and *tale,* prefacing *Manciple* with pou).

105 **Whan . . . adoun**: Chaucer probably drew the general notion of Phoebus Apollo's life on earth from Ovid, perhaps *Met.* (the ultimate origin for the Middle Ages of the tale itself) 1.438ff. or 2.531-632. Possibly he was also influenced by *Ars amatoria* 2.239-40, according to Norton-Smith (1974:151), who suggests that this couplet may have provided a link. The sources, ancient and modern, are briefly mentioned by all major editions, discussed in detail with relevant selections from texts by Work in Bryan and Dempster (1941:699-722), and discussed with more recent suggestions in Critical Commentary.

    in this erthe: UR's *in yearth* is clearly a misreading of ST's *in pearth* (ST does not distinguish between *y* and *p.*

109 **Phitoun the serpent**: Python. See *Met.* 1.438-51. Apollo was known by the sobriquet Pythian. Isidore of Seville, in his *Etymologiae* 8.54, explains that the Pythian games were instituted in honor of Apollo's victory over Python, repeating the story of Ovid but specifically deriving the name of the games from Apollo.

110 **Slepynge agayne the sonne**: Hazelton (1963:9) takes this to be parodic, sug-

And many another noble worthy dede
He with his bowe wroghte, as men may rede.
Pleyen he koude on every mynstralcye,
And syngen, that it was a melodye
To heren of his clere voys the soun.   115
Certes the kyng of Thebes, Amphioun,
That with his syngyng walled that citee,
Koude nevere syngen half so wel as he.

---

111 **another]** a Ad³+   **noble worthy]** n. *(b+)* CX¹; w. n. La Pw+
112 **wroghte]** broghte Cp Gg *(corr.* Gg₁*)* La   **men]** ȝe Gg+
113 **Pleyen]** Pleynge La   **on]** of Cp La+
115 **heren]** harken Pw+
117 **syngyng]** song *(b+)* CX¹-SP³   **that]** the Ad³ *(b+)* CX¹-TR

---

gesting that Phoebus's feat was of no great daring. The fact that there is no such description in any of Chaucer's possible sources lends some credibility to Hazelton's interpretation, but not enough to sustain his overall theory of parody. The sources that Chaucer might have known, particularly Ovid, treat the episode as a great victory over a huge monster: ". . . *maxime Python* / . . . *incognita serpens*" (*Met.* 1.438-39). It seems to be the case, as McCall argues (1979: passim, but particularly pp. 123-53), that classical myth is always reduced by Chaucer to comic or pathetic dimensions, but not deliberately parodied: ". . . Chaucer was far more interested in people than in gods, in this world than in an airy mythology of antiquity" (p. 157). Marshall (1979) made the interesting observation that Chaucer's description of the python sleeping "agayn" the sun may be an alchemical reference, for ". . . a serpent . . . superimposed upon the sun illustrates the *Mercurias noster,* the *prima materia* of the alchemical process" (p. 18). He agrees with Spector (1957) in seeing a relation between the *ManPT* and *CYT.*

    sonne: RB's *soone* is simply a misprint.

    113-18 Harwood observes (1972:269) that Chaucer pays far more attention to Phoebus's musical abilities than do his possible "sources." McCall (1979:129) compares this part of Phoebus's description in particular to the descriptions of his kin, who are "'hende' Nicholas with his 'gay sautrie,' Absolon with his 'giterne' and 'quynyble,' and the Canterbury Squire, 'syngynge . . . al the day.'"

    116 **the kyng of Thebes Amphioun:** A story well known in the Middle Ages, and there is likely no particular source that Chaucer used; he refers to it also in *MerT* 1716. It is found in Horace's *Ars p.* 1.394: ". . . dictus et Amphion, Thebanae conditor urbis saxa movere sono testudinis et prece blanda ducere quo vellet" (". . . it is said that Amphion, builder of the city of Thebes, could move stones by the sound of his lyre and lead them wherever he wished by the sound of his supplicating spell"); and in Statius, *Thebaid* 1.7-11: "longa retro series, trepidum si Martis operti agricolam infandis condentem proelia sulcis expediam penitusque sequar, quo carmine muris iusserit Amphion Tyrios accedere montes, unde graves irae cognata in moenia Baccho" ("far in antiquity runs the tale, should I tell of the diligent begetter of hidden war, seeding battles in the unhallowed earth, and searching further,

97

Ther to he was the semelieste man
That is, or was, sith that the world bigan.　　　　　　　　　120
What nedeth it hise fetures to discryve?
For in this world was noon so fair on lyve.
He was ther with fulfild of gentillesse,
Of honour, and of parfit worthynesse.

119　**Ther]** And t. (Dl) SP²-UR
120　**that]** *om. (b)* Cp Ha⁴ La Pw+ CX¹-WR
121　**hise]** is Pw　　**fetures]** feture (Tc²) CX¹-SP³ TR; fortune Ha⁴　　**to]** for t. *(b)* La+ CX¹
122　**was noon]** w. ther n. (Tc²) CX¹,² WN PN²; w. t. no man ~ PN¹; is noon Ha⁴+ WR; n'is non ~ TR
123　**gentillesse]** gentilnesse Cp Pw+ CX¹-UR

---

tell with what song Amphion commanded the Tyrian mountains move to create a city's walls, whence came Bacchus's grievous wrath against his kindred towers"; and according to Boccaccio, *Genealogie deorum gentilium libri* (1951:1.274), Amphion was so skilled in the art of music ("Anphyon musice artis adeo peritus fuit") that with it he constructed the Theban walls ("Thebanos muros construxit"). Although SK (5.434) simply gives "Cf. Horace, *De Arte Poetica* 1.394," in view of the fact that Chaucer's direct borrowing from Horace has never been convincingly demonstrated (Lounsbury 1892:2.261; Siebert 1912:304-307; Shannon 1929:359-60), it is rather more probable that Chaucer derived the story, if he derived it from any particular source, from Statius or Boccaccio. The detail of Amphion as *king* of Thebes Chaucer probably derived from medieval sources, particularly Boccaccio's *Genealogie* (see Wise 1911:59). Chaucer would have known of Amphion as a musician from Ovid *Met.* 6.177-79 (Shannon 1929:319). Perhaps, just perhaps, there was an association in Chaucer's mind between the Bacchus who presides over *ManP* (invoked by the Host, line 116), and Thebes, which was traditionally hated by Bacchus (see *Thebaid,* cited above). Clogan (1964) suggests that Chaucer may have been acquainted with the *scolia* of the *Thebaid,* though he does not mention *ManT* in this connection.

119　**Ther:** The only MS authority for *And ther to* in SP²-UR is Dl; UR could have derived the reading from either (UR's *ManT* text is heavily influenced by Dl, which is *Out* for *ManP*); since line 119 is the only instance of possible Dl origin for *ManPT* in SP², the probable explanation is that SP² was merely "smoothing."

122　**was noon:** TR's *n'is non* has no MS or printed-edition authority and is clearly a silent emendation.

123　**gentillesse:** MR's *Corpus of Variants* does not list *gentilnesse* as a variant of *gentillesse,* treating it as the same word; it is apparent to me, however, that Chaucer always uses *gentillesse* in a technical sense and avoids confusion with *gentilnesse,* a term of broader implications for him. § Chaucer's use of this word in this form is very interesting. The most authoritative MSS of *CT* almost always spell it this way, and the *MED* citations of *gentilnesse* in Chaucer are almost always from the less dependable MSS. In view of the Manciple's concern with the precise use of language, the term is perhaps worth more attention than it has received (see Elliott 1974:112). According to Coghill (1971:7) it is "the

This Phebus that was flour of bachelrye,   109r   125
As wel in fredom as in chivalrye,
For his desport, in signe eek of victorie
Of Phitoun, so as telleth us the storie,
Was wont to beren in his hand a bowe.
Now hadde this Phebus in his hous a crowe,   130

---

   125   **of]** ob La
   127   **his]** to Ha⁴ WR; *om. (b)* Cp La Pw+   **in]** and i. Pw+   **eek]** *om.* En¹ Ha⁴+
UR WR
   128   **Of]** O En¹+
   129   **wont]** worpy Cp La+
   130   **hadde]** hap Pw+   **this]** pat En¹+

---

quality that Chaucer most deeply admired." Burnley (1979:151-70) surveys Chaucer's employment of the ideal of "gentillesse" in his works and concludes that, although it is not a monolithic concept, it generally consists of the capacity for "pitee," sensitivity, "mesure" in behavior: "The company of the *gentil* is defined by union of affect, mutuality of will, *pitee, grace, mercy* and love" (p. 159). The character of the "vileyn" is just the opposite. Burnley remarks that Chaucer's "gentillesse" is somewhat similar to the theological doctrine of grace: ". . . where faith calls forth grace unmerited. *Gentillesse,* too, deals in beneficence rather than rights" (p. 159). He remarks further that "gentillesse" is Chaucer's usual translation of *nobilitas.* Burnley does not discuss *ManPT* in light of this ideal, but one can assume that, ironically or not, such are the ideals implied in the Manciple's use of the term "gentillesse." See Birney (1960) for an extensive comment on the irony of the term as used by the Manciple. The concept is treated at length by Brewer (1968), Coghill (1971), and Gaylord (1964), among others.

   125   **bachelrye:** Knighthood; Chaucer has, of course, made Phoebus into a medieval knight, and, as McCall says (1979:130), as far as the Manciple can tell, ". . . the god is a complete gentleman."

   126   **fredom . . . chivalrye:** The word "fredom" combines into one from the meanings "nobility" and "generosity" (Davis:1979), and "chivalrye" would seem to mean simply knighthood. The Manciple is loading his description of Phoebus with all the terms which he has heard and read about even if seldom seen in practice. He would seem to be idealizing Phoebus rather than mocking him as Hazelton argues (1963).

   129   **in his hand a bowe:** Hazelton (1963:8-9) sees this detail as parodic, in that the bow and arrow were not the weapons of chivalry. It is, however, as he recognizes, in most of the sources that Chaucer might have known, and he does not suggest that Chaucer might have substituted the lance and broadsword. Indeed, that would have been parodic. The mixture of classical myth and medieval detail is common everywhere, and there is nothing essentially ridiculous in Phoebus's being described as a true knight and armed with the arrows that were his trademark.

   130   **crowe:** Instead of the traditional raven of the classical myth. However, *The Seven Sages of Rome* is about a crow, and Chaucer seems to have been a bit confused about the traditional characteristics of the bird; cf. *PF,* in which the characterizations of the crow and raven in Alanus's *De planctu naturae* are reversed. See Harrison 1956:4, and the discussion of sources in Critical Commentary.

Which in a cage he fostred many a day,
And taughte it speke, as men teche a jay.
Whit was this crowe as is a snow whit swan,
And contrefete the speche of every man
He kowde, whan he sholde telle a tale.   135
Ther with in al this world no nyghtyngale
Ne koude, by an hondred thousand deel,
Syngen so wonder myrily and weel.

   Now hadde this Phebus in his hous a wyf
Which that he lovede moore than his lyf,   140
And nyght and day dide evere his diligence
Hire for to plese and doon hire reverence,
Save oonly that, the sothe if I shal sayn,

---

131   **Which]** With Ad³ *(b)* CX¹-SP³   **in a]** i. La+   **cage he fostred]** c. yfostrid (Tc²) CX¹-SP³

132   **it]** in ~ SP³;   **speke]** to s. Pw+ UR; speche ~ WN TH¹-SP³   **as]** a. that Cp En¹+   **teche]** doon Ha⁴ Pw+ WR; techeþ La

133   **is]** *om.* El+   **snow]** mylke ~ PN¹; *om.* Pw+ TH¹-SP³

134   **contrefete]** countirfetid *(b)* Cp Gg La Pw+ CX¹-PN²

135   **whan]** w. as ~ SP²,³; w. that ~ UR   **sholde telle]** t. s. *(En³)* UR

136   **Ther with in al this world no]** T. was i. a. t. w. n. *(b+)* CX¹-UR; T. is wiþenne t. w. n. Ha⁴+ WR; T. w. i. a. þe w. n. Cp; T. w. i. a. t. londe per nys no Pw

137   **Ne]** That Pw+

138   **wonder]** wonderly *(b)* Cp La+ CX¹-SP³; *om.* Pw+   **myrily]** mery La Pw+ WN TH¹-SP³   **and]** a. eke so Pw+

140   **his]** h. owne Cp La Pw+ UR

141   **evere]** e. mor Ha⁴+ WR   **his]** *om.* Ha⁴ PW+ WR

142   **for to]** t. El *(corr.* El,*)*   **hire]** *om.* Pw+

143   **that the sothe if I shal]** t. t. s. that I s. El Gg+; if t. s. t. I s. Cp En¹ Ha⁴

---

132   **teche:** MR's *Corpus of Variants* omits La's variant *techeþ*.

133   **Whit . . . swan:** Chaucer and Gower, as RB² (p. 764) observes, liken the crow only to the swan, whereas Ovid compares him to swans, doves, and geese (*Met.* 2.536-39).

135   **whan he sholde telle a tale:** UR's *whan that he tellin should* has no MS authority for the additon of *that* and perhaps relies for the inversion upon Ry¹.

139   **a wyf:** Chaucer does not name her, but, according to Ovid (*Met.* 2.542), she was Coronis of Larissa; she is also named in the *Ovide moralisé* (lines 2146-47); all the analogues that Chaucer might have known develop her character to some extent (Severs 1952:3-4). Chaucer, in making Phebus's wife behave as she does, without any sympathetic treatment (he "suppresses" the fact that she is pregnant, for instance), is condemning the idea of courtly love, according to Schlauch (1937:210-11).

143   **that . . . shal:** Hg in its reading *that the sothe if I shal* is supported by only

Jalous he was, and wolde han kept hire fayn.
For hym were looth byjaped for to be,   145
And so is every wight in swich degree;
But al for naught, for it availeth noght.

La+ WR SK-PR; the s. yf I s. Ad³ *(b+)* CX¹ PN¹; yif I pe sop s. Pw+ TH¹-UR FI; yf t. s. yf I s. CX² WN PN²; i. that I t. s. (Mm) TR

   145   **byjaped]** iapid *(b)* La+ CX¹-SP³; i iaped Pw+ UR TR
   146   **is]** *om.* Cp La Pw+   **wight]** man wolde Pw+
   147   **for naught]** in ydel El Gg+ SK RB¹ RB² FI   **availeth]** auaylid *(b+)* CX¹-PN²

---

one other MS, Ps, and by no printed editions. Hg, however, makes excellent sense to me, both semantically and syntactically, and it is not emended. El's *that the soth that I shal* is also supported meagerly, by only two MSS, Gg Ha³. The El Gg reading, interestingly, is very close to the Hg, and although speculation is fruitless, it is quite possible that the versions represent an original, at some remove, that had been corrected, without the effect of the correction being totally clear. TR's *if that I the soth shal* seems derived from MS Mm. FI takes his reading from Bo², here with Pw, and joined in the editions by TH¹-UR.

   147   **for naught:** El and Gg's *in ydel* was adopted by SK and Pollard (1898) and by RB for both editions. MR, however, printed Hg, as has PR. El would seem authentic, whether a first or second thought of Chaucer's one cannot, of course, say; there is something, however, in the repetition of *naught* in the line that is more emphatic and suitable for the repetitious Manciple, and so on a basis of style and my own judgment I retain Hg's *for naught.*

   Marginal gloss: Verum quid prodest diligens custodia cum uxor impudica seruari non possit pudica non debeat feda enim custos est castitatis necessitas pulcra [cito?] adamatur feda facile concupiscit difficile custoditur quod plures amant Hg. This is a slightly shortened form of a passage in Jerome's *Epistola adversus Jovinianum* (1.47), an extract, Jerome tells us, from Theophrastus *Liber aureolus de nuptiis* (Migne, *PL* 23:290): "Verum quid prodest etiam diligens custodia, cum uxor seruari impudica non possit, pudica non debeat? Infida enim custos est castitatis necessitas: et illa uere pudica dicenda est, cui licuit peccare, si uoluit. Pulchra cito adamatur, foeda facile concupiscit. Difficile custoditur, quod plures amant" ("Indeed, what profits diligent custody when a dishonest wife may not be watched over and an honest one ought not be? For necessity is an untrustworthy guardian, and truly only a woman may be said to be honest who has been given freedom to sin if she has wished. A beautiful woman quickly attracts lovers, and an ugly one easily becomes wanton. It is difficult to guard what many desire"). Hg's scribe has mistakenly written *feda* for *Infida,* anticipating the *feda (foeda)* in the following sentence. The glossator omitted the second half of the second sentence (or may have been using a text from which it was missing). It is odd that El, so much more finished a MS, does not have this gloss. Chaucer in his poem has neatly translated the first sentence in lines 148-51. The general point of the passage from Jerome is encapsulated in lines 152-53. The sentence beginning "Pulchra cito adamatur" is expanded beautifully by the Wife of Bath in her *Prologue,* lines 257-68, with the point that attractive women are pursued by all and ugly women pursue all men: "For as a spaynel she wol on hym lepe" (line 267). MR in their discussion of the glosses (3.483-527) conclude that very few of the *CT* glosses were Chaucer's work and do not comment on the possibility that this gloss in Hg may have been Chaucerian. Silvia (1965) argues forcefully that the glosses from Jerome in

A good wyf that is clene in werk and thoght
Sholde nat be kept in noon awayt, certayn;
And trewely the labour is in vayn   150
To kepe a shrewe, for it wol nat be.
This holde I for a verray nycetee,
To spille labour for to kepe wyves:
Thus writen olde clerkes in hir lyves.
    But now to purpos as I first bigan.   155
This worthy Phebus dooth al that he kan

---

148   **in]** of El *(b)* Cp En¹ Ha⁴ La Pw+ CX¹-FI
149   **awayt]** awe *(b+)* CX¹
150   **labour]** more it *(b+)* CX¹   **in]** *om.* (Ra²) UR
152   **nycetee]** vanytee Gg+
153   **labour]** a l. La+   **wyves]** our w. ~ SP²,³ UR
154   **writen olde clerkes]** o. c. w. Ha⁴+ WR

El and Hg, in particular, may have been Chaucer's own work, though he does not deal with the *ManT* gloss. Certainly Chaucer knew intimately the section of the *Epistola* from which the above passage is taken; not only is the material above cited from *WBT* taken from it, but his exempla in *FranT* are taken from the pages immediately preceding it (Dempster [1937]; Sledd [1947]; Baker [1961]); further use by Chaucer of the extract from Theophrastus quoted here by Jerome is found in *MerT* 1294, where "Theofraste" is cited; it is impossible to believe that Chaucer could have known all this material from any other source, though bits and pieces, of course, are frequently found elsewhere, for the *Epistola* was one of the most influential works on medieval writers. SK in his notes (5.296-313) gives a series of references for *WBT* in addition to the one cited above that demonstrate the dependence of that work upon Jerome (and, through Jerome, Theophrastus), a heavy dependence upon what is really a rather short portion of the *Epistola,* a few pages before the end of the first section. Further, the remark of the old hag in *WBT* 1215-16, "For filthe and elde, also moot I thee, / Been grete wardeyns upon chastitee," may well be derived, as SK surmises (5.322), from an old French proverb, but it seems to catch up perfectly the ironic tone of the Theophrastus-Jerome comment upon necessity as a guardian of chastity. In my opinion the Hg *ManT* gloss is quite likely to have been Chaucerian in origin. For a general discussion of the antifeminist literature available to Chaucer, see Pratt (1962).

    148 **in:** The overwhelming support given El's *of* against Hg's *in* by all printed editions is impressive; however, both words seem equally authentic and mean the same thing, and since a single unimportant word is involved, I see no reason to emend. Hg's reading is supported by, in addition to the MSS in the collations, seven others.

    150 **in:** UR's omission is supported by only one MS, Ra², and by no printed editions; a compositorial error is probable.

    152 **verray nycetee:** The essence or height of folly.

    153 **wyves:** The *our wyues* of SP²,³ clearly is a compositor's addition or an editorial bit of tinkering that UR picked up; it exists in no MSS or other printed editions.

    154 **olde clerkes:** I.e., Theophrastus and Jerome.

To plesen hire, wenynge for swich plesaunce,
And for his manhode and his governaunce,
That no man sholde han put hym from hire grace.
But God it woot ther may no man embrace 160
As to destreyne a thyng which that nature
Hath naturelly set in a creature.
   Take any bryd, and put it in a cage,

---

157 **for]** that El En¹ Gg+; by Cp Ha⁴ La Pw+ WR SK MR PR; thorow *(b+)* CX¹-TR
158 **and]** a. for Ad³ *(b+)* CX¹-SP³
159 **han]** *om. (b+)* CX¹-TR   **hym]** hire Gg+   **hire]** his En¹+
161 **destreyne]** destroy Ha⁴ Pw+ WR; discryue La+   **which]** þe w. Ha⁴ WR
163 **bryd]** thyng Gg+   **it]** hym *(b)* Ha⁴+ CX¹-WR

---

157   **for:** Hg's reading is supported by Ad³ of the base-ten MSS and by three others; of the major printed editions only Koch (1915—and curiously, since he is primarily printing El), RB¹,², and FI follow Hg. MR followed SK in adopting the Ha⁴ *by,* and PR prints *by* also.

160-62: The analogues for this passage are several. It is a version of Horace *Epist.* 1.10.24: "Naturam expelles furca, tamen usque recurret [medieval and early editions generally read *expellas*]" ("You may expel Nature with a pitchfork, yet she will always quickly return"). Chaucer, as I have noted, was unlikely to have known Horace in the original, except perhaps as a *flosculus.* Plessow (1929:74-75), as had SK (5.439-40) cited the *Roman de la Rose* (Langlois 1922:4.14019-30): "Car Horaces neïs raconte, / Qui bien set que tel chose monte: / Qui voudrait une fourche prendre / Pour sei de Nature defendre, / E la bouterait hors de sei, / Revendrait ele, bien le sai. / Toujourz Nature recourra, / Ja pour abit ne demourra. / Que vaut ce? Toute creature / Veaut retourner a sa nature; / Ja nou laira pour violence / De force ne de couvenance" ("As Horace says, who knew well what such things meant, 'Who would wish to take up a pitchfork to defend himself against Nature and thrust her away would find that she would soon return.' That I know well. For ever Nature returns, and clerical cloth will not deter her. Why go on about such an obvious thing? Every creature will return to its nature, nor is able to give it up, neither by violence nor by covenant"). This passage is preceded in the *Roman de la Rose* by the exemplum of the caged bird (lines 13941-58) that follows in the *ManT.* John of Salisbury's *Polycraticus* (3.8; Webb 1909: 1.191) also quotes the line from Horace, as Hamilton observed (1903:143-44). Gower's *Confessio Amantis,* which seems to provide Chaucer with a subject for parody during the last part of *ManT* also quotes Horace: "What nature hath set in hir lawe / Ther mai no manner miht with drawe" (*Lib.* 3.355-56; 1900:1.235).

163   **Take any bryd:** TR (2.508) observed that this figure is found in both the *Roman de la Rose* and Boethius; in the *Roman* it precedes the passage cited above (Langlois 1922: 4.13941-53): "Li oisillons dou vert boschage, / Quant il est pris e mis en cage, / Nourriz mout ententivement / Laienz delicieusement, / E chante, tant con sera vis, / De cueur gai, ce vous est avis, / Si desierre il les bois ramez / Qu'il a naturelment amez, / E voudrait seur les arbres estre, / Ja si bien nou savra l'en paistre; / Toujourz i pense e s'estudie /

A recouvrer sa franche vie. / Sa viande a ses piez demarche, / O l'ardeur qui son cueur li charche, / E va par sa cage traçant, / A grant angoisse pourchaçant. / Coment fenestre ou pertuis truisse / Par quei voler au bois s'en puisse" ("The bird which is from the green woods captured and placed in a cage, and nourished with care, and fed with delicious food, may sing happily in your opinion; but it yearns for the boughs of the trees which it naturally loves, and wishes to be there however well it may be cared for. Always it thinks of ways to recover its freedom. With all the ardor of its heart it tramples its food beneath its feet and seeks with agony throughout its cage for a window or some means through which it will be able to fly back to the woods"). SK (5.440), following TR, asserts that Chaucer is, however, following Boethius, and Plessow (1929:75) agrees; see Whiting 1968, B300. The passage is in *De cons.* 3, m.2 (1973:238): "Quae canit altis garrula ramis / Ales, caueae clauditur antro: / Huic licet inlita pocula melle, / Largasque dapes dulci studio / Ludens hominum cura minis-tret, / Si tamen, arto saliens texto, / Nemorum gratas viderit umbras; / Sparsas pedibus proterit escas, / Silvas tantum maesta requirit, / Silvas dulci voci susurrat." This is trans-lated by Chaucer (RB[2], p. 343): "And the janglynge brid that syngeth on the heghe braunches (that is to seyn, in the wode), and after is enclosed in a streyt cage, although that the pleyinge bysynes of men yiveth hem honyed drynkes and large metes with swete studye, yit natheles yif thilke bryd skippynge out of hir streyte cage seith the agreable schadwes of the wodes, sche defouleth with hir feet hir metes ischad, and seketh mornynge oonly the wode, and twytereth desyrynge the wode with hir swete voys." Chaucer also used the illustration of the caged bird in *SqT* (lines 610-20); in that poem he seems to have been following Boethius (Fansler 1914:219), and TR (2.508), SK (5.440), and RB[2] (p. 764) agree that in *ManT* Chaucer was following the *Roman*. Koeppel (1891-92:261-62) concludes, by comparing the passage in *SqT* (lines 610-20):

> "Men loven of propre kynde newfangelnesse
> As bryddes doon that men in cages feede.
> For theigh thow nyght and day take of hem hede,
> And strawe hir cages faire and softe as sylk,
> And yeve hem sugre, hony, breed and milk,
> Yet right anon as that hir dore is uppe
> He with his feet wol sporne down his cuppe
> And to the wode he wole and wormes ete.
> So newfangel been they of hir mete,
> And loven novelries of propre kynde,
> No gentilesse of blood may hem bynde."

and the exemplum of the cat in *ManT* 175-82 that *ManT* was written before *SqT* and that Chaucer may have glanced at his earlier poem, recalled the *milk/sylk* rhyme, and used it for the bird exemplum, which it does not fit as well as it does the cat exemplum in *ManT*. SK (5.440) also remarks upon this curiosity but draws no conclusions from it. Jefferson (1917:148) observes that in *ManT*, as in *SqT*, the "discussion is to prove that men, by in-stinct, follow their 'likerous appetyt.' The *Consolatio*, in the corresponding discussion, at-tempts to prove just the opposite, that men, by nature, seek the highest good." Economou (1975:679-83) makes much the same observation, pointing out that, whereas Boethius deals with human nature generally, in *ManT* the image of the bird in the cage is "invested with the notion that there exists a similarity between the instincts of lower creatures and the lubriciousness of a certain kind of woman" (p. 681). In *SqT* the image illustrates the change-ability of the tercelet. Economou goes on to call attention to a "submerged" use of the image

And do al thyn entente and thy corage
[To] fostre it tendrely with mete and drynke,   109v   165
Of alle deyntees that thow kanst bithynke,
And kepe it al so clenly as thow may,
Al though his cage of gold be never so gay,
Yet hath this bryd, by twenty thousand fold,
Levere in a forest that is rude and cold   170
Gon ete wormes and swich wrecchednesse.
For evere this bryd wol doon his bisynesse
To eschape out of his cage if he may.

---

165   **To**] *om.* Hg *(torn leaf)*
166   **Of alle**] And with a. pe Ha⁴+ WR; O. a. pe (Dl+) UR   **that thow**] thou Ha⁴
La+ WR   **bithynke**] pink Ha⁴+
167   **al so**] as En¹ La+   **clenly**] kyndly Ha⁴+ WR   **thow**] he Pw+
168   **his**] he h. La; the ~ TH¹-TR
169   **hath**] had En¹+ TH¹-TR   **twenty**] .xx. Hg+
170   **Levere**] L. to be Ha⁴+ WR   **in a forest**] i. f. Ha⁴+ WR   **that is**] *om.* Ha⁴+
WR   **rude**] wild *(b)* Cp La Pw+ CX¹-PN² TR WR MR; wyd Ha⁴+ WN TH¹-UR
172   **evere**] er ~ UR
173   **eschape**] scape Ha⁴+ WR   **if**] i. pat En¹+; when *(b)* Cp Ha⁴ La+ CX¹-SP³ WR;
whan that ~ UR TR

---

in *MilT* 3221-26 combined with the description of Alisoun as like a swallow sitting on a
barn.
    163   *Marginal glosses:* Exemplum de volucre El Ad³; Similitudo de Aue Cn Ma Ln;
de natura auium per similitudine En³ Ll¹; Exemplum Se.
    168   **his:** The reading *the* has no extant MS or early printed-edition authority and was
probably a compositorial error first introduced in TH¹ that survived through TR, being first
"corrected" by WR. MR's *Corpus of Variants* misses La's *he his.*
    169   **hath:** The reading *had* introduced in TH¹ (and reprinted through TR) possibly
suggests that TH¹ had access to one of the ten MSS extant that contain this variant, but
more probably it is an error.
    170   **rude:** The words *rude* (Hg El Ad³ En¹ Gg and others) and *wild* (Cp La Pw and
others) are both almost without doubt authentic (MR, 2.449 accept this). The Hg reading was
adopted (through Gg) by SK and also by RB¹,² and PR. MR chose *wild,* which seems to me
a strange choice since the phrase "wild and cold" has the ring of a cliché, and it seems more
likely that it was rejected in revision. The fact that the three very best MSS, overall, Hg
El Gg, have *rude* should be decisive. The reading *wyd* found only in Ha⁴ and two others
seems a scribal error (missing the *l* in *wyld* is an easy mistake) and, although WN may have
derived it from one of these MSS, a more obvious explanation is that it was there, too, an
error, whence it was picked up in TH¹ and continued through UR. WR corrects Ha⁴ by La.
    172   *Spurious lines:* Ther to a bide hym thenkith a grete distresse Mg; As by nature to
hym apropred ys Lc.
    173   **if:** RB² in his textual notes (p. 897) makes a point of distinguishing his reading
yif (derived from Gg) from RB¹ *if,* the significance of which is not clear.

His libertee this bryd desireth ay.

Lat take a cat, and fostre hym wel with milk 175
And tendre flessh, and make his couche of silk,
And lat hym seen a mous go by the wal,
Anon he weyveth milk and flessh and al,
And every deyntee that is in that hous,
Swich appetit hath he to ete a mous. 180
Lo, heere hath lust his domynacioun,

---

174 this] þe *(b)* Cp Ha⁴ La Pw+ CX¹-WR
175 cat] cok *(deleted* Pw₁) c. Pw   hym] hir *(b+)* CX¹-TR   wel] *om. (b+)* CX¹-TR
176 **And**] An Cp   his] hir *(b+)* CX¹-TR   couche] bed Ha⁴+ WR
177 **hym**] hir (Tc²) CX¹-TR
178 **Anon**] And a. Cp La Pw+   he] she (Tc²+) CX¹-TR   **milk and flessh**] m. f. Cp La Pw+; f. a. couche (Tc²) CX¹-UR
179 **that is**] which i. Ha⁴ WR   that] þe Pw+
180 **hath he**] he hath El; h. she Cp Ha⁴ (Tc²+) CX¹-TR   a] þe *(b)* En¹ Ha⁴+ CX¹-TR
181 **heere**] he Cp La+   lust] kind (En³+) TR-WR   his] hir (En³+) TR
domynacioun] dampnacioun Cp La+

175-82 **Lat take a cat:** The exemplum of the cat seems, to all commentators (TR 2.508; SK 5.440; RB², p. 764, etc.), in the context of the other similar passages, to be taken from the *Roman* (lines 14039-48; 1922:4): "'Qui prendrait, beaus fiz, un chaton / Qui onques rate ne raton / Veü n'avrait, puis fust nourriz / Senz ja voeir rat ne souriz, / Lonc tens, par ententive cure, / De delicieuse pasture, / E puis veïst souriz venir, / N'est riens qui le peüst tenir, / Se l'en le laissait eschaper, / Qu'il ne l'alast tantost haper'" ("'If one should take, fair son, a cat which had been brought up without seeing a male or a female rat, nor a mouse, and feed him well for a long time with attentive care delicious food, and then allow a mouse to appear, there is nothing that will restrain the cat, if it is allowed to escape, from running to seize his prey, and it doesn't matter whether the cat is hungry or not'"). Rowland (1971: 105-107) on *ManT* 162-80 remarks that the Manciple is "asserting that animal instincts cannot be suppressed. . . . Superficially the Manciple's remarks bear some resemblance to the Franklyn's, and both men are to tell tales involving a husband, a wife and her admirer. But the Franklyn, while claiming that 'love wol nat been constreyned by maistrye. . . . Wommen, of kynde, desiren libertee' (FranklT . . . 764-768), finds that *gentilesse* ensures marital fidelity and love. The Manciple regards love only as an animal appetite" (p. 106). Rowland agrees with Economou that the Manciple believes that "women have a natural taste for sexual depravity" (p. 196).

175 *Marginal glosses:* Exemplum de Murelego El Ad³; De mureligo Cn Ma Ln; De Natura Cati En³; Exemplum Se.

181 **Lo . . . domynacioun:** Cf. *ManT* 57.

lust: TR's reading *kind* for *lust* is clearly drawn from either En³ or Ad¹, his use of them having already been noted; the same is true for his reading of *hir* for *his* in the same line. WR follows in the first instance but not in the second.

And appetit flemeth discrecioun.
    A she wolf hath also a vileyns kynde.
The lewedeste wolf that she may fynde,
And leest of reputacioun, that wol she take   185
In tyme whan hire lust to han a make.

---

183   **A she wolf hath also**] As þe w. h. a. *(b)* Cp La Pw+ CX[1]; Also a s. w. h. Ha[4]+
WR   **a**] so ~ SP[3]   **vileyns**] dyuers Gg+ vylanous (En[3]+) TH[1]-UR
184   **that**] t. euer ~ SP[2]-UR
185   **And**] Or El Ad[3] *(b)* Cp En[1] Ha[4] La Pw+ CX[1]-FI   **leest**] lewedest La   **that**]
him Ha[4]+ WR; *om.* ~ UR TR SK RB[1] RB[2]
186   **whan**] w. that En[1]+ UR

---

183   **A she wolf:** SK (5.440), following TR (2.508), asserts that this exemplum is taken from the *Roman* (lines 7761-66; 1921:3): "Le vaillant ome arriere boute / E prent le pire de la route; / La nourrist ses amours e couve, / Tout autresince come la louve, / Cui sa folie tant empire / Qu'el prent adès des lous le pire" ("The fool will quickly reject the worthy man and choose the worst of all the rout; she will incubate and nourish her love in the manner of the she wolf, whose folly is so lewd that she will choose the worst of all the pack"). Plessow (1929:78) also cites this parallel, but Emerson (1922:146-47) observes that the passage is in an entirely different part of the *Roman* from the lines referred to in the note on *ManT* 175-82 and that Chaucer's reference may have been drawn from a much fuller account in *The Master of Game* (chap. 7, pp. 54-55). Rowland (1971:107) suggests Ovid as another parallel (*Ars amandi* 3.419-22). But Reid (1955:16-19) demonstrates how widespread was this bit of folklore in its form as an exemplum and concludes that it is rather unlikely that Chaucer had actually drawn upon any particular "source" for the figure. See Whiting (1968, W448). Scattergood (1970:244-46) provides another parallel in an unpublished ME poem.

    vileyns: TH[1]-UR read *vylanous,* and this may have simply been a compositorial error, the reading of En[3] and others, or a transformation of the word into its then current form.

    vileyns kynde: the nature of a villain, a base nature. The genitive of *vileyn,* though as SK (5.440) and RB[2] (p. 764) note, it came to be used as an adjective *(OED, villains),* and from it developed the adverb *vileynsly* (e.g., *ParsT* 154). SK offers (5.440) the analogy of the noun *wonders* (gen.) becoming the adjective *wonders* (later *wondrous*). Other examples of Chaucer's use of the adjective *vileyns* (in the sense "base") are *WBT* 1158, 1268; and *ParsT* 556.

    Marginal gloss: Exemplum de lupo El Ad[3]; De lupo Ad[1] Cn Ma Ln En[3] Tc[2]; Exemplum Se.

185   **And:** Only Hg and two minor MSS read *And* here, the rest giving *Or;* all printed editions read *Or.* The single word has no real importance for the text or commentary, and so I retain the Hg *And,* believing that it makes for better emphasis, the *Or* lessening the sweeping effect of the figure.

    that: All MSS and all early printed editions have either *that* or *him;* UR omitted to print either word, and all important editions after UR followed his lead until Pollard (1898) restored *that.* MR followed suit, though RB[1] had omitted it, and RB[2] omitted it also. PR and FI have now once more restored *that.*

Alle this ensamples speke I by thise men
That ben untrewe, but no thyng by wommen.
For men han evere a likerous appetit
On lower thyng to parformen hir delit   190
Than on hire wyves, be they never so faire,
Ne never so trewe, ne so debonaire.
Flessh is so newfangel, with meschaunce,
That we ne konne in no thyng han plesaunce
That sowneth in to vertu any while.   195

---

187   thise] þis Ha⁴ WR   speke] tel Ha⁴+ WR   thise] þis Ha⁴ La+ WR; those ~ SP²,³

188   but] and El *(b)* Cp Gg Ha⁴ La Pw+ CX¹-FI

190   thyng] pink La

192   ne so] ne nevere s. Gg+ PN¹

193   Flessh] The f. (Dl) UR

194   ne] *om.* Ha⁴+ WR   in] *om.* Pw+

195   in to] vn t. *(b+)* CX¹-TR; i. Pw+

---

187   **thise:** MR's *Corpus of Variants* omits *þis* for both occurrences of the word in the line in Ha⁴. This may have been regarded simply as a spelling variation, but WR's *this* suggests that he did not read it (from Ha⁴) as a plural.

by thise men: Lumiansky (1947:560-62) observes that lines 187-95 contain a brief statement of the idea that is the framework of *LGW* and also appears in the concluding passage of *TC* (5.1772-85). Lumiansky also notes what is clearly true (1955:239), that the Manciple's claim to imply only wicked men by his exempla is ridiculous.

Marginal glosses: per antifrasim quedam figura que est per contrarium, with minor variations, *Cn En³,* but not in base-MSS. Nota Ln.

188   **but:** Hg's reading is supported by only Ad³ of the base-ten and seven other MSS, and by no printed editions; again, since *but* for *and* makes clear sense and achieves more emphatic contrast, I have retained the Hg reading.

190   **thyng:** MR's *Corpus of Variants* misses La's *pink*.

192   **so:** PN¹'s *neuer so* may reflect any of a number of MSS (including Gg), but is more probably an editorial addition since it is not found in CX¹,² and since PN² removes it.

193-95   Makarewicz (1953:114-15) suggests that this passage on man's weakness for the *newfangel* may be "poetic renditions" (p. 114) of Saint Augustine's thought in a passage of the *Sermo in Monte* 1.2.9 (Migne, *PL* 34.1233). The passage cited, however, is a very general and extensive one on man's weakness for the carnal, and the view expressed is found so generally that parallels of this sort are of limited interest. SK (5.385) argues that the word *newefangel* is of four syllables here; this is not required in my view, and the Hg spelling *newfangel* is retained. SK (5.385-86) calls attention to Chaucer's use of the noun *newefangelnesse* in *Anel* 141, *LGWP* 154, and other appearances in ME. The adjective simply means "eager for new and different things."

193   **Flesshe:** UR's *The flesh* has support in only one MS, Dl, and there can be little doubt that in this case Dl is the source.

194   **Ne:** MR's *Corpus of Variants* overlooks the omission of *ne* in Ha⁴.

This Phebus, which that thoughte up on no gile,
Deceyved was, for al his jolitee.
For under hym another hadde she,
A man of litel reputacioun,
Nat worth to Phebus in comparisoun.   200
The moore harm is, it happeth ofte so,
Of which ther cometh muchel harm and wo.
And so bifel, whan Phebus was absent,
His wyf anon hath for hire lemman sent.
Hir lemman? Certes, this [is] a knavyssh speche!   110r   205

---

196   **This**] Thus ~ CX[1]-PN[2]; Now this ~ SP[2,3]   **which that**] w. *(b)* CX[1,2] WN-SP[3]
up on] on Gg+; *om. (b+)* CX[1]-SP[3]
   198   **under**] bysyde (Dl) UR   **another**] a. love (Dl) UR
   200   **to Phebus**] t. hym *(b+)* CX[1]   **in**] i. no (Ne +) CX[1]
   201   **The**] *om.* Ad[3] Ha[4]+ WR   **is it**] it is it Cp Ha[4] WR   **happeth ofte**] o. h.
Gg+
   202   **muchel**] bope Ha[4] WR
   203   **whan**] that Gg+
   204   **for hire**] forth his Gg+
   205   **this**] that *(b)*+ CX[1]-TR   **is**] *om.* Hg

---

198   **under:** UR's *bysyde* seems derived from Dl, the only MS with this reading.
        another: UR's addition of *love* is clearly from Dl, again unique, and is an unlikely editorial addition.
205   **lemman:** This word, from OE *leof-man,* meaning "dear one" or "sweetheart," also had a baser meaning, "wench" or "mistress" (see *OED;* Davis et al. 1979). In the former sense it was also applied to the Virgin Mary and to Christ himself (*MED* s.v. *lemman* 2, 3) in the usual transference caused probably by the tradition of the Song of Songs. Its interest here arises from the fact that it is the excuse for a long digression by the Manciple on the necessity of calling things by their right names in context. It is fairly clear that Chaucer generally uses the word with what Ross (1972:134) calls "an aura of the illicit and the delicious." Chaucer does not seem to use the word to refer to one's marital partner. Lumiansky (1955:239) argues that *lemman* would not have been regarded as a "bad" word, and the Manciple's apology is an act of exaggerated and ignorant gentility. Donner (1955:247) sees the apology as arising from the Manciple's recollection that the Host has allowed him to tell a tale instead of the Cook, fearing the coarseness of the Cook. Hussey (1971:24-25) emphasizes the Manciple's use of the word in scornful opposition to *fin amour,* and it "demolishes any romantic and aristocratic associations" with the idea of "lady." "So much for fashionable adultery" (p. 26). Scattergood (1974:141) detects an "odor of" what Whiting (1968:284) calls "class bitterness" in the Manciple's insistence upon *lemman.* Campbell notes (1972:143) that, having overcome this linguistic problem, the Manciple goes on to use the word *swyve* (line 256) without apology (though one may remember that the scribe of Hg and El seems to have felt apologetic about the latter word). Knight (1973:176) has a fine rhetorical analysis exposing the way in which

109

Foryeveth it me, and that I yow biseche.
The wise Plato seith, as ye may rede,
The word moot nede acorde with the dede.
If men shal telle proprely a thyng,

---

206   and] *om. (b+)* CX[1]
207   rede] here r. Pw+
208   The] *om.* Pw (*corr.* Pw₁)
209   shal] sholde ~ PN[1] WN TH[1]-UR   **telle proprely**] p. t. En[1]+

---

lemman sets off the *digressio* with its analogies, which form a dual *amplificatio.* Plessow (1929:22-23) provides a technical rhetorical sketch of the whole passage of lines 100-33.

    this is: Hg's *this* instead of *this is* is perhaps a scribal (or supervisory) contraction of *this is* instead of the scribal slip that I assumed in my discussion of Hg in the Textual Commentary. Indeed, it may even be authorial, for the contraction would reduce the line to ten syllables. But since Hg is supported by no other MS or printed edition, and since the Hg reading would give trouble to a modern reader, I have emended.

    207-10   The saying is a commonplace; cf. *GP* 724 (see SK 5.57, who has a solid note on the idea where it appears in *GP*). It is in Boethius's *De cons. phil.* 3, pr. 12, which in Chaucer's translation reads ". . . sith thow hast lernyd by the sentence of Plato that nedes the wordis moot be cosynes to the thinges of which thei speken" (RB[2], p. 357). Two passages in the *Roman* give the same saying (Langlois 1921:3.7099-7102): "Car Platons lisait en s'escole / Que donee nous fu parole / Pour faire noz vouleirs entendre, / Pour enseignier e pour aprendre" ("For Plato was accustomed in school to say that words were given us to make us wish to understand and to teach as well as to learn"); and (Langlois 1922:4.15190-92): "Li diz deit le fait resembler; / Car les voiz aus choses veisines / Deivent estre a leur faiz cousines" ("He must make his tale resemble the facts; the neighboring words must at least be cousins to the deeds"). Fansler (1914:222) compares the Manciple's defense of his language with that of Reason in the *Roman* (lines 6987-7184) for having used the word "coilles" (testicles). Huppé (1964:28-29) has aptly commented, though not in connection with *ManT,* that when Plato made this famous remark he was not thinking in terms of "realism" in a literary sense. Elliott (1974:268-422) argues at length that the concept of words' relations to things may have contributed to the strong sense of individuality in Chaucer's works. Scattergood (1974:142-43) in a somewhat different vein observes that, although Chaucer does not identify himself with the Manciple, through the Manciple's mouth he reveals some of his own concern with the danger inherent in the relationship between words and things, particularly for a servant in society to attempt the "truth," and quotes Chaucer's ballade *Truth* to this point. Knight (1973:182) remarks the ironic inappropriateness of this theme to the shifty Manciple. Gruber (1973:44) concludes that Chaucer, as a poet, seems to "know what his characters do not, that the word is anything . . . but 'cousin' to the deed." Reiss (1979:76) dismisses the Manciple's theoretical pretensions thus: ". . . what had been a matter of virtue in Plato is perverted by [the Manciple] to a matter of manners." The appropriateness of this theme to the Manciple's story and character is naturally of interest to most critics, and is discussed in the Critical Commentary.

    209   **shal:** Any one of a number of MSS (none of them important ones) may lie behind

110

The word moot cosyn be to the werkyng.   210
I am a boystous man, right thus seye I,
Ther nys no difference, trewely,
Bitwix a wyf that is of heigh degree,
If of hire body deshoneste she be,
And a poore wenche, oother than this—   215
If it so be they werke bothe amys—
But that the gentile, in estat above,

---

210   **cosyn be]** acorde Ha⁴+ WR   **to the]** wiþ þe þing Ha⁴ WR
211   **am]** am a. El (*corr.* El₁)   **man]** *om.* Ha⁴+
212   **nys]** is *(b)* Cp Gg Ha⁴ La+ CX¹-WR   **no]** noon other En¹+; but litil (Tc²)
CX¹-UR
213   **Bitwix]** Bitwene En¹+
215   **And a]** A. any ~ TR   **poore]** pouerer La; p. sely ~ UR   **oother]** any o. ~
SP²,³
216   **If it]** I. En¹ Ha⁴+ WR   **they]** þe En¹+
217   **But that the]** B. for t. ~ TH¹-TR; B. the Ha⁴+   **in]** is i. *(b)* Cp La Pw+
CX¹-TR   **estat]** hire e. El+; hir staat Gg; staat *(b)* Cp Pw+ CX¹-PN² UR

---

sholde in PN¹, which was picked up by WN and, though corrected in PN², continued in TH¹-UR; it was probably, however, a typesetter's error.

210   **cosyn be to the:** The curious readings of Ha⁴ here (with some other MSS), followed by WR, are simply the result of a fusion by the scribe of lines 208 and 210, with *thing* picked up again from line 209.

211   **boystous:** "rude," "coarse," f. OF boisteus (limping, rough), cf. *MED* 1a. Chaucer also uses the word (adv. form) for "plain" in *ClT* 791, with perhaps an overtone of "cruel." The word also carried the meaning "unlearned" (cf. *Mum and the Sothsegger,* line 50). All seem implied here.

215   **And . . . this:** SK remarks (5.441) that the line is deficient metrically and approves TR's reading *any* for *a,* though he himself does not adopt it. TR, however, had confessed (2.508-509) that his reading of *any* for *a* in line 224 was conjecture only (though he adopted UR's *or ellis a* for the edition of 1798), and we may assume that TR's *any* in line 215 is likewise only a conjecture, for it has no MS authority. See Textual Commentary.

wenche: Ross (1972:236) says that in Chaucer's time this was a more insulting term than *lemman;* but Tolkien (1934:52) asserts that *wench* was a respectable word for "girl" in Chaucer's time. Donaldson (1970:25n.), however, believes that the word did not convey respectability in Chaucer's eyes.

216   **If it:** MR's *Corpus of Variants* misses Ha⁴'s omission of *it,* as well as the En¹ reading *þe* for *they* in the same line.

217   **estat:** Curiously, the El *hire estaat,* supported by three other MSS and no printed editions, is printed by Pollard (1898), though not by SK.

She shal be clepid his lady as in love;
And for that oother is a poore womman,
She shal be clepid his wenche or his lemman.   220
And, God it woot, myn owene deere brother,
Men leyn that oon as lowe as lyth that oother.
    Right so bitwix a titlelees tiraunt
And an outlawe, or a theef erraunt,
The same I seye, ther is no difference.   225
To Alisandre was told this sentence,

---

218   **clepid]** called (Ps) TH¹-UR   **as in]** and his *(b+)* CX¹-TR
219   **oother]** toþer La TH¹-SP¹,³ UR   *Out:* SP²
220   **clepid]** called (Ps) TH¹-UR   **or]** and Ha⁴ Pw+ UR TR
222   **Men leyn that oon as lowe]** M. l. a. l. t. o. *(b+)* CX¹-TR; M. l. þe tone a. l.
La; M. sayne p. o. lith a. l. Pw+   **as lyth]** a. doþ Pw+; a. *(b)* Ha⁴+ CX¹-UR
223   **bitwix]** betwene En¹+   **a titlelees]** an open (Tc²) CX¹; articles Ha⁴+
224   **outlawe]** houlawe Pw   **or a theef]** o. t. Ad³; and a t. La Pw+; o. elles a. t.
~ UR TR²; o. any t. ~ TR¹
225   **is]** nys Pw+
226   **was told]** t. w. En¹ Ha⁴+ TR WR SK   **this]** his Ad³+; þat Pw+

---

218   **clepid:** Only one MS, Ps, reads *called* here and in line 220; rather than assume
that TH¹ shows the influence of Ps, it seems better to assume simple modernizing here and
elsewhere, which is carried through UR.
222   **Men leyn that oon as lowe:** MR's *Corpus of Variants* misses La's *Men leyn þe
tone as lowe.* § Literally, "Men place or rank that one as low as they rank that other," but
there is clearly a pun on "lay," to have sexual relations with. See Baum (1956:238) and Ross
(1972:130). Cf. *MilT* 3269-70: "For any lord to leggen in his bedde / Or yet for any good
yeman to wedde." Davis does not remark the double entendre. Elliott notes (1974:208) that
the Manciple's excursus is an effective debunking of the high-flown ideas of *fin amour* as
revealed in the posturing of May in *MerT;* Kean also (1972:2.164) remarks that *ManT* 221-
22 are "unkindly appropriate to May." Fyler (1979:154-55) suggests, on a more theoretical
level, that the Manciple's "reductionist impulses answer the specialist's argot" of *CYT*.
223   **titlelees tiraunt:** Tyrant without legal right or title.
      Interlinear gloss: sine titulo (*above* titlelees) Hg. The words are in a cramped hand
but are apparently by the scribe of Hg; they appear in no other MSS.
224   **or a theef:** The second edition of TR (1798) has *or elles a theef* in one of the
infrequent variations between the first two editions. In his notes, reprinted in the second
edition, TR expresses his admiration of UR's reading, though "from conjecture only" (1798:
2.508), saying, "I should have adopted it in preference to my own, if I had taken notice of it
in time" (p. 509); it was adopted for the second edition. TR's first-edition reading is unique.
226   **To Alisandre:** One of the best-known exempla of the Middle Ages. It would have
been familiar to Chaucer in many "sources"; SK (5.441) and RB² (p. 764) cite, among others,
the *Gesta Romanorum* (chap. 146); John of Salisbury's *Polycraticus* (3.14; 1909:1.224-25),
and, earlier, Augustine's *De civ. D.* (4. 4), and Cicero's *Rep.* (3.12).

That, for the tiraunt is of gretter myght
By force of meyne for to sleen doun right,
And brennen hous and hoom, and make al playn,
Lo, ther fore is he clepid a capitayn.   230
And for the outlawe hath but smal meynee,
And may nat doon so gret an harm as he,
Ne brynge a contree to so gret meschief,
Men clepen hym an outlawe or a theef.
But, for I am a man noght textuel,   235
I wol noght telle of textes never a del.
I wol go to my tale, as I bigan.
    Whan Phebus wyf hadde sent for hire lemman,
Anon they wroghte al hire lust volage.
The white crowe, that heng ay in the cage,   240
Biheld hir werk, and seyde never a word.
And whan that hoom was come Phebus the lord,

---

227   **That]** But (Tc¹)+ TR WR
228   **for]** *om. (b)* La+ CX¹-SP³   **to]** *om.* Pw+   **right]** aright ~ PN¹
230   **is he]** h. i. La+ i. Pw+   **clepid]** clepe La; called (En³+) WN TH¹-UR
231   **the]** an Ha⁴+ WR   **but]** so Ha⁴+ WR
232   **an]** a ~ SP¹; *om. (b+)* CX¹
234   **clepen]** call ~ WN TH¹-UR   **or a]** o. elles an La
235   **textuel]** texted wel Cp Ha⁴ La+ WR; text wel Pw+
236   **telle]** *om.* (Ne +) CX¹   **textes]** Tytus Cp La Pw+; this trete (Tc²) CX¹
238   **wyf]** *om.* Cp (*corr.* Cp₂) La (*corr.* La₁) Pw+   **hadde]** hath Gg+
239   **Anon]** And En¹+   **al]** as Ad³   **lust]** wil Ha⁴+ WR
240   **The]** This *(b)* Cp Ha⁴ La Pw+ CX¹-WR   **ay]** alway Ha⁴+ WR
242   **that]** *om. (b+)* CX¹-SP³

---

227   **That:** The reading *But* is found in only two MSS, Mc and Tc¹; TR clearly drew upon Tc¹ (1798:1.xvi), and WR followed.

230   **clepid:** MR's *Corpus of Variants* omits La's *clepe.*

235   **textuel:** Learned in the texts of the authorities. Nor, as Lounsbury noted (1892: 2.421), is the Parson (*ParsP* 57) "textueel." There is no reason why either use of the word should be ironic, for both characters are concerned with their sermons, not with scholarly disputation, as Fyler (1979:154-55) concludes. Harwood argues (1972:279) that the Parson, unlike the Manciple, is both sincere and accurate in his disclaimer of textuality.

239   **lust volage:** Wild, heedless (volatile) lust. SK (5.441) calls our attention to *Rom* 1284: "With herte wylde, and thought volage." Davis et al. (1979) glosses *volage* as "foolish" in *Rom,* and it may well have that common sense in *ManT* as well; but something needs to be added to "foolish" to recover the Manciple's harsh, critical tone.

This crowe sang "Cokkow! Cokkow! Cokkow!"
 "What, bryd!" quod Phebus, "What song syngestow?
[N]e were thow wont so myrily to synge   110v   245
That to myn herte it was a rejoysynge
To here thy voys? Allas, what song is this?"
 "By God," quod he, "I synge nat amys!
Phebus," quod he, "for al thy worthynesse,
For al thy beautee and thy gentillesse,   250

---

243   This] The En[1]+   Cokkow Cokkow Cokkow] C. C. *(b+)* CX[1]
244   song] *om. (b+)* CX[1]-SP[3]   syngestow] s. now (Gl+) TR WR
245   Ne] e Hg *(torn leaf); om.* (Bo[1]+) SP[2],[3]   wont] not w. *(b)* CX[1]-UR; wone Gg
246   a] *om.* (Bo[2]+) TH[3]-SP[3]
247   thy] this (Ne +) CX[1]-PN[2]   song] ioye Gg+
250   and] a. al Ad[3]+   gentillesse] gentilnesse *(b)* Cp Gg Ha[4] La Pw+ CX[1]-UR

---

243   **Cokkow:** The clear meaning of the "word of fear" in Chaucer's time is shown in *PF* 358: ". . . the cukkow ever unkynde," in which *unkynde* is used in its frequent double sense of "misallying" and "cruel." For *cokkow—cuckold* see *OED* and *MED,* as well as SK (5.441). The crow, we remember, could counterfeit the voice of any bird, and hence the word is repeated twice, in imitation of the repetitive song of the cuckoo. That there are many jokes lying in the word and the circumstances of its use cannot be in doubt: the musical genius of Phoebus answered by the song of the cuckoo, which Phoebus is unable to recognize, the bird whose business is to provide entertainment having been himself entertained, etc. It is difficult to see in the crow's harsh song the sympathetic and sensitive bird that Cadbury (1964) and others have argued him to be. Birney (1960) remarks (1960:267) that "in the crow's accents at this moment it is difficult to hear the white bird of Phoebus Apollo that outsang the nightingale, but it is easy to catch the sardonic tone of that un-gentle pilgrim who could not restrain himself from jeering at anyone who has been made a fool of, whether it be a drunken cook or a college of lawyers." Knight (1973:177-78) argues against Birney's interpretation (1960) of the Manciple as "lewed" on the basis of this passage, suggesting instead that he is a master of dramatic contrast and narrative development: ". . . when he goes on to say 'What wol ye moore?' (257). . . . He asks this in the confidence that he has led us skillfully up to the crisis of the story" (p. 178). Knight analyzes the crow's speech as "a skilled performance at, perhaps, the upper limit of the middle style (p. 178). See Ross (1972:217) for an observation upon the possibly equivocal subject-object relationship in line 256.

244   **syngestow:** TR's *singest thou now* has little MS authority, and he seems to have followed Ra[2] (1798.1.xv); WR followed TR rather than his base MS, Ha[4].

245   **Ne:** Several MSS omit *Ne,* but it is more likely that SP[2],[3] omit because of error; all previous printed editions have *Ne.*

    wont: MR's *Corpus of Variants* omits Gg's *wone.*

246   **a:** Although there is MS authority for omitting *a,* the fact that TH[1],[2] included it suggests strongly that the first omission from printed editions by TH[3] was simply a typesetting error that ST (largely set up from TH[3]) and SP[1-3] followed.

250   **gentillesse:** MR's CV does not treat *gentilnesse* as a variant on *gentillesse.* See note to line 123.

For al thy song and al thy mynstralcye,
For al thy waityng, blered is thyn eye
With oon of litel reputacioun,
Nat worth to thee, in comparisoun,
The montaunce of a gnat, so mote I thryve!   255
For in thy bed thy wif I sey hym swyve."
What wol ye moore? The crowe anon hym tolde,
By sadde toknes and by wordes bolde,
How that his wyf hadde doon hire lecherye,
Hym to gret shame and to gret vileynye,   260
And tolde hym ofte he say it with hise eyen.
    This Phebus gan aweyward for to wryen,

---

251   song] songes Ha⁴ UR WR   and al] and El *(b)* Gg Ha⁴+ CX¹ WN TH¹-WR
254   in] as i. Cp Ha⁴ La Pw+ UR-FI; i. no *(b+)* CX¹   comparisoun] computacioun
Gg+
255   I] *om.* La
256   in] on El *(b)* Cp En¹ Gg Ha⁴ La Pw+ CX¹-FI   swyve] etc. Hg; swy etc. El
257   ye] you ~ ST-TR
258   sadde] ful s. ~ SP²,³
262   wryen] prien He+ CX¹-SP¹ UR

---

252   **waityng:** Normally "watching," and so glossed, but perhaps there is an allowable double meaning here, "attendance" (as opposed to "spying") in a courtly sense (*OED* 10a, 1d).
    blered: In addition to the ordinary meaning of "deceived" when used with *eye,* we might have, as complementary to the second meaning suggested for *waityng* above, the sense "made dim with tears" (in anticipation) as in *OED* 2a or b (*OED* 2c is "deceived").
254   **in:** All major printed editions since UR read *as in;* the MS authority for *in* is very strong, including not only Hg and El but Ad³ and Gg. The chief MSS that read *as in* are Cp Ha⁴ La Pw, the testimony of which, while valuable, is decidedly subordinate normally to that of the Hg El tradition. Fifteen other MSS agree with Hg El, and in such a small matter I prefer to maintain the Hg El reading rather than change for the sake of an extra syllable.
255   **mountaunce:** Amount (value).
256   **swyve:** The curious reticence of the scribe of Hg El is shown by Hg's refusal to write *swyve,* writing only *etc.,* and El's *swy et cetera.*
    Marginal glosses: Nota malum quid El Ad³; also Tc² at line 247.
257   **ye:** The *you* of ST-TR was apparently a bit of modernization.
258   **sadde toknes:** Serious, believable evidence.
260   **Hym . . . vileynye:** Cf. *Ovide moralisé* 2352, "La vilonnie et la grant honte" (Bryan and Dempster, 1941:705). The meaning would be that Phoebus has been shamed and treated *as* a "villeyn," basely, not that he has been debased.
262   **to wryen:** A phrase that much confused the scribes meaning "to turn aside," with

And thoughte his sorweful herte brast atwo.
His bowe he bente, and sette ther inne a flo,
And in his ire his wyf thanne hath he slayn.   265
This is th'effect, ther nys namoore to sayn.
For sorwe of which he brak his mynstralcye,
Bothe harpe and lute, and gyterne and sawtrye,
And eek he brak hise arwes and his bowe,

---

263   **And**] Hym Cp Ha⁴ He La Pw+ CX¹-SK MR PR FI   **sorweful**] woful ~ CX²-
TR; *om.* He+ CX¹   **brast**] abrast La   **atwo**] on tuo Ha⁴; in tuo La
264   **bente**] hent Ad³+
265   **his wyf thanne hath he**] pan hap he his w. Cp La+; he hath his w. Ha⁴ He+
CX¹-WR; hap he h. w. Pw+   **slayn**] islayn Ha³ He+ UR-WR
266   **nys**] is El Cp En¹ Gg Ha⁴ He La+ CX¹-RB¹ RB² PR FI
267   **of which**] *om.* He+ CX¹; wherof ~ CX²-SP³; then ~ UR
268   **and lute**] *om.* Ha⁴+   **and gyterne**] g. Cp En¹ Gg Ha⁴ He La Pw+ CX¹-WR
MR PR

---

the probable implication "to conceal his emotions." Curiously, SP²,³ have the correct *wryen*
instead of the *pryen* of earlier printed editions, but UR follows the earlier error.

263   **And:** All major printed editions except Pollard and RB¹,² read *Hym* in defiance of
very strong MS authority for Hg's *And*. In addition to Hg El Ad³ Gg, all the MSS of the
a group read *And*. Both words make good sense in context, *thoughte* being either reflexive
or nonreflexive, and so the present edition retains Hg's *And*.

   sorweful: There is no extant MS authority for CX²'s *woful*, which was continued
through TR; CX¹ and the *b* group omit.

   atwo: MR's *Corpus of Variants* omits Ha⁴'s *on tuo*.

265   **hath he slayn:** Chaucer omits here the fact that Coronis was pregnant with
Phoebus's child, a circumstance that is very prominent in Ovid's account and in the *Ovide
moralisé,* as well as in Machaut (Bryan and Dempster 1941: 702, 706, 714; Stillwell 1940),
and in those poems provides the reason for Phoebus's hasty repentance (see Shannon 1929:
325; Harwood 1972:270). The pathos of Coronis's plea would seem to have been deliberately
omitted by Chaucer. Severs (1952:3-6) was apparently the first to remark upon Chaucer's
unsympathetic treatment of Phoebus's wife during the course of perhaps the most important
essay ever written upon the poem.

266   **is:** Only Hg Ad³ Pw among the base-ten MSS read *nys,* the rest having *is;* all
previous printed editions except MR read *is.* MR, however, confuse the issue by treating *is*
as the base lemma in the *Corpus of Variants* (8.165), perhaps indicating that their printing
of *nys* in the text was an error.

   Spurious line: Also forsop with myght and eek with mayn *En³ Hk.*

267   **of which:** The *b* tradition, including CX¹, omits *of which;* CX² emends to *wherof*
(on the authority of no extant MS), and was followed until SP³. UR emends to *then,* again
on no MS authority.

268   **and lute:** All printed editions except SK, RB¹,² FI follow the reading of most of

And after that thus spak he to the crowe: 270
    "Traytour," quod he, "with tonge of scorpioun,
Thow hast me broght to my confusioun!
Allas that I was wroght! Why nere I ded?
O deere wyf! O gemme of lustihed,
That were to me so sad and eek so trewe,   275
Now lystow ded with face pale of hewe,
Ful giltlees, that dorste I swere, ywys!
O rakel hand, to doon so foule amys!
O trouble wit! O ire recchelees,

---

273   I] *om.* ~ WN   wroght] born Ha⁴+ WR
274   O gemme of] G. o. En¹+; O g. o (Mm) CX²-SP³; O g. o. all (Dl) UR
276   pale] all p. ~ UR
277   I] *om.* La
278   rakel] rachel La   hand] hounde Cp La Pw+
279   trouble] troublyd (Bo¹) WN TH¹-TR   recchelees] wretchelesse UR; o recche-
lees MR *(misprint)*

---

the MSS, omitting *and.* SK RB¹,² FI follow Hg El Ad³ (and two other MSS), and the present
edition likewise follows.

271   **scorpioun:** A reference to the traditional notion that the scorpion was equipped
both with a flattering, beguiling tongue and a stinging tail—a traditional figure of betrayal.
SK (5.441) calls our attention to Chaucer's use of the figure in *MLT* 404 and *MerT* 2057-
60, and to *BD* 636-41. That the figure was usually conceived of as feminine is clear in
that all Chaucer's references except *ManT* are applied to a feminine figure, the "Sowdanesse"
in *MLT* and to Fortune, a female figure, in the other appearances. This conventional way
of seeing the scorpion as female or as applied to a female figure is well illustrated by Vincent
of Beauvais in his *Spec. nat.* 20.160, where he quotes in turn from the *Liber de naturis
rerum* (as quoted by SK 5.365): "Scorpio blandum et quasi virgineum dicitur vultum habere,
sed habet in cauda nodosa venenatum aculeum, quo pungit et inficit proximantem" ("The
scorpion is said to have a pleasing and attractive face like that of a young woman, but has
in its jointed tail a venomous sting whereby it punctures and poisons that which is nearest").
Also the *Ayenbyte of Inwyt* (Morris 1866:62) ". . . the scorpioun, thet maketh uayr mid the
heauede, and enueymeth mid the tayle." It is also in Aesop's *Fables* 4.3. It is a commonplace
though powerful figure, and there is little likelihood that Chaucer needed to find it anywhere.

274   **O gemme of:** CX²'s change to *O gemme o* has the authority of only one MS,
Mm, and probably was simply a typesetting error that was followed through SP³. UR's *O
gemme of all* is clearly derived from D1, the only MS with this reading.

    gemme of lustihed: A curious figure. *OED* compares it with *BD* 27-28; Davis
et al. (1979) defines *lustihed* as "pleasure," and RB² as "delight." There is apparently no
sexual connotation in the word here (see Ross 1972:114).

278   **rakel:** Rash. As SK observes (5.441), the word was afterward altered to *rake-hell,*
and then shortened to *rake,* the noun form.

279   **trouble:** An adjective derived from the past participle. WN's *troublyd* has the au-

117

That unavysed smytest giltlees!   280
O wantrust, ful of fals suspecioun,
Where was thy wit and thy discrecioun?
O every man, be war of rakelnesse!
Ne trowe ye no thyng with outen strong witnesse.
Smyt nat to soone er that ye witen why,   111r   285
And beth avysed wel and sobrely
Er ye do any execucioun
Up on youre ire for suspecioun.
    Allas! A thousand folk hath rakel ire
Fully fordoon, or broght hem in the myre.   290

---

280   **smytest**] smyteth El+ RB[1] RB[2] FI; synnest He+ CX[1]-PN[2]
281   **fals**] *om.* He+ CX[1]
283   **O**] of La   **rakelnesse**] rekelnesse Cp He+ CX[1]-UR; rechelnesse La+ PN[1];
rechelesnesse Pw+
284   **ye**] *om.* El Ad[3] Cp En[1] Gg Ha[4] He La+ CX[1]-FI   **strong**] gret Gg Ha[4]+ WR;
om. He+ CX[1]
285   **soone**] sore Gg+   **that**] *om.* (Ne) Pw+ CX[1]-SP[1]   **ye witen**] þou wit Cp Ha[4]
He La Pw+ CX[1]-WR
286   **And beth**] But b. En[1]+; A. be Cp Ha[4] He La Pw+ CX[1]-UR   **sobrely**] sikerly
He+ CX[1]-TR
288   **for**] through ~ UR
289   **hath**] han *or* have Cp En[1] Gg La Pw+ CX[1]-PN[2]   **rakel**] for r. En[1]; rachel La
290   **Fully fordoon or**] F. f. and El Gg He+ CX[1]-RB[1] RB[2] FI; Fordoon or dun hath
Ha[4]+ WR

---

thority of Bo[1] only, and was probably a typesetter's error picked up by TH[1]-TR.
        O ire: The apostrophe is to be compared with the denunciations of wrath in
SumT 2005-89, and *ParsT* 537-650, particularly lines 560-65.
        280   **smytest**: Hg's reading is supported by all MSS except El (and three others), which
have *smyteth,* and is followed by all printed editions except Pollard (1898), Koch (1915),
and RB[1,2] and FI. PR returns to the Hg reading.
        284   **ye**: Hg is supported here by only a single MS, Py, and by no printed editions. But
here Phoebus is using a plural pronoun in variation (for *every man*), controlling the next
four lines, following a singular invocative addressing the abstractions of the preceding lines.
The *ye* here may be merely an anticipation, and it adds an extra syllable to the line. But the
rhetorical shift and emphasis here lead me to believe that Chaucer originally intended the
plural pronoun, though he may have later smoothed it away. At any rate, it is significant
enough for the rhetorical pattern, and it is witnessed by Hg, and so I retain *ye*.
        290   **Fully fordoon or**: All major printed editions until MR followed the El Gg sub-
stitution of *and* for *or*. Although RB[1,2] read *and*, PR adopts Hg's *or*, which is supported by all
important MSS except El Gg. FI returns to *and*. There seems little to choose between the

Allas! For sorwe I wol my selven sle!"
   And to the crowe, "O false theef," seyde he,
"I wol thee quyte anon thy false tale.
Thow songe whilom lyk a nyghtyngale;
Now shaltow, false theef, thy song forgon,   295
And eek thy white fetheres everichon,
Ne nevere in al thy lyf ne shaltow speke.
Thus shal men on a traytour ben awreke.
Thow and thyn ofspryng evere shul be blake,
Ne nevere swete noyse shul ye make,   300
But evere crye agayn tempest and rayn,

---

292   **seyde**] quod Gg+
293   **thee**] *om.* He+ CX[1]-SP[1]
294   **songe**] songist ~ UR   **lyk**] as Ha[4]+ SP[2,3] WR   **a**] an ~ CX[1,2] PN[2]; any Ha[4]
SP[2,3] TR WR
295   **Now shaltow**] Thowe n. s. He
296   **And**] *om.* Cp La (Ne) Pw+ CX[1]-PN[2]   **eek**] also (Dl) UR
297   **ne**] *om.* Cp La (Ne) Pw+ CX[1]-UR
298   **traytour**] fals peef Ha[4] WR   **awreke**] ywreke La Pw+; wreke (Bo[2]+) PN[1]
299   **ofspryng**] hospreinge Cp La Pw   **evere**] *om.* Gg+
300   **nevere**] n. after ~ SP[2]-UR   **noyse**] voys El
301   **crye**] criyng ~ ST SP[1]

---

two, though the Hg reading seems preferable as meaning "destroyed or damaged," a more appropriate parallelism than "destroyed and damaged," which is merely repetitious. The version *Fordoon or dun hath* is clearly a confused remembrance of the *ManP*'s *Don is in the myre* (line 5), but this reading of Ha[4], shared with Ld[1], does indicate that in the mind of one or two scribes the coming full circle from *ManP* to *ManT* may not have been ignored. SK well remarked (5.442), "This is one of the many signs of the untrustworthiness of this grossly over-rated MS."
      fordoon: Destroyed totally.
    294-300   Harwood (1972:270) remarks that, whereas in the analogues of *ManT,* and in Chaucer's most probable sources, the dramatic point to the *Tale* is the changing of the crow's color from white to black (the plucking out of the feathers and exposing the black skin, one would suppose), Chaucer, on the other hand, places much more emphasis upon Phoebus's removing the song and speech of the crow. This is, of course, quite in keeping with the Manciple's moral that if one misuses speech he is likely to lose it.
    296   **eek:** UR's *also* is clearly drawn from Dl, the only extant MS authority.
    298   **awreke:** PN[1] reads *wreke,* which has MS authority (Bo[2] Ld[1] etc.), but this is probably a typesetting error.
    299   **ofspryng:** MR's *Corpus of Variants* omits *hospreinge* of Cp La Pw. Furnivall's Six-Text edition prints *offspryng* in the transcription of Hg.
    301   **But . . . rayn:** Cf. *PF* 363. SK (1.520-21) remarks that Chaucer here and in the

In tokenynge that thurgh thee my wyf is slayn."
And to the crowe he stirte, and that anon,
And pulled hise white fetheres everichon,
And made hym blak, and refte hym al his song,   305
And eek his speche, and out at dore hym slong
Un to the devel, which I hym bitake;
And for this cas ben alle crowes blake.
    Lordynges, by this ensample I yow preye,

---

302   **In tokenynge**] I. tokyn (Ne+) CX¹-TR   **that**] *om.* Ad³+   **is**] was Cp Ha⁴ WR

304   **pulled**] p. of He+ CX¹-UR   **white**] *om.* Ad³+   **everichon**] of e. En¹+

305   **al**] of a. ~ SP²,³

306   **at**] a. pe Cp En¹ Gg He La Pw+ CX¹-PN¹   **slong**] flong ~ TR

307   **which**] to whoom Pw+

308   **cas**] cause Ha⁴+ PN¹ TH¹-WR

309   **this ensample**] these ensamples (Mc+) PN¹   **I**] I wol (Tc²) CX¹-UR

PF mistranslates Virgil "precisely as Batman does" (*Batman uppon Bartholomew* 12.9). Batman translates "Nunc plena cornix pluuium uocat improbe uoce (*Georg.* 1.388) thus: "That is to understande, Nowe the Crowe calleth rayne with an eleinge voyce." Chaucer in *PF* refers to the crow as "with vois of care." The only references to tempest and rain in the Phoebus analogues are, curiously, in *The Seven Sages of Rome* and the *Integumenta Ovidii* (Bryan and Dempster 1941:716-19). In the former we are told that there had been "rain and ponder briʒt" (p. 718, line 2252), but it is very unlikely that Chaucer drew anything in particular from this poem (for another opinion see Cadbury 1964). In the *Integumenta Ovidii* (text taken from MS Lansdowne 728, fol. 54; Bryan and Dempster 1941:716), we learn that the Raven (Crow) is sacred to Phoebus for his vocal abilities and his ability to presage tempests (which is what Virgil says): "Item de coruo: Coruus Ioui [*sic*] sacratus dicitur quia quadraginta quatuor vocum interpretacLones habet et ad Phebum pertinet vocum interpretacio, vel quia futuras presignet tempestates sicut et Phebus" ("The Raven is said to be sacred to Jove [undoubtedly an error for Phoebus] because he possesses forty-four different interpretations of the voices [of others], which art of imitation of voice belongs to Phoebus, as well as the fact that he is able to presage tempests, an art likewise in the power of Phoebus").

    crye: ST's unsupported reading *criyng* is probably a compositor's error, in which *cryen* has been confused with the present participle.

    306 **slong**: TR's *flong,* unsupported by MSS or printed editions, is probably a typographical error caused by the similarity of *s* and *f.* SK (5.442) remarks upon TR's error of emendation and gives numerous examples of *slong* used in Chaucer's time, particularly in alliterative lines.

    309 **this ensample**: The reading *these ensamples* in PN¹ is not without MS authority, but it is most probably an error, corrected by PN².

Beth war, and taketh kepe what I seye: 310
Ne telleth nevere no man in youre lyf
How that another man hath dight his wyf;
He wol yow haten mortally, certeyn.
    Daun Salomon, as wise clerkes seyn,
Techeth a man to kepen his tonge wel.   315
But, as I seyde, I nam nat textuel.
But nathelees, thus taughte me my Dame:

---

310   **Beth**] Be He+ CX¹-SP³   **taketh**] take He+ CX¹-SP³   **what**] w. þat Cp En¹
Gg La Pw+ UR RB¹ RB²   **I**] ye Ad³ Cp En¹ Ha⁴ Pw+ TR WR MR RB² PR FI
311   **no man**] m. Ha⁴+ TR WR   **in**] i. al En¹ Ha⁴+ WR; *om.* Pw+
312   **How**] How h. Ad³ (*corr.* Ad³₁)   **dight**] swyued La+   **his**] þi Pw
314   **Daun**] *om.* (Ne +) CX¹   **wise**] thes w. (Tc¹) UR
316   **nam**] am El Ad³ Cp Ha⁴ La Pw+ CX²-FI   **textuel**] text wel Cp La Pw+; texted
w. Ha⁴ WR   *Out:* CX¹
317   **me**] *om.* En¹

---

310   **I:** The reading *ye* was ignored in the early printed editions, though it is found in several major MSS (Ad³ Cp En¹ Ha⁴ Pw); it was introduced by TR, followed by WR (after Ha⁴). SK and RB¹ kept *I*, but MR adopted *ye*, followed by RB² PR FI. It is simply a question of interpretation, and either could be right (both are probably authorial); the decision does to some extent determine punctuation, however, the colon here more naturally following *I;* with *ye* the next line is another clause in a parallel series. I prefer the personally admonitory Manciple and retain Hg's *I.* For the contrary argument see MR (4.526).

311-13   Mustanoja (1965) has proposed that a passage in a Latin poem attributed to Abelard, "Carmen ad astralabium filium," might have been the original for the advice against telling a husband of his wife's infidelity in these lines of *ManT.* It is highly unlikely that Chaucer knew of the poem, but it is useful to know that this particular piece of wisdom literature is documented in the Middle Ages.

312   **dight:** "Treated," "done by" (*OED,* 1), here, of course, "lain with," "had intercourse with" as well (*OED,* 4b); see Ross (1972:78-79).

314   **Daun Salomon:** SK (5.442) and RB² (p. 764) cite Prov. 21.23: "Qui custodit os suum et linguam suam / Custodit ab angustiis animam suam" ("Whoso keepeth his mouth and his tongue keepeth his soul from troubles"); and Ps. 34.13: "Prohibe linguam tuam a malo, / Et labia tua ne loquantur dolum" ("Keep thy tongue from evil, and thy lips from speaking guile").

    wise: UR's *thes wise* is probably drawn from Dl's *this wise,* "corrected" by UR; Tc¹ has UR's reading, but there is no clear indication that UR used this MS.

316   *Spurious line:* This is al and som and euery del He.

317   **thus taughte me my Dame:** RB² (p. 764) cites the parallel in *WBP* 576: "My dame taughte me that soutiltee" (not in Hg). Tupper (1915:264-65) claims that these moral passages are directed at the Cook by the Manciple; Spector (1957:25) disagrees, arguing instead that they are aimed at the Canon's Yeoman and that *ManT* 357-60 is an appraisal of *CYT.*

"My sone, thenk on the crowe, a goddes name.
My sone, keep wel thy tonge and kepe thy freend.
A wikke tonge is worse than a feend.   320
My sone, from a feend men may hem blesse.
My sone, God of his endelees goodnesse
Walled a tonge with teeth and lippes eke,

---

318   **a]** on El+; in Ha⁴+ WR
320   **than]** t. is (Lc+) UR
321   **a]** any ~ UR   **hem]** hym He+
323   **Walled]** Wallep En²+

---

318   **My sone:** This formula of address, which appears eight more times, is a tradi-
tional one from wisdom literature, found in Prov. 2.1, 3.1, and 5.1, as many scholars have
pointed out (Plessow 1929:85-86). Tatlock (1935:296), however, argues that the formula is
not really similar to those of Proverbs but is rather more so to the *Disticha Catonis, Proverbs
of Alfred,* etc. Hazelton states (1960:378) that this vocative formula appears only once in
the *Disticha Catonis,* though it is found in all the *glossulae* on the "Virtutem primam" *topos.*
He further argues that the repeated use of the formula in *ManT* emphasizes the parodic
nature of the *Tale.* He asserts that it is a parody of similar passages in Gower's *Confessio
Amantis,* which, he maintains, was written earlier than Chaucer's poem. Whittock (1968:285)
states that "My sone" is repeated in the *Confessio* only a few times, however, and that these
occurrences are spaced far apart. In fact, I must observe, Gower used the formula frequently
(52 times in the first book of the *Confessio*), and these are clustered together between the
tales so that the repetitions of the same formula 52 times in 3,446 lines, while not appearing
statistically great, nevertheless occurring as they do in passages of from 30 to 80 lines,
have quite a noticeable and monotonous effect. Something of the same vocative formula is
found ("Ma dame" here) as well in the *Roman* (cf. lines 4617-4808 of *Rom*); see the note
by TR (2.509) on his line 17278: "In the *Rom. de la R.* ver 7399. this precept is quoted
from *Ptolomee,* Au commencer de *l'Almageste.*" SK elaborates (5.442): ". . . we may further
compare a passage in Le Roman de la Rose, 7069, which professes to follow Ptolemy's
Almagest. We find similar pieces of advice in Middle English, with such titles as 'How the
Good Wife taught her Daughter,' and 'How the Wise man taught his Son'; but these are
probably later than the time of Chaucer." SK also refers to Albertano of Brescia's *De arte
loquendi et tacendi.* See note to line 325 below; Elliot suggests (1954:511-12) that the device
"My sone" enables the Manciple to recall the wandering attention of the Cook. Trask (1977:
114) observes that the "My sone" formula underlines the Manciple's moral simpleness and his
reliance upon his mother for his language.
          a: Pollard (1898) alone follows El (and many others), printing *on.*
319   **keep wel thy tonge and kepe thy freend:** See Whiting (1968, T373).
320   **A wikke tonge:** One of several proverbial expressions and comparisons in *ManT*
that can in no sense be traced to any one source (see Whiting 1968, T402; Haeckel 1890:
52).
          than: UR's *than is* is probably an emendation; though there are two MSS with the
reading (Lc Mg), there is no evidence that UR used them.
          Spurious line before line 321: For many a man hit doth shend Mc.

For man sholde hym avyse what he speeke.
[My] sone, ful ofte for to muche speche 111v 325
Hath many a man ben spilt, as clerkes teche;
But for litel speche avysely
Is no man shent, to speke generally.
My sone, thy tonge sholdestow restreyne
At alle tymes, but whan thow doost thy peyne 330
To speke of God in honour and prayere.
The firste vertu, sone, if thow wolt leere,

---

324   **man]** a m. En[1]+   **sholde]** schal Ha[4]+ WR
325   **My]** *om.* Hg *(leaf torn)*   **ful]** to He
326   **Hath]** *first letter torn in* Hg
327   **litel]** a l. Ha[4]+ TR-SK   **avysely]** spoken a. (Tc[2]) CX[1]-UR
328   **Is]** I Gg+
330   **tymes]** tyme Cp Ha[4] He La Pw+ CX[1]-PN[2] TR-SK
331   **in honour and prayere]** i. h. here (Ne+) CX[1]
332   **sone]** my s. (Dl) UR   **if]** is i. Ad[3]

325-28   Hazelton (1960:377) and others have noted that these lines are a paraphrase of the second verse of Dionysius Cato *Disticha Catonis* 1.12 (1952:44): "Nam nulli tacuisse nocet, nocet esse (saepe) lucutum." The first verse of the distich is the famous "Rumores fuge, ne incipias nouus auctor haberi," which Chaucer paraphrases in *ManT* 359-60. Koeppel (1891:44-46), cited by SK (5.442), argues that Chaucer was drawing directly upon Albertano of Brescia's *De arte loquendi et tacendi,* which also quotes Cato and which contains much of the material in the conclusion of *ManT,* and his argument was apparently accepted by SK. RB[2] (p. 764) observes, however, that the parallels in Albertano's treatise are widely scattered and not always close to Chaucer. They are plausible, though, when combined with the father-son vocative formulas of Albertano, paralleled by the mother-son formula of the advice in *ManT.* At any rate, Albertano and Cato are probably the "clerkes" referred to in line 326.

327   **litel:** Ha[4]'s reading *a litel* is taken by WR, who was also influenced by TR, which had the same reading, taken from En[1]. SK printed *a litel,* but has not been followed by any major edition.

329-31   RB[2] (p. 764) cites a passage in the *Roman* which professes to follow Ptolemy's *Almagest* (1921:3.7037-43): "Langue deit estre refrenee, / Car nous lisons de Tholomee / Une parole mout oneste, / Au comencier de l'*Almageste:* / Que sages est cil qui met peine / A ce que sa langue refreine, / Forz, senz plus, quant de Deu parole" ("The tongue should be bridled, as we read in Ptolemy's most noble words early on in the *Almagest:* 'Most wise is that one who is at pains to hold his tongue except, of course, when he speaks of God'").

330   **tymes:** Again TR derived his reading *tyme* from En[1], and WR the same from Ha[4]. SK also printed *tyme,* apparently following TR, but Pollard (1898) printed *tymes,* as have all others.

332-33   **The firste vertu:** The passage is a translation of *Disticha Catonis* 1.3a: "Virtutem primam esse puto conpescere linguam," as noted first by TR (2.509). Albertano

Is to restreyne and kepe wel thy tonge.
Thus lernen children whan that they ben yonge.
My sone, of muchel spekyng yvele avysed,   335
Ther lasse spekyng hadde ynow suffised,

---

334 **lernen**] lernede Gg   **children**] clerkes Ha⁴+ WR   **that**] *om.* Cp He La
Pw+ CX¹-SP³   **they**] þe La
335 **yvele avysed**] unauysed He+ CX¹-UR
336 **Ther**] T. whan ~ UR

---

quotes this (1869:xcvi), as noted by SK (5.443), following Koeppel (1891), and it is also
found in the *Roman,* as SK observes (1921:3.12179-83): "Sire, la vertu prumeraine, / La
plus grant, la plus souveraine / Que nus morteus on puisse aveir / Par science ne par aveir, /
C'est de sa langue refrener" ("Sire, [said Abstinence], the first virtue, the greatest and most
sovereign that mortal man may have, whether acquired by learning or by inheritance, is to
restrain his tongue"). Chaucer himself had translated the verse broadly in *TC* (3.294-96),
called to our attention by SK (5.443; RB², p. 424): "For which thise wise clerkes that ben
dede / Han evere thus proverbed to us yonge, / That 'firste vertu is to kepe tonge.'" Hazelton
(1960:377) argues that Chaucer probably drew upon the original for these passages rather
than upon Albertano, as Koeppel (1891:45-46) had proposed, or upon the *Roman,* as Fansler
had claimed (1914:200-202). Lounsbury remarks (1892:2.359) upon the fact that in both
ManT and *TC* Chaucer emphasizes the learning of the proverb by the young, perhaps in-
dicating its school-text origins. There were many earlier, similar *sententiae,* and Boas (1952:
36-37) cites Horace (*Epist.* 1.1.41-42) with others. Hazelton cites (1960:377), from the
glossulae of the *Disticha Catonis,* Prov. 13:3: "Qui custodit os suum custodit animam suam /
Custodit ab angustiis animam suam" (actually something of a paraphrase of Prov. 13:3, the
original reading somewhat differently; in the King James translation it is "He that keepeth
his mouth keepeth his life: but he that openeth wide his lips shall have destruction." But as
Hazelton remarks, the "Virtutem primam" had become a *topos,* and, from whatever source,
if any, that Chaucer may have drawn it, about half the lines of the conclusion to *ManT*
render either Cato's distichs or related materials commonly found in commentaries upon
them (1960:378). Hazelton also here cites Deschamps's *balade* "Pour sa langue refrener"
and the ME poem "See Much, Say Little, and Learn to Suffer in Time" (Brown 1939:279-80),
which depend upon Cato's "Virtutem primam" for their key texts. See Whiting (1968, V41).
See Critical Commentary for further discussion of these matters.

332   **sone:** Again, UR's *my sone* is derived from the unique authority Dl.

333   *Marginal glosses:* Virtutem primam esse puta compescere linguam Cn Ma; Virtu-
tem primam esse et cetera Ad¹ En³; Virtutem primam Se.

334   **they:** MR's *Corpus of Variants* misses La's þe.

335-38   As SK notes (5.443), this is a paraphrase of Prov. 10:19: "In multiloquio non
deerit peccatum" ("In the multitude of words there wanteth not sin"). SK also calls attention
(5.443) to Albertano, who uses this text. Albertano (1869:cxv), in fact, has the exact wording
that is found in marginal glosses of Ad¹ En³ Gg Ha³: ". . . in multiloquio non deest pec-
catum." Also of interest is the *Ovide moralisé* (Bryan and Dempster 1941:708): "En jenglerie
a grant pechié" (line 2522). See Whiting (1968, S608).

335   **of . . . avysed:** See Whiting (1968, S591).

Comth muchel harm; thus was me told and taught.
In muchel speche synne wanteth naught.
Wostow wher of a rakel tonge serveth?
Right as a swerd forkitteth and forkerveth   340
An arm atwo, my deere sone, right so
A tonge kitteth frendship al atwo.
A janglere is to God abhomynable.
Rede Salomon, so wys and honurable;
Rede David in his psalmes, rede Senekke.   345
My sone, spek noght, but with thyn hed thow bekke.
Dissimule as thow were deef if that thow heere

---

337   **thus]** it Gg+   **told and]** *om.* He+ CX¹-SP³
338   **speche]** specheþ La; speche ther ~ SP²,³; s. t. ne ~ UR; s. ne En¹+
339   **Wostow]** Wost þou nat En¹; Wost Ha⁴   **wher of]** wherfore He+ CX¹-UR
a] *om.* Gg+
340   **as]** *om.* Ha⁴+   **a]** *om.* La+   **forkerveth]** kerueþ En¹ Ha⁴+
341   **An]** And La   **atwo]** on two Gg+ TH¹-UR; or to (Ha³+) WN
342   **frendship al]** a. f. He; f. Pw+
345   **in his]** and h. Cp He La Pw+ CX¹-PN²
346   **but]** ne He+ CX¹-SP³   **thow]** *om.* (Bo¹+) TH¹-SP³
347   **deef]** deed Ha⁴+ WR   **that]** *om.* He+

---

337   *Marginal glosses:* In multiloquio non deest peccatum Ad¹ En³ Gg Ha³; In multi-
tudo Se.

338   **speche:** UR's *speche ther ne* is doubly derived: he gets the spurious *ther* from SP²,³
and the *ne* from Dl.

340   **Right as a swerd:** Cf., as SK notes (5.443), Ps. 57.4: ". . . et lingua eorum
gladius acutus" (". . . and their tongue a sharp sword"). See Whiting (1968, T385).

344-45   **Rede Salomon:** SK (5.443) and Plessow (1929:88-90) cite exempla from
Solomon, David, and "Senekke" that might have been in Chaucer's mind. Of particular
interest is Prov. 6:16-17, where a lying tongue is said to be one of the seven things abom-
inable to the Lord (cf. *ManT* 334): "Sex sunt quae odit Dominus, / et septimum detestatur
anima ejus: oculos sublimes, linguam mendacem" ("These six things doth the Lord hate:
yea, seven are an abomination unto him: A proud look, a lying tongue"). General exhor-
tations against jangling are also found in Prov. 10:31, 32; 18:20; Ps. 9 (10):7; 11:3; 51:4;
63:3-5; 120:3. The reference to Seneca is most likely to the *De ira*, from which stories in
SumT are probably taken (1.18.3-6, 3.14.1-6, 3.21.1-3, all printed in Bryan and Dempster
1941:286-87). It is, of course, possible that Chaucer had in mind works that were vaguely
attributed to Seneca. SK (5.204-205) remarks upon a number of instances in which Chaucer
in *Mel* refers to Seneca when actually the source is either Publilius Syrus's *Sententiae* or
Martinus Dumiensis's *Formula honestae vitae* (Chaucer is here, of course, following his French
source).

346   **thow:** There is a good deal of MS authority for TH¹'s omission of this word,
but it is most probably an error, continued through SP³.

A janglere speke of perilous matere.
    The Flemyng seith, and lerne it if thee leste,
That litel janglyng causeth muchel reste.   350
My sone, if thow no wikked word hast seyd,
Thee thar nat drede for to be biwreyd;
But he that hath mysseyd, I dar wel sayn,
He may by no wey clepe his word agayn.
Thyng that is sayd is sayd, and forth it gooth,   355
Though hym repente, or be hym leef or looth.
He is his thral to whom that he hath sayd

---

348   **A]** The He+ CX¹-SP³   **speke]** speketh He La+ CX¹-SP³
349   **and]** *om.* (Tc²+) CX¹-SP³   **it]** *om.* He La+ CX¹-SP³ TR   **if thee]** yf that thowe He+ CX¹-SP³; i. that thee ~ TR
350   **muchel]** grete ~ PN¹
352   **thar]** ther Pw; dar En¹ He+ CX¹-SP³; therof ~ UR   **drede]** d. the Gg+   **for]** *om.* He+   **biwreyd]** be wryede Ad³+
356   **be hym]** h. b. He+ CX¹-SP¹; b. he Pw+; b. (Gl+) SP²,³   **leef or]** neuer so Cp Ha⁴ He La Pw+ CX¹-WR MR RB² PR FI
357   **his thral to whom that]** thralle to hym t. w. (Tc²) CX¹-SP³

---

349   **The Flemyng seith:** Since Chaucer tells us that this is a Flemish saying, it seems pointless to look among similar English sayings, for all, in any case, were traditional. Grauls and Vanderheijden (1934:746) cite an exactly parallel Flemish proverb, "Luttel onderwinds maakt groote rust" ("Little jangling makes great peace"), which they trace back to the fifteenth century, and it is undoubtedly much older. See Skeat 1910, no. 290. Cf. Chaucer *CkP* 4357 and Whiting (1968, J13).
    if thee: TR's *if that thee* is probably a misreading.
350   **muchel:** Since there is no extant MS authority, one must consider PN¹'s *grete* simply a modernizing slip, corrected in PN².
355-56   This is a *flosculus* from Horace *Epist.* 1.18.71: ". . . et semel emissum volat irrevocabile verbum," as SK observes (5.443), using a slightly different text with *fugit* instead of *volat* (the meaning is unchanged: "The word once let fly is unrecallable"). Koeppel (1891) suggests that Chaucer may have derived it from Albertano (1869:xcviii), who quotes Horace, or from the *Roman:* "Mais parole une feiz volee / Ne peut puis estre repeler" (Langlois 1922: 4.16545-46). Hazelton (1960:378) points out that the line is found in many later *glossulae* of the *Disticha Catonis.* See Whiting (1968, W605).
356   **leef or:** The reading *neuer so* of Cp Ha⁴ He La Pw and others was used exclusively in the printed editions until SK (and Pollard 1898 and Koch 1915), and RB¹ adopted the Hg El *leef or.* MR restored *neuer so,* and RB² PR and FI (Bo²) have followed. I see no reason to abandon a sensible and metrically "superior" reading from the very best MSS for *ManT,* Hg El Ad³ Gg. MR (4.526) conclude that no decision is possible on textual grounds.
357   **He is his thral:** A common observation—Koeppel (1891:45) and SK (5.443)

A tale of which he is now yvele apayd.
My sone, be war, and be noon auctour newe
Of tidynges, wher they ben false or trewe.   360
Wher so thow come, amonges heye or lowe,
Kepe wel thy tonge, and thynk up on the crowe."

Here is ended the Manciples tale of the crowe.

---

358   **of which**] for w. (Tc²) CX¹-UR; w. that He+   **now**] *om.* He   **yvele**] ill
~ UR   **apayd**] payd Cp+
   359   **My sone be war**] B. w. m. s. He   **noon**] nouʒt Cp Pw+
   360   **wher**] wheither El Cp En¹ Gg Ha⁴ La Pw+ CX¹-FI
   361   **come**] comest Ha⁴+ WR
   362   **up on**] o. He+ CX¹-SP³

---

cite Albertano (1869:cvi): "Consilium vel secretum tuum absconditum quasi in carcere tuo est reclusum; revelatum vero te in carcere suo tenet ligatum" ("Your counsel or hidden secret should be shut up as if in your prison; once revealed indeed it holds you bound as if in its prison"). As RB² observes (p. 765), the parallel is not exact. It seems close enough, however, given Chaucer's at least indirect familiarity with Albertano's treatises. See Whiting (1968, W626), citing Barclay's *Ship of Fools*.

358   **apayd**: MR's *Corpus of Variants* omits Cp's *payd*.

359-60   This is a rough translation of Dionysius Cato *(Disticha Catonis* 1.12a; 1952:44): "Rumores fuge, ne incipias novus auctor haberi." TR noted this (2.509) and remarked that Chaucer may have read it, in view of his own wording, "*Rumoris* fuge . . . ." That this is the ultimate source seems clear enough, but it also is supported by various glosses in MSS of *CT*: Ad¹ Cn En³ Mg quote Cato in full here as given above, and Se has "Caton R. f. et cetera" (see note to line 360), indicating the great familiarity of the passage. Fyler (1979: 155) calls our attention to the similarity of this passage to several in *HF,* particularly to the conclusion of that poem.

360   *Marginal glosses:* Rumores fuge ne incipias nouus auctor haberi Ad¹ Cn En³ Mg; Caton R. f. et cetera Se.

Bibliographical Index

Included in the Bibliographical Index are all books, articles, and editions referred to in this volume, as well as some works not cited. It is intended in the course of the completion of the *Variorum Chaucer* to compile an overall bibliography of Chaucer. Many of the large-scale treatments which are normally included in bibliographies but which contain nothing or only a passing comment on *The Manciple's Prologue* or *Tale* are not collected here.

Alanus de Insulis 1855. *Liber de planctu naturae.* In J.-P. Migne, ed. *Patrologiae Latinae,* vol. 210, cols. 431-82. Paris: J.-P. Migne.

Albertano of Brescia (Albertanus Brixiensis) 1869. *De arte loquendi et tacendi.* In T. Sundby, ed. *Brunetto Latinos levnet og Skrifter.* Copenhagen: J. Lund.

——— 1873. *Liber consolationis et consilii, ex quo hausta est fabula de Melibeo et Prudentia.* Ed. Thor Sundby. Copenhagen: Høst and Sons.

Alderson, William L., and Arnold C. Henderson 1970. *Chaucer and Augustan Scholarship.* University of California Publications, English Studies, no. 35. Berkeley: University of California Press.

Baker, Donald C. 1961. A Crux in Chaucer's *Franklin's Tale:* Dorigen's Complaint. *JEGP* 60:56-64.

——— 1981. The Evolution of Bradshaw's Idea of the Order of the *Canterbury Tales. ChauN* 3 (Winter):2-6.

Baugh, Albert C., ed. 1963. *Chaucer's Major Poetry.* New York: Appleton-Century-Crofts.

Baum, Paull F. 1956. Chaucer's Puns. *PMLA* 71:225-46.

——— 1958. Chaucer's Puns: A Supplementary List. *PMLA* 73:167-70.

——— 1961. *Chaucer's Verse.* Durham, N.C.: Duke University Press.

Benson, Larry D. 1981. The Order of the *Canterbury Tales. SAC* 3:77-117.

Bersuire, Pierre (Petrus Berchorius) 1933. *Ovidius moralizatus.* Ed. F. Ghisalberti. In "L'Ovidius moralizatus" de Pierre Bersuire. *SRo.* 33:5-136.

Birney, Earle 1960. Chaucer's "Gentil" Manciple and His "Gentil" Tale. *NM* 21:257-67.

Blake, N. F. 1967. Caxton and Chaucer. *LeedsSE,* n.s. 1:19-36.

——— 1969. *Caxton and His World.* London: André Deutsch.

——— 1979. The Relationship Between the Hengwrt and the Ellesmere Manuscripts of the *Canterbury Tales. E&S,* n.s., 32:1-18.

Boas, M. 1952. See Cato 1952.

Boccaccio, G. 1951. *Genealogie deorum gentilium libri.* Ed. V. Romano. Scrittori d'Italia. 2 vols. Bari: Giusseppe Laterza e Figli.

Boethius (Anicius Manlius Severinus Boethius) 1973: *Tractates: De consolatione phi-*

losophiae. Trans. and ed. H. F. Stewart, E. K. Rand, and S. J. Tester. Loeb Classical Library. Cambridge, Mass.: Harvard University Press.

Boyd, B. 1973. *Chaucer and the Medieval Book.* San Marino, Calif.: Henry E. Huntington Library.

Brewer, D. S., ed. 1966. *Chaucer and Chaucerians: Critical Studies in Middle English Literature.* London: Nelson.

——— 1968. Class Distinction in Chaucer. *Speculum* 43:290-305.

———, ed. 1973. *Chaucer.* 3d ed. London: Longmans. 1st ed., 1953; 2d ed., 1960.

——— 1978. *Chaucer: The Critical Heritage.* 2 vols. London: Henley; Boston: Routledge and Kegan Paul.

Brink, Bernhard ten 1883-93. *History of English Literature.* 2 vols. in 3. New York: Holt.

Brodie, A. H. 1971. Hodge of Ware and Geber's Cook. *NM* 72:62-68.

Bronson, B. H. 1940. Chaucer's Art in Relation to His Audience. In *Five Studies in Literature.* University of California Publications in English, no. 8. Berkeley: University of California.

Brown, Carleton, ed. 1939. *Religious Lyrics of the XVth Century.* Oxford: Oxford University Press.

Brown, E. 1980. Word Play in the Prologue to the *Manciple's Tale* 98. *ChauN* 2 (2):11-12.

Brusendorff, Aage 1925. *The Chaucer Tradition.* London: Oxford University Press; Copenhagen: V. Pio-Branner.

Bryan, W. F., and Germaine Dempster, eds. 1941. *Sources and Analogues of Chaucer's Canterbury Tales.* Chicago: University of Chicago Press. Reprint. New York: Humanities Press, 1958. J. A. Work edited the section dealing with *ManT.*

Burlin, R. B. 1977. *Chaucerian Fiction.* Princeton, N.J.: Princeton University Press.

Burnley, J. D. 1979. *Chaucer's Language and the Philosopher's Tradition.* Chaucer Studies, no. 2. Ipswich: D. S. Brewer; Totowa, N.J.: Rowman and Littlefield.

Cadbury, W. 1964. Manipulation of Sources and Meaning of the *Manciple's Tale. PQ* 43:538-48.

Campbell, J. 1972. Polonius Among the Pilgrims. *ChauR* 7:140-46.

Cato (Dionysius Cato) 1952. *Disticha Catonis.* Ed. M. Boas. Amsterdam: North-Holland Publishing Co.

Caxton, William, ed. 1478 [*The Canterbury Tales*]. Westminster. *STC* 5082.

———, ed. 1484. [*The Canterbury Tales*]. Westminster. *STC* 5083.

Chute, Marchette 1949. *Geoffrey Chaucer of England.* New York: Dutton.

Clogan, P. 1964. Chaucer and the *Thebaid* Scolia. *SP* 61:599-615.

Coghill, Neville 1949. *The Poet Chaucer.* Oxford: Oxford University Press. 2d ed., 1967.

——— 1966. Chaucer's Narrative Art. In Brewer, ed. 1966, pp. 114-39.

Corsa, Helen Storm 1964. *Chaucer: Poet of Mirth and Morality.* Notre Dame, Ind.: University of Notre Dame Press.

Cowper, J. M. 1868. Chaucer's Bob-Up-And-Down. *Athenaeum,* Dec. 26, 1868, p. 886.

Crawford, William R. 1967. *Bibliography of Chaucer, 1954-63.* Seattle: University of Washington Press.

——— 1971. *Chaucer's Idea of What Is Noble.* Presidential Address, 1971. London: English Association.

Davidson, A. E. 1979. The Logic of Confusion in Chaucer's *Manciple's Tale. AnM* 19: 5-12.

Davis, Norman, et al., eds. 1979. *A Chaucer Glossary.* Oxford: Clarendon Press.

Dempster, Germaine 1932. *Dramatic Irony in Chaucer.* Stanford Publications in Language and Literature, vol. 4 no. 3. Stanford, Calif.: Stanford University Press.

—— 1937. Chaucer at Work on the Complaint in the *Franklin's Tale. MLN* 52:16-23.

—— 1946. Manly's Conception of the Early History of the *Canterbury Tales. PMLA* 56:379-415.

—— 1948. A Chapter of the Manuscript History of the *Canterbury Tales. PMLA* 63: 456-84.

—— 1949. The Fifteenth-Century Editors of the *Canterbury Tales* and the Problem of Tale Order. *PMLA* 64:1123-42.

—— 1951. The Early History of the Manuscripts of the *Canterbury Tales.* Paper delivered to Rocky Mountain Modern Language Association, Boulder, Colorado, October, 1951. Dempster papers, Norlin Library, University of Colorado.

Deschamps, Eustache 1878-1903. *Oeuvres complètes.* ed. H.-E. Queux de Saint-Hilaire and Gaston Raynaud. 11 vols. SATF. Paris: Various publishers.

Donaldson, E. Talbot 1958. *Chaucer's Poetry. An Anthology for the Modern Reader.* New York: Ronald.

—— 1970. *Speaking of Chaucer.* London: Athlone.

Donner, M. J. 1955. The Unity of Chaucer's Manciple Fragment. *MLN* 70:245-49.

Doyle, A. I., and M. B. Parkes 1978. The Production of Copies of the *Canterbury Tales* and the *Confessio Amantis* in the Early Fifteenth Century. In M. B. Parkes and Andrew Watson, eds. *Medieval Scribes, Manuscripts, and Libraries: Essays Presented to N. R. Ker.* London: Scolar Press, pp. 163-212.

—— and —— 1979. Paleographical Introduction. In Ruggiers, ed. 1979.

Dunn, T. R. 1940. *The Manuscript Source of Caxton's Second Edition of the Canterbury Tales.* Chicago: University of Chicago Press.

Economou, George D. 1975. Chaucer's Use of the Bird in the Cage Imagery in the *Canterbury Tales. PQ* 54:669-83.

Eliason, Norman E. 1972. *The Language of Chaucer's Poetry.* Anglistica, vol. 17. Copenhagen: Rosenkilde and Begger.

Elliott, J. D. 1954. The Moral of the *Manciple's Tale. N&Q* 199:511-12.

Elliott, Ralph W. V. 1974. *Chaucer's English.* London: André Deutsch.

Emerson, Oliver Farrar 1922. Chaucer and Medieval Hunting. *RR* 13:115-20.

Everett, Dorothy 1950. Some Reflections on Chaucer's "Art Poetical." *PBA* 36:131-54. Reprinted in P. M. Kean, ed. *Essays on Middle English Literature by Dorothy Everett.* Oxford: Oxford University Press, 1955.

Fansler, D. 1914. *Chaucer and the Roman de la Rose.* New York: Columbia University Press. Reprint. Gloucester, Mass.: Peter Smith, 1965.

Faral, Edmond, ed. 1924. *Les Arts poétiques du XIIe et du XIIIe siècle: recherches et documents sur la technique littéraire du Moyen Age.* Bibliothèque de l'École des hautes études, fasc. 238. Paris: Librairie H. Champion. Reprint. 1958.

Fisher, John H. 1965. *John Gower: Moral Philosopher and Friend of Chaucer.* New York: New York University Press.

———— ed. 1977. *The Complete Poetry and Prose of Geoffrey Chaucer.* New York: Holt, Rinehart, and Winston. [FI]

Fletcher, Bradford Y. 1978. Printer's Copy for Stow's Chaucer. *SB* 31:184-201.

French, Robert Dudley 1947. *A Chaucer Handbook.* 2d ed. New York: Appleton-Century-Crofts.

Fulk, R. D. 1979. Reinterpreting the *Manciple's Tale. JEGP* 78:485-93.

Furnivall, Frederick J. 1868. *A Temporary Preface to the Chaucer Society's Six-Text Edition of Chaucer's Canterbury Tales.* Chaucer Society. 2d ser., no. 3. London: Trübner.

————, ed. 1868-79. *The Six-Text Edition of the Canterbury Tales.* Chaucer Society. 4 vols. 1st ser., no. 1; n.s., nos. 14-15, 25, 30-31, 37, 49. London: Trübner.

———— 1871. Letter. *Athenaeum* 2:495.

————, E. Brock, and W. A. Clouston, eds. 1872-87. *Originals and Analogues of Some of Chaucer's Canterbury Tales.* Chaucer Society. 2d ser., nos. 7, 10, 15, 20, 22. London: Trübner.

Fyler, J. M. 1979. *Chaucer and Ovid.* New Haven, Conn.: Yale University Press.

Garbáty, Thomas J. 1978. Wynkyn de Worde's "Sir Thopas" and Other Tales. *SB* 31: 57-67.

Gardner, John 1977*a*. *The Life and Times of Geoffrey Chaucer.* New York: Knopf.

———— 1977*b*. *The Poetry of Chaucer.* Carbondale, Ill.: Southern Illinois University Press.

Gaylord, Alan T. 1964. *Gentillesse* in Chaucer's *Troilus. SP* 61:19-34.

Gower, John 1900-1901. *The English Works of John Gower.* ed. George Campbell Maccaulay. 2 vols. EETS, e.s., nos. 81, 82. Oxford: Oxford University Press. Reprint. 1957.

Gradon, P. 1971. *Form and Style in Early English Literature.* London: Methuen.

Grauls, J., and J. H. Vanderheijden 1934. Two Flemish Proverbs in Chaucer's *Canterbury Tales. RBPH* 13:745-49.

Greg, W. W. 1924. Early Printed Editions of the Canterbury Tales. *PMLA* 39:737-61.

Griffith, D. D. 1926. *A Bibliography of Chaucer, 1908-1924.* Seattle: University of Washington Press.

———— 1955. *A Bibliography of Chaucer, 1908-1953.* Seattle: University of Washington Press.

Gruber, L. C. 1973. *The Manciple's Tale:* One Key to Chaucer's Language. In L. C. Gruber and W. C. Johnson, eds. *New Views on Chaucer: Essays in Generative Criticism.* Denver, Colo.: Society for New Language Study, pp. 43-50.

Hadow, G. E. 1914. *Chaucer and His Time.* London: Thornton, Butterworth.

Haeckel, W. 1890. *Das Sprichwort bei Chaucer.* Erlanger Beiträge zur Englischen Philologie, no. 8. Erlangen and Leipzig.

Hamilton, G. L. 1903. *The Indebtedness of Chaucer's* Troilus and Criseyde *to Guido delle Colonne's* Historia Trojana. New York: Columbia University Press.

Hammond, Eleanor P. 1908. *Chaucer: A Bibliographical Manual.* New York: Macmillan. Reprint. New York: Peter Smith, 1933.

Harrison, T. P. 1956. *They Tell of Birds.* Austin: University of Texas Press.

Harwood, B. J. 1972. Language and the Real: Chaucer's Manciple. *ChauR* 6:268-79.

Hazelton, Richard 1960. Chaucer and Cato. *Speculum* 35:357-80.

——— 1963. The "Manciple's Tale": Parody and Critique. *JEGP* 62:1-31.

Hench, Atcheson L. 1950. Printer's Copy for Tyrwhitt's Chaucer. *SB* 3:265-66.

Herrtage, S. J. H., ed. 1879. *The Early English Versions of the* Gesta Romanorum. EETS, e.s., no. 33. Oxford: Oxford University Press. Reprint. 1962.

Hetherington, John R. 1964. Chaucer 1532-1602: Notes and Facsimile Texts. Type-written. [Birmingham]: Author. Rev. ed. 1967.

Hieronymus, Eusebius [Saint Jerome] 1883. *Epistola adversus Jovinianum.* In J.-P. Migne, ed. *Patrologiae Latinae,* vol. 23, cols. 222-352. Paris: J.-P. Migne.

Hoffman, Richard L. 1964. *Ovid and the* Canterbury Tales. Philadelphia: University of Pennsylvania Press.

Horace (Quintus Horatius Flaccus) 1936. *Satires, Epistles, Ars Poetica.* Trans. and ed. H. R. Fairclough. Loeb Classical Library. Cambridge, Mass.: Harvard University Press.

Howard, Donald R. 1976. *The Idea of the* Canterbury Tales. Berkeley: University of California Press.

Howard, Edwin J. 1964. *Geoffrey Chaucer.* Boston: Twayne.

Hulbert, J. R. 1948. The *Canterbury Tales* and Their Narrators. *SP* 45:565-77.

Huppé, Bernard F. 1964. *A Reading of the* Canterbury Tales. Albany: State University of New York Press.

Hussey, S. S. 1971. *Chaucer: An Introduction.* London: Methuen.

Jefferson, B. L. 1917. *Chaucer and the* Consolation of Philosophy *of Boethius.* Princeton, N.J.: Princeton University Press.

Jerome, Saint. See Hieronymus 1883.

Jordan, Robert M. 1964. Chaucer's Sense of Illusion: Roadside Drama Reconsidered. *ELH* 29:19-33.

Kalendrier 1925. Bertrand Guégan, ed. *Le grant kalendrier & côpost des bergiers auecq leur astrologie, et plusieurs aultres choses.* [Troyes: Nicolas le Rouge, 1529]; Paris: Payot.

Kean, P. M. 1972. *Chaucer and the Making of English Poetry.* 2 vols. London: Routledge and Kegan Paul.

Kearny, M. 1978. Much Ado in a "Litel Toun." *Innisfree,* pp. 30-41.

Knight, S. 1973. *Rymyng Craftily: Meaning in Chaucer's Poetry.* London and Sydney: Angus and Robertson.

Koch, John, ed. 1915. *Chaucer: Canterbury Tales: Nach dem Ellesmere MS mit Lesarten, Anmerkungen, und einem Glossar.* Heidelberg: C. Winter.

——— 1923. Chaucers Belesenheit in den römischen Klassikern. *Englische Studien* 57: 8-84.

———, and F. J. Furnivall, eds. 1898. *Parallel-Text Specimens, Pt. V: The Pardoner's Prolog and Tale, a Six-Text, from three MSS and three Black Letters.* Chaucer Society, no. 91. London: Trübner.

Koeppel, E. 1891. Chaucer und Albertanus Brixiensis. *Archiv* 86:29-46.

——— 1891-92. Chauceriana. *Anglia* 14:227-67.

Langlois, Ernest, ed. 1914-24. *Guillaume de Lorris et Jean de Meun: Le Roman de la Rose.* 5 vols. SATF, no. 63. Paris: Various publishers.

Lawrence, William W. 1950. *Chaucer and the* Canterbury Tales. New York: Columbia University Press.

Lorris, Guillaume de, and Jean de Meun. See Langlois, ed. 1914-24.

Lossing, M. L. S. 1938. The Order of the *Canterbury Tales:* A Fresh Relation Between A and B Types of MSS. *JEGP* 37:153-63.

Lounsbury, Thomas R. 1892. *Studies in Chaucer.* 3 vols. New York: Harper.

Lowes, John Livingston 1915. Chaucer and the Seven Deadly Sins. *PMLA* 30:237-71.

Lumiansky, R. M. 1947. Chaucer and the Idea of Unfaithful Men. *MLN* 62:560-62.

———— 1955. *Of Sondry Folk: The Dramatic Principle in the* Canterbury Tales. Austin: University of Texas Press.

Lyon, E. D. 1937. Roger de Ware, Cook. *MLN* 52:491-94.

McCall, J. P. 1979. *Chaucer Among the Gods.* University Park: Pennsylvania State University Press.

MacDonald, Donald 1966. Proverbs, *Sententiae,* and *Exempla* in Chaucer's Comic Tales: The Function of Comic Misapplication. *Speculum* 41:453-65.

Machaut, Guillaume de 1908-21. *Oeuvres de Guillaume de Machaut.* Ed. E. Hoepffner. 3 vols. SATF. Paris: Various publishers.

MacLaine, A. H. 1964. *The Student's Comprehensive Guide to the* Canterbury Tales. Great Neck, N.J.: Barron's.

Makarewicz, M. R. 1953. *The Patristic Influence on Chaucer.* Washington, D.C.: Catholic University of America Press.

Malone, Kemp 1951. *Chapters on Chaucer.* Baltimore, Md.: Johns Hopkins University Press.

Manly, John M. 1913. What Is the House of Fame? In *Anniversary Papers in Honor of G. L. Kittredge.* Boston: Ginn, pp. 73-81.

———— 1926*a*. Chaucer and the Rhetoricians. *PBA* 12:95-113.

———— 1926*b. Some New Light on Chaucer.* New York: Holt. Reprint. New York: Peter Smith, 1952.

————, ed. 1928. The Canterbury Tales, *by Geoffrey Chaucer.* New York: Holt.

———— 1931. Tales of the Homeward Journey. *SP* 28:613-17.

————, and Edith Rickert 1939. The "Hengwrt" Manuscript of Chaucer's *Canterbury Tales. NLWJ* 1:59-75.

————, and Edith Rickert, eds. 1940. *The Text of the Canterbury Tales: Studied on the Basis of All Known Manuscripts.* 8 vols. Chicago: University of Chicago Press.

Marshall, D. F. 1979. A Note on Chaucer's *Manciple's Tale* 105-10. *ChauN* 1 (1):17-18.

The Master of Game [Edward, second duke of York] 1909. Ed. W. A. and F. Baillie-Grohman. London: Chatto and Windus.

Morris, Richard, ed. 1866. *Dan Michel's Ayenbite of Inwyt.* EETS, o.s., no. 23. London: Trübner.

Murphy, James J. 1964. A New Look at Chaucer and the Rhetoricians. *RES,* n.s. 15: 1-20.

Muscatine, Charles 1957. *Chaucer and the French Tradition: A Study in Style and Meaning.* Berkeley and Los Angeles: University of California Press.

Mustanoja, Tauno F. 1965. Chaucer's *Manciple's Tale,* Lines 311-13. In J. B. Bessinger, Jr., and R. P. Creed, eds. *Franciplegius: Medieval and Linguistic Studies in Honor of Francis Peabody Magoun, Jr.* New York: New York University Press, pp. 250-54.

Naunin, T. 1929. *Einfluss der Mittelalterlichen Rhetorik auf Chaucers Dichtung.* Bonn: Bonn University Dissertations.

Norton-Smith, John 1974. *Geoffrey Chaucer.* London: Routledge and Kegan Paul.

Ovid [Publius Ovidius Naso] 1916. *Metamorphoses.* Trans. and ed. F. J. Miller. 2 vols. Loeb Classical Library. Cambridge, Mass.: Harvard University Press.

Owen, Charles A., Jr. 1951. The Plan of the Canterbury Pilgrimage. *PMLA* 66:820-26.

——— 1958. The Development of the *Canterbury Tales. JEGP* 57:449-76.

——— 1959. The Earliest Plan of the *Canterbury Tales. MS* 21:202-10.

——— 1977. *Pilgrimage and Storytelling in the Canterbury Tales: The Dialectic of "Ernest" and "Game."* Norman: University of Oklahoma Press.

Pace, George B. 1968. Speght's Chaucer and MS GG.4.27. *SB* 21:225-35.

Parkes, M. B. 1976. The Influence of the Conception of *Ordinatio* and *Compilatio* on the Development of the Book. In J. J. G. Alexander and M. T. Gibson, eds. *Medieval Learning and Literature: Essays Presented to Richard William Hunt.* Oxford: Clarendon Press, pp. 115-41.

———, and Richard Beadle, eds. 1979-80. Introduction to *Geoffrey Chaucer: Poetical Works: A Facsimile of Cambridge University Library Gg.4.27.* 3 vols. Cambridge: Brewer.

Payne, Robert O. 1963. *The Key of Remembrance: A Study of Chaucer's Poetics.* New Haven, Conn.: Yale University Press.

Pearcy, Roy J. 1974. Does the *Manciple's Prologue* Contain a Reference to Hell's Mouth? *ELN* 11:167-75.

Pichaske, D. R., and L. Sweetland 1977. Chaucer and the Medieval Monarch: Harry Bailly in the *Canterbury Tales. ChauR* 11:179-200.

Plessow, G. 1929. *Des Haushälters Erzählung aus den Canterbury-Geschichten Gottfried Chaucers.* Trübners Philologische Bibliothek, vol. 12. Berlin: de Gruyter.

Pollard, Alfred W., et al., eds. 1898. *The Works of Geoffrey Chaucer.* Globe edition. London: Macmillan.

Pratt, Robert A. 1951. The Order of the *Canterbury Tales. PMLA* 66:1141-67.

——— 1962. Jankyn's Book of Wikked Wyves: Medieval Antimatrimonial Propaganda in the Universities. *AnM* 3:5-27.

———, ed. 1974. *The Tales of Canterbury, Complete, Geoffrey Chaucer.* Boston: Houghton Mifflin.

Pynson, Richard, ed. 1492 [*The Canterbury Tales*]. London: Pynson. *STC* 5084.

———, ed. 1526. *Here begynneth the boke of Caunterbury tales dilygently and truely corrected and newly printed.* London. *STC* 5086. Pt. 3 of an edition of the works.

Ramsey, R. Vance 1982. The Hengwrt and Ellesmere Manuscripts of the *Canterbury Tales:* Different Scribes. *SB* 35:133-53.

Reid, T. B. W. 1955. The She-Wolf's Mate. *MÆ* 24:16-19.

Reiss, E. 1979. Chaucer and Medieval Irony. *SAC* 1:67-82.

Rickert, E. 1932. Chaucer's Hodge of Ware. *TLS,* October 20, 1932, p. 761.

Robbins, R. H., ed. 1975. *Chaucer at Albany.* New York: Burt Franklin.

Robinson, F. N., ed. 1933. *The Works of Geoffrey Chaucer.* Boston: Houghton Mifflin. 2d ed. 1957.

Roman de la Rose. See Langlois, ed. 1914-24.

Root, Robert Kilburn 1922. *The Poetry of Chaucer: A Guide to Its Study and Appreciation.* Rev. ed. Boston: Houghton Mifflin. Originally published 1906.

——— 1929. The *Manciple's Prologue. MLN* 44:493-96.

Ross, Thomas W. 1972. *Chaucer's Bawdy.* New York: Dutton.

Rowland, Beryl, ed. 1968. *Companion to Chaucer Studies.* New York: Oxford University Press. Rev. ed., 1979.

———— 1972. *Blind Beasts: Chaucer's Animal World.* Kent, Ohio: Kent State University Press.

Ruggiers, Paul G. 1965. *The Art of the* Canterbury Tales. Madison, Wis.: University of Wisconsin Press. Reprint. 1967.

————, ed. 1979. *The Canterbury Tales: A Facsimile and Transcription of the Hengwrt Manuscript, with Variants from the Ellesmere Manuscript.* Introductions by Donald C. Baker and by A. I. Doyle and M. B. Parkes. Vol. 1 of the *Variorum Chaucer.* Norman: University of Oklahoma Press; Folkestone: Dawson.

Rydland, Kurt 1972. The Meaning of "Variant Reading" in the Manly-Rickert *Canterbury Tales. NM* 73:805-14.

"S." 1932. The Little Town of Bob-up-and-Down. *N&Q* 167:26.

Samuels, M. L. 1983. The Scribe of the Hengwrt and Ellesmere Manuscripts of *The Canterbury Tales. SAC* 5:000.

Scattergood, V. J. 1970. The Debate Between Nurture and Kynde: An Unpublished Middle English Poem. *N&Q* 215:244-46.

———— 1974. The Manciple's Manner of Speaking. *EIC* 24:124-46.

Schlauch, M. 1937. Chaucer's *Merchant's Tale* and Courtly Love. *ELH* 4:201-12.

Seneca [Lucius Annaeus Seneca] 1928. *Moral Essays.* Trans. and ed. J. W. Bashore. 3 vols. Loeb Classical Library. Cambridge, Mass.: Harvard University Press.

Severs, J. Burke 1952. Is the *Manciple's Tale* a Success? *JEGP* 51:1-16.

Shannon, E. F. 1929. *Chaucer and the Roman Poets.* Cambridge, Mass.: Harvard University Press.

Siebert, H. 1916. Chaucer and Horace. *MLN* 31:304-307.

Silvia, Daniel S. 1965. Glosses to the *Canterbury Tales* from St. Jerome's *Epistola adversus Jovinianum. SP* 62:28-39.

Skeat, Walter W., ed. 1894. *The Complete Works of Geoffrey Chaucer.* 6 vols. Oxford: Clarendon Press.

———— 1909. *The Eight-Text Edition of the Canterbury Tales with Remarks on the Classification of the Manuscripts.* Chaucer Society, 2d ser., no. 43. London: Kegan Paul, Trench and Trübner, 1909 for 1905.

———— 1910. *Early English Proverbs.* Oxford: Clarendon Press.

Slaughter, E. 1957. *Virtue According to Love—in Chaucer.* New York: Bookman Associates, 1957.

Sledd, James 1947. Dorigen's Complaint. *MP* 45:36-45.

Southworth, James G. 1954. *Verses of Cadence: Introduction to the Prosody of Chaucer and His Followers.* Westport, Conn.: Greenwood Press.

Spector, R. D. 1957. Chaucer's "The Manciple's Tale." *N&Q* 4:25.

Speght, Thomas, ed. 1598. *The Workes of our Antient and Lerned English Poet, Geffrey Chaucer, newly Printed.* London: Adam Islip for Bonham Norton. *STC* 5077.

————, ed. 1602. *The Workes of Our Ancient and learned English Poet, Geffrey Chaucer, newly Printed.* London: Adam Islip. *STC* 5080.

————, ed. 1687. *The Works of our Ancient, Learned, & Excellent Poet, Jeffrey Chaucer.* London.

Speirs, John 1951. *Chaucer the Maker.* London: Faber. 2d ed., 1960.

Spurgeon, Caroline F. E. 1911. *Chaucer devant la critique en Angleterre et en France depuis son temps jusqu'a nos jours.* Paris: Hachette.

Statius [Publius Papinius Statius] 1928. *Thebaid* (with *Silvae*). Trans. and ed. J. H. Mozley. 2 vols. Loeb Classical Library. Cambridge, Mass.: Harvard University Press.

Steadman, John M. 1963. Venus' *Citole* in Chaucer's *Knight's Tale* and Berchorius. *Speculum* 38:620-24.

Stillwell, Gardiner 1940. Analogues to Chaucer's *Manciple's Tale* in the *Ovide moralisé* and Machaut's *Voir-Dit. PQ* 19:133-38.

Stow[e], John, ed. 1561. *The Workes of Geffrey Chaucer, newlie printed, with divers addicions whiche were never in print before.* London: Jhon Kyngston for Jhon Wight.

Strutt, J. 1867. *The Sports and Pastimes of the People of England.* London: Tegg.

Tatlock, John S. P. 1907. *Development and Chronology of Chaucer's Works.* Chaucer Society, 2d ser., no. 37. London: Oxford University Press. Reprint. Gloucester, Mass.: Peter Smith, 1965.

——— 1935*a*. The *Canterbury Tales* in 1400. *PMLA* 50:100-39.

——— 1935*b*. The Date of the *Troilus:* and Minor Chauceriana. *MLN* 50:277-96.

———, and Arthur G. Kennedy 1927. *A Concordance to the Complete Works of Geoffrey Chaucer and to the* Romaunt of the Rose. Washington, D.C. Carnegie Institution.

Thynne, William, ed. 1532. *The Workes of Geffray Chaucer newly printed with dyvers workes whiche were never in print before.* London: Thomas Godfray. *STC* 5068.

———, ed. 1542. *The workes of Geffray Chaucer newly printed, wyth dyvers workes whych were never in print before.* London: Wylyam Bonham. *STC* 5069.

———, ed. Ca. 1545. *The workes of Geffray Chaucer newly printed, with dyvers workes whiche were never in print before.* London: Thomas Petit. *STC* 5076.

Tolkien, J. R. R. 1934. Chaucer as a Philologist: *The Reeve's Tale. TPS,* pp. 1-70.

Trask, R. M. 1977. The Manciple's Problem. *SSF* 14:109-16.

Tupper, Frederick 1914. Chaucer and the Seven Deadly Sins. *PMLA* 29:93-128.

——— 1915. The Quarrels of the Canterbury Pilgrims. *JEGP* 14:256-70.

——— 1916. Chaucer's Sins and Sinners. *JEGP* 15:56-106.

——— 1926. *Types of Society in Medieval Literature.* New York: Holt.

Tyrwhitt, Thomas, ed. 1775-78. *The Canterbury Tales of Chaucer.* 5 vols. London. 2d ed. Oxford, 1798. 2 vols.

Urry, John, et al., eds. 1721. *The Works of Geoffrey Chaucer, Compared with the Former Editions, and many valuable MSS.* London: For Bernard Lintot.

Ussery, H. E. 1971. *Chaucer's Physician: Medicine and Literature in Fourteenth Century England.* Tulane Studies in English, no. 19.

Wagenknecht, Edward 1968. *The Personality of Chaucer.* Norman: University of Oklahoma Press.

Webb, C. C. J., ed. 1909. *Joannis Saresberiensis Episcopi Carnotensis Policratici sive de Nugis Curialium et Vestigiis Philosophorum.* 2 vols. Oxford: Clarendon.

Whiting, B. J. 1934. *Chaucer's Use of Proverbs.* Harvard Studies in Comparative Literature, vol. 11. Cambridge, Mass.: Harvard University Press.

——— 1968. *Proverbs, Sentences, and Proverbial Phrases from English Writings Mainly Before 1500.* Cambridge, Mass.: Harvard University Press.

Whittock, Trevor 1968. *A Reading of the* Canterbury Tales. Cambridge: Cambridge University Press.

Wilkins, E. H. 1957. Descriptions of Pagan Divinities from Petrarch to Chaucer. *Speculum* 32:511-22.

Wimsatt, James I. 1968. *Chaucer and the French Love Poets.* Chapel Hill: University of North Carolina Press.

Wise, B. A. 1911. *The Influence of Statius upon Chaucer.* Baltimore, Md.: Furst.

Worde, Wynkyn de, ed. 1498. *The boke of Chaucer named Caunterbury tales.* Westminster.

Wordsworth, William 1958. Letter to Dora Wordsworth. In *Poetical Works of William Wordsworth.* 2d ed. Ed. E. de Selincourt and H. Darbishire. Oxford: Oxford University Press. Vol. 4, app. B.

Work, J. A. 1932*a*. The *Manciple's Prologue. SP* 29:11-14.

———— 1932*b*. The Position of the Tales of the Manciple and the Parson on Chaucer's Canterbury Pilgrimage. *JEGP* 31:62-65.

———— 1941. The *Manciple's Tale.* In Bryan and Dempster, pp. 699-722.

Wright, H. G. 1959. Thomas Speght as a Lexicographer and Annotator of Chaucer's Works. *ES* 40:194-208.

Wright, Thomas, ed. 1847-51. *The Canterbury Tales of Geoffrey Chaucer. A New Text with Illustrative Notes.* 3 vols. For the Percy Society. London.

————, ed. 1906. *The Book of the Knight of La Tour Landry.* EETS, o.s., no. 33. Rev. ed. London: Oxford University Press.

Zacher, C. K. 1976. *Curiosity and Pilgrimage.* Baltimore, Md.: Johns Hopkins University Press.

General Index

Designed by Bill Cason, *The Manciple's Tale* was composed by the University of Oklahoma Press in various sizes of Garamond. Handset Nicolini Broadpen was used for the display type, with decorative Victorian initial letters on the title page. Color separation and presswork were provided by University of Oklahoma Printing Services. The paper used for this volume is 70-pound Glatfelter A50. Binding was provided by Ellis Bindery.

THE VARIORUM CHAUCER

UNIVERSITY OF OKLAHOMA PRESS : NORMAN